PIRATE
HUNTERS

TREASURE, OBSESSION, and the SEARCH

for a LEGENDARY PIRATE SHIP

ROBERT KURSON

First published in the United States of America in 2015 by Random House, an imprint and division of Penguin Random House LLC, New York.

This edition published in the United Kingdom in 2015 by
Elliott and Thompson Limited
27 John Street, London WC1N 2BX
www.eandtbooks.com

ISBN: 978-1-78396-219-8

910.452

Text copyright © 2015 by Robert Kurson
Maps copyright © 2015 by David Lindroth Inc.

Image Credits:
iStock (frontispiece), Todd Ehrhardt (p. 182), Robert Kurson (p. 249), Howard Ehrenberg (pp. 8, 251, 268), Library of Congress (p. 86), John Mattera (pp. 18, 67, 259, 269), courtesy of the National Library of Jamaica (p. 255), Joe Porter (p. 12), Grateful acknowledgment is made to Paul Cox for permission to reprint the map of Port Royal (p. 48) by Oliver Cox, drawn subsequently as part of the report proposal "Upgrading and Renewing the Historic City of Port Royal, Jamaica," June 1984. Reprinted by permission.

9 8 7 6 5 4 3 2 1

A catalogue record for this book is available from the British Library.

Cover design by James Nunn
Typeset by Marie Doherty

Printed by CPI Group (UK) Ltd, Croydon, CR0 4YY

*For Amy,
my treasure found*

*Now and then we had a hope that if
we lived and were good,
God would permit us to be pirates.*

MARK TWAIN

Pirates could happen to anyone.

TOM STOPPARD

AUTHOR'S NOTE

Early one January morning in 2012, I received an international call from an unknown number. It was coming from the Dominican Republic, but I didn't know anyone in that country, I had never been there in my life. The voice on the line, however, was unmistakable.

"If you like pirates, meet me in New Jersey."

The caller was John Chatterton, one of the heroes of my book *Shadow Divers*, a true story about two weekend scuba divers who discover a World War II German U-boat sunk off the coast of New Jersey, and their obsessive and deadly quest to identify the wreck. I hadn't spoken to Chatterton in more than a year, but knew his New York–tinged baritone right away.

"What kind of pirates?" I asked.

"Seventeenth century. Caribbean. The real deal."

Just the mention of pirates sat me straight up in my seat. But the timing for a trip from Chicago to New Jersey could not have been worse. It was snowing. I was researching a new book. And I was just winding down from the holidays. But I'd learned something from Chatterton the first time around—if there's a window to go, you go. An hour later, I was on I-94 headed east.

Late that night, I pulled into Scotty's Steakhouse in Springfield, New Jersey. I hadn't seen Chatterton for three years, but he looked younger than I remembered. He was sixty now, but appeared in better shape than men half his age. He introduced me to his friend John Mattera, a man of about fifty with a broad smile and a Staten Island accent. I'd met Mattera years earlier, and remembered he'd worked as an executive bodyguard. His arms still looked the part.

We ordered drinks and caught up on family, then Chatterton got down to business.

"How much do you know about the Golden Age of Piracy?" he asked.

As it turned out, I knew quite a bit. Years earlier, at a used bookstore, I'd picked up a tiny paperback called *The Buccaneers of America* by Alexandre Exquemelin, a true account of pirate life by a man who'd sailed aboard real pirate ships and had chronicled the exploits of Captain Henry Morgan. The book, considered a classic, couldn't have been more than two hundred pages. I had paid two dollars and taken it to lunch with me down the street.

I never got to the food.

Exquemelin's pirates were wilder than in any movie, more treacherous than in any novel. They conquered entire cities, devised ingenious methods for plundering, and struck terror into the hearts of their enemies, sometimes without raising a sword. By a single act alone—perhaps by eating the still-beating heart of a merchant captain who refused to surrender—they broadcast their reputations across oceans. Even their downtime was epic, so packed with debauchery and fast living it would have spun the heads of modern millionaire rock stars. And yet, these pirates lived by a code of conduct and honor so far ahead of its time it made them nearly invincible.

They also left no trail. Only one pirate ship had ever been discovered and positively identified in the centuries since the buccaneers prowled the oceans: the *Whydah*, found in waters off Cape Cod in 1984. Nothing was harder to find underwater—or maybe in all the world—than a pirate ship. It was as if every trace of the buccaneers had disappeared.

I read every pirate book I could find after devouring Exquemelin, asked at rare coin shops to see silver pieces of eight, and even drove cross-country to explore a museum exhibit on the *Whydah*. So I knew about the Golden Age, which lasted from about 1650 to 1720.

"Good," Mattera said. "Because we just spent a year living in the seventeenth century."

For the next three hours, the men told me of their quest to find a great pirate ship—a journey filled with danger, diving, and mystery. They talked about researching the history of pirates in libraries and archives around the globe. They described using cutting-edge technology and tracking down ancient maps and manuscripts. They told stories about learning from wise elders, and doing battle with cutthroats and rivals. And they told me about their search for a pirate captain more notorious than Blackbeard and more daring than William Kidd, a real-life Jack Sparrow, a man who'd been legend but whose story had been lost to time: the buccaneer Joseph Bannister.

I pressed the men for more details and asked questions until the restaurant closed. In the parking lot, they told me they'd be happy to talk further, but that a person couldn't truly understand what they'd been through without seeing for himself where it all had happened.

Two weeks later, I met Chatterton and Mattera in the Colonial Zone in Santo Domingo, the oldest permanent settlement in the New World. We walked down the cobblestoned Calle Las Damas, the first paved road in the Americas. To my right, I could see the home of conquistador Nicolás de Ovando, built in 1502, complete with dungeons; to my left, the oldest church in the New World. After breakfast, the men took me to a sixteenth-century coral block structure. This was the laboratory at the Oficina Nacional de Patrimonio Cultural Subacuático, the place where artifacts discovered by treasure hunters were cataloged and divvied up.

I didn't know where to look first. On one table was a nine-foot gold chain from the seventeenth century. On another was a set of slave manacles and an egg-shaped box made of pure silver. In a cement tank, lying in water, was an anchor used by Christopher Columbus. In the States, the anchor would have been protected by Plexiglas and guarded by lasers. Here, I was free to reach in and touch it, and I did. Time disappeared with the contact. This is what Columbus's world felt like. Now I was feeling it, too.

Near the exit, I was shown to a final table, this one piled high with hundreds of pieces of eight, all from the seventeenth century. I scooped up as many of the silver coins as would fit in my hands, then let them spill onto the table. They made a sound I'd never heard before but somehow had known my whole life, a waterfall of muted chimes, dense and deep and old. This was the song that had called to the pirates. This was the sound of treasure.

That night, the men drove me to the north coast of the country, where they'd launched their search for the *Golden Fleece*, the greatest pirate ship that had ever sailed. In New Jersey, they had told me the outline of the story. Here, on a sticky hot night in which even the moon seemed to sweat, I heard more—about how difficult the quest had become for Chatterton and Mattera, how much they'd risked to undertake it, how they were still paying the price for going on this hunt for history, and for getting into the mind of a great leader and adventurer, the pirate Joseph Bannister. And I could feel, in between the swashbuckling details of their tale, how they'd been searching for more than a pirate ship all along.

When I got home, I didn't feel much like going back to work on my old project. Instead, I woke my two young sons and told them the pirate story. Then, I decided to tell it to you.

MAP

of the

CARIBBEAN

BASIN

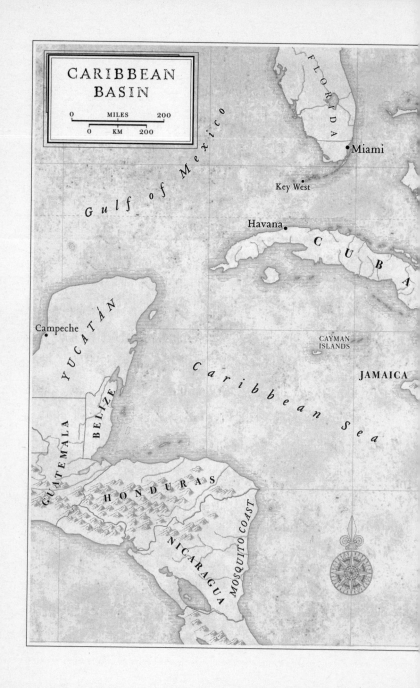

Chapter 1

THE GREATEST
PIRATE STORY EVER

John Chatterton and John Mattera were days away from launching a quest they'd been planning for two years, a search for the treasure ship *San Bartolomé*, sunk in the seventeenth century and worth a hundred million dollars or more. To find it, they'd moved to the Dominican Republic and risked everything they owned and held dear. The discovery would make them rich beyond their dreams and engrave their names in the history books. *The New York Times* would profile them. Museums would hold black-tie affairs in their honor. Best of all, they knew just where to look.

And then their phone rang.

On the line was Tracy Bowden, a sixty-nine-year-old treasure hunter and a legend in the business. He said he had something big to discuss and asked if the men might fly to Miami to hear him out.

Chatterton and Mattera didn't have two minutes to spare in advance of their quest for the *San Bartolomé*. They'd vowed never to let anything put them off track. But there was an urgency in Bowden's voice they hadn't heard in the year since they'd met him, and Miami was just a two-hour flight from Santo Domingo; they could be there and back the same day. If nothing else, Bowden told great stories, and in treasure hunting, stories were the next best thing to gold. So, one morning in early 2008, they packed day bags and booked tickets, and went on their way. The treasure on board the *San Bartolomé* had been lost for four hundred years. It could wait another few hours for them to come find it.

In Miami, they rented a car and set out for Bowden's house. He wasn't like any other treasure hunter they'd met. He seemed to work in the shadows, shunning publicity and almost never teaming up with others. He didn't boast or issue bullshit claims. And he used little of the modern technology that had revolutionized underwater salvage, relying instead on old drawings, aging equipment, and his own decades-old notes to find wrecked ships loaded with silver and gold.

During his career, Bowden had discovered not one but two Spanish treasure galleons, and he'd done groundbreaking work on a third, yet neither Chatterton nor Mattera could judge how wealthy he'd become. His home in the Dominican Republic was hardly larger than a garage, and his salvage boat, the *Dolphin*, was good but not grand. As a successful treasure hunter, Bowden should have been able to live in a palace, a place with solid gold doorknobs and a moat. But as Chatterton and Mattera pulled into the driveway, they had to double-check the address. The house, while lovely, looked no different than any other in this ordinary suburban subdivision.

Inside, Bowden offered them coffee, but they hardly heard him. Everywhere they looked they saw treasure. In one room were silver coins embedded in coral; in another, centuries-old brass navigational instruments that museums would have paid a fortune to own. The china in Bowden's dining room was seventeenth-century Delftware, still as blue and white as the day it was made, and a match for a priceless set Mattera had seen in the Metropolitan Museum of Art in New York.

Bowden showed them other coins and artifacts, each with a story, each from a shipwreck he'd worked. He let them handle everything; touch was important, he said, otherwise a person could never really know this stuff. Finally, Mattera excused himself to use the bathroom. He stopped when he walked in the door.

Piled high in the bathtub were plastic bags filled with silver pieces of eight, all from the seventeenth century. He lifted one of the bags from the tub and inspected the contents through the flimsy plastic. For years, he'd seen silver coins like these sell for a thousand dollars apiece at auction. By his count, there were at least one hundred bags in the tub, and fifty coins to a bag. Mattera had never been quick at math, but he made this calculation right away. In a single bathtub, he was looking at five million dollars in treasure, all bundled in the cheapest baggies he'd ever seen, not even with Ziploc tops.

Returning to the living room, Mattera quick-stepped over to Chatterton and whispered in his ear.

"Take a leak."

"Huh?"

"Just do it. Go to the bathroom."

Chatterton shrugged. They were partners. So he went.

He returned a few minutes later, eyes bulging.

Bowden asked the men to join him at the dining room table, then got down to business. He'd done it all in his thirty-plus-year career—worked three galleons, a slave ship, and a legendary warship from the American Revolution. He'd been featured—twice—in *National Geographic* (Mattera had read the first of those stories when he was sixteen, then read it over and over again). He'd recovered world-class treasures and priceless artifacts. But there was something he wanted different from any of that—something rare beyond measure, a prize he'd been seeking for decades.

"Have you heard of Joseph Bannister?" he asked.

The men shook their heads.

Bannister, Bowden explained, was a well-respected seventeenth-century English sea captain in charge of transporting cargos between London and Jamaica. One day, for no reason anyone could explain, he stole the great ship he commanded, the *Golden Fleece*, and embarked on a pirating rampage, a genuine good guy gone bad in the 1680s, the Golden Age of Piracy. In just a few years, he became one of the most wanted men in the Caribbean. The harder the English tried to stop him, the more ingeniously he defied them. Soon, he'd become an international terror. The Brits swore they'd stop at nothing to hunt him down and hang him.

The Royal Navy pursued him on the open seas and used the full force of its might to try to find him. In those days, no one eluded a manhunt like that. But Bannister did. And his crimes got bolder and bolder. Finally, two navy warships pinned the pirate captain down, trapping him and his ship on an inescapable island. At the sight of a single frigate like these, most pirate captains threw up their hands and surrendered. Confronted by two? Even the toughest would drop to his knees and pray.

Not Bannister.

He and his crew manned cannons and rifles, and they waged an all-out battle against the two Royal Navy warships. The fighting lasted for two days. Bannister's ship, the *Golden Fleece*, was sunk in the combat. But Bannister won the war. Battered, and with many men dead and wounded, the navy ships limped back to Jamaica, and Bannister made his escape. It was a stunning defeat for the English and made Bannister a legend. Through the ages, however, his name had been lost to time.

"This is the greatest pirate story ever," Bowden said. "And no one knows about it. I want the *Golden Fleece*. And I think you guys can help find her."

Bowden did not have to explain the rarity of finding a pirate ship. Both Chatterton and Mattera knew that only one had ever been discovered and positively identified—the *Whydah*—lost in 1717 off Cape Cod and recovered by explorer Barry Clifford in 1984. The discovery had inspired books, documentaries, and an exhibit that continued to tour major museums more than twenty years after the find. It was clear, after the *Whydah* came up, that the world couldn't get enough of real pirates. Now Bowden was talking about going after a pirate ship captained by a man who sounded even more daring than the swashbucklers in Hollywood movies.

But that wasn't the only big news. Bowden also believed he knew the wreck's location. History was clear that the *Golden Fleece* had sunk off Cayo Levantado, a small island on the north coast of the Dominican Republic. Chatterton and Mattera knew the place; it was shimmering with white sandy beaches, and home to a five-star resort. For years, it had been known as Bacardi Island, used by the rum maker in ads to depict a paradise on earth. It was a manageable area to work.

Bannister's story had been legend in its day, but few people seem to have searched for the wreck. The late Dominican dictator Rafael Trujillo was rumored to have sent divers to Cayo Levantado as recently as the 1960s, but his men came up empty. Bowden picked up the search in 1984 but had found little more than modern debris at the island. In recent months, he'd come to believe that without the use of state-of-the-art equipment such as side-scan sonar and magnetometers, the *Golden Fleece* might never be found. Bowden had never gone in for technology like that; he'd stayed loyal to the time-tested ways that had made him. But he couldn't deny that guys like Chatterton and Mattera were the future. He knew they'd spent two years of their lives and a fortune to master the modern equipment, and he'd seen them make it work as they trained to hunt for their own galleon.

So, he offered them a deal.

He would give them 20 percent of the *Golden Fleece* if they found the pirate wreck for him. There might be gold, silver, and jewels aboard. There might be swords, muskets, pirate beads, peg legs, and daggers. Even skeletons. Or there might be nothing at all. In any case, Bowden wanted something bigger than treasure. He wanted Bannister, the greatest pirate of them all.

Bowden didn't require an answer on the spot. He knew Chatterton and Mattera were about to embark on their own journey. He admired their guts and vision—it reminded him of when he'd thrown over his own safe American life to seek his Caribbean fortune. But Bannister's *Golden Fleece* was once in a lifetime. Think it over, he told them, and give me your answer soon.

Pulling out of Bowden's driveway, the two partners said almost nothing, but each was thinking the same thing. Between them, they'd dived the most famous and fascinating shipwrecks in the world—*Titanic, Andrea Doria, Lusitania*, a mystery German U-boat, *Britannic, Arizona*—but neither could imagine anything cooler or rarer than a Golden Age pirate ship, especially one captained by a gentleman sailor turned rogue who had defeated the Royal Navy in battle. Every diver, at some deep level in his soul, dreamed of discovering a pirate ship. Yet, it never seemed to happen to anyone. Ever. Now, Chatterton and Mattera were being given a chance to find one as thrilling as any history had known.

Yet, both men knew they could never accept Bowden's offer.

They had trained for two years to find treasure, spent hundreds of thousands of dollars on boats and equipment, pledged their lives' savings to the cause. They'd put together a crew, researched at archives in Spain, consulted legends and gurus, nearly got into gunfights in wild but beautiful places, survived an attack by shadowy rivals. It all had led them to a target few others knew about, a galleon called the *San Bartolomé*, sunk in a hurricane in 1556 on the Dominican south coast, and still filled with mountains of treasure. They knew she was there. They'd come too far to turn their backs on her now.

In another era, the two partners might have delayed their search for this treasure ship, but time was running out for treasure hunters now. Governments and archaeologists had pressured many of the countries richest in treasure wrecks—Jamaica, Mexico, Cuba, the Bahamas, Bermuda—to outlaw private salvage. Just a few years earlier, the United Nations Educational, Scientific and Cultural Organization (UNESCO) established an international treaty effectively holding that shipwrecks more than one hundred years old belonged to the nations that lost them, not to the person who found them. Already, several countries had adopted the treaty. The Dominican Republic had managed to hold out thus far, but it was just a matter of time before it signed on, too. In 2008, if a person intended to hunt treasure in that country, that person had to go now.

Time was running out on the divers, too. Chatterton was fifty-seven, Mattera forty-six. Both were much older than most participants in deepwater-wreck diving, a sport that pushed the body to its limits and could paralyze or kill a person for the slightest mistake. Most got out of the game by forty; those who stayed longer often just dipped their toes on the weekends. But galleon hunting was no part-time job. To do it, Chatterton and Mattera had to be ready to spend full days in the water, perhaps for weeks or even months on end. They couldn't afford to grow older by searching for a pirate ship that very well might not be there.

And there was no guarantee they could afford a pirate ship search, in any case. Both men had begun life as blue-collar workers; neither was independently wealthy. Together, they'd invested nearly a million dollars to hunt for a galleon. If they detoured now for a pirate ship, they risked expending what remained of their funds to find a wreck that might have no treasure at all.

So, it was clear they needed to call Bowden to thank him for the pirate opportunity, and then to politely decline. Yet, even as they arrived at the Miami airport, neither man could reach for his phone.

In just ten years, John Chatterton had gone from being an underwater construction worker to perhaps the most famous living scuba diver in the world. He hadn't done it by being a great swimmer or

John Chatterton

by exploring beautiful coral reefs. He did it by going inside the most dangerous and deadly shipwrecks on earth.

These places were steel labyrinths, twisted like balloon animals by nature's temper and the ravages of time. Many lay at depths never intended for humans, where water pressure could collapse vital organs, and the buildup of nitrogen could disorient the mind and turn blood to foam. If a person stayed in the sport for a season, he would see fellow divers hallucinate underwater, get lost inside wrecks, become tangled in wire and cable. If he stayed longer, he would see them succumb to crippling nerve damage, become paralyzed, or drown. And that's if it didn't happen to him first. In his twenty years as a deepwater-wreck diver, Chatterton had seen nine men die, including a father and son, and one of his best friends.

He didn't risk these wrecks for the usual reasons—to stockpile artifacts, bragging rights, or mentions in dive magazines. In fact, he gave away much of the rare china and other relics he found, even when the stuff had great value. He pushed inside these wrecks because he believed, as he had since volunteering to fight on the front lines in Vietnam, that the only way to see what really mattered in life was to go to the places that were hardest to reach. After the war, he found those places to be made of steel and sunk hundreds of feet underwater.

Over the next decade, Chatterton went to dozens of the most dangerous wrecks, often penetrating into places thought too difficult, or deadly, for a human being to reach. By the time he was thirty-five, some veterans of the sport were calling him the greatest shipwreck diver they'd ever seen.

In 1997, Chatterton and dive partner Richie Kohler solved an international mystery by identifying a World War II German U-boat sunk off the coast of New Jersey. Three divers died during the six-year odyssey; Chatterton lost his marriage and his money, and several times he nearly lost his life. When people asked why he'd been willing to risk it—the sub had no gold or priceless artifacts aboard, just an identifying number—he told them the U-boat was his moment, that once-in-a-lifetime chance a person gets, if he's lucky, to see who he really is. For that reason, he would have rather died than turn his back on the wreck just because it got difficult, just because it couldn't be done.

The U-boat brought Chatterton and Kohler international acclaim. By 2004, they'd been featured in a book and in documentaries, and had become hosts of a popular television show on the History Channel. Chatterton, handsome and tall, and with a beautiful baritone voice, was paid to do speeches and endorse products. For the first time since Jacques Cousteau, a scuba diver had emerged from the sea and into the mainstream. People recognized him on the street. Kids asked for his autograph. Women sent him their pictures.

Most wreck divers, especially those past fifty, would have hung it up then and called it a career. But Chatterton kept pushing—body, technology, and nature—to go deeper into oceans and farther into wrecks. He saw more divers die. He reached even more places no one had ever gone.

His last big adventure had come in 2005, when he and Kohler put together an expedition to *Titanic*. The trip produced new insight into the ship's sinking, but in the end it hadn't pushed Chatterton to his limits. The location of the wreck was already known. The ship was sunk in thousands of feet of water, which meant he could do no more than remain in the Russian submersible that had delivered him to the site. Others had been there first.

After returning home from *Titanic*, Chatterton began to look for a new shipwreck project, something harder and rarer than anything he'd done. For more than a year, he came up empty.

Accountants and lawyers urged him to retire and invest his money. Relax. He redoubled his efforts. He couldn't pretend to be happy when Kohler announced he was going back to work in his family's glass-repair business. How could a man fix broken windows at Burger King after he'd pushed into a World War II German U-boat that no one in the world knew was there?

And yet, he wondered if Kohler might not have it right. Great wrecks were rare; a person could search for decades and never find another. Chatterton was fifty-six then. He didn't have decades anymore.

That's when he connected with Mattera. They'd met once or twice in the early 1980s, but hadn't spoken for twenty-five years. At a dive seminar in 2006, the men reacquainted; by the end of the weekend, they'd pledged their lives and their savings to an idea: They could find a Spanish galleon in Dominican waters, one of the last places on earth left to hunt treasure ships. And that they would find one, whatever it took.

Mattera's life was bigger than Hollywood even before he could drive. A butcher's son from Staten Island, he started risky businesses as a teenager that earned hundreds of thousands of dollars, and owned social clubs and taverns he was too young by law to enter. At twenty-three, he became embroiled in a historic war between factions of New York's Gambino crime family. One of his options was to plunge headfirst into the violence. His other option was even crazier—to become a cop. Mattera made his choice, and joined law enforcement. By thirty, he was a highly paid personal bodyguard, protecting celebrities and tycoons.

All the while, history and diving had been Mattera's salvation. In his younger years, when his life might have gone either way, he

John Mattera

found his center in history books, which he devoured by the dozens, and in libraries, where he camped out for days. To Mattera, history was more than just a collection of old stories; it was an insight into human nature, a crystal ball that told as much about the future as it did about the past. And he learned to scuba dive, not to look at pretty fish in tropical resorts, but to go deep into cold oceans, where a person could swim inside the wrecks and touch history for himself.

Mattera's first trip had been to the *Oregon*, a luxury liner sunk in 1886 in water deep enough to kill an experienced diver. He was just fourteen. Minors were forbidden on dive charters, so he showed up at the dock one morning with a case of beer and a cooler full of sandwiches from his father's butcher shop. He bribed the captain with this bounty, and an hour later he was on the high seas, bunking next to a rogues' gallery of bikers, dive gang members, and other hardened souls who were the pioneers of East Coast wreck diving. For three days, he pounded out portholes on the *Oregon*, looking for clues that would add to his understanding of her sinking. The trip hooked him. No matter where life took him after that—to high-tech shooting schools, to third-world countries doing contract work for the U.S. government, to glamorous international locales working security detail for celebrity clients—he came back to history and diving, the two things in a risky world that always told him the truth.

At forty, he sold his security company. It was a mistake—the money was too good to pass up and his partner wanted to sell—but there he was, with a big bank account and, for the first time in his life, nowhere to go at five every morning. Since boyhood, he'd dreamed of living somewhere warm enough to read his books outside at night, surrounded on all sides by shipwrecks. He'd done work in the Dominican Republic, loved its people and its history. And the shipwrecks were everywhere—this is where Columbus had landed, the gateway to the New World. A few months later, he moved to Santo Domingo, the Dominican capital, and began a life of leisure.

It lasted all of two months. Mattera was blue-collar—he needed to work, so he opened Pirate's Cove, a dive resort on the country's south coast, and began taking paying customers to centuries-old shipwrecks in the area. Few tourists, however, seemed interested in these living pieces of history; clients preferred to stay close to the resort, where the coral was pretty and the scotch on the rocks was never more than a few minutes away. Mattera continued to smile and show his guests a good time. At night, he took refuge in his books.

This time, he began reading a different kind of story—of popes and kings, explorers and conquistadors, and fearless captains who'd perished at sea. These were the stories of the galleons, the legendary Spanish treasure ships from the sixteenth and seventeenth centuries that carried vast fortunes from the New World back to Spain. The Dominican Republic—then called the island of Hispaniola—was the crossroads of it all.

Mattera put together a plan. Whatever the cost, he would go find a galleon of his own. The monetary reward would be staggering—he could buy his beloved New York Mets and have several treasure chests left over. More important, discovering a galleon would be historic, and for that he was willing to risk all he had.

That's when Chatterton showed up at a dive workshop Mattera was sponsoring at Pirate's Cove. The men hadn't seen each other in decades, but it took just a seaside lunch for Mattera to remember what he admired about the guy. Chatterton was in love with shipwrecks, but he bothered only with those that mattered to history and were difficult to work. Once he committed to a wreck, he never let go, no matter how deep or tangled the ship, and that was true even if it might cost him his life. More than anything, Chatterton believed in rare things; to him, "hard to find" equaled beauty, and he was willing to search the world for beautiful things no one else could find.

Standing in line at Miami's airport, the men marveled at the pirate story Bowden had told them, and especially about that badass captain, Joseph Bannister. Imagine a proper English gentleman stealing the ship he'd been trusted to sail, going on a whirlwind crime spree, then doing battle with two Royal Navy warships. And winning. You didn't even see stuff like that in the Johnny Depp movies.

In the terminal, they stopped at gift shops to pick up something for Chatterton's wife, Carla, and Mattera's fiancée, Carolina.

When they got to their gate, they knew it was time to call Bowden. They would be up-front with him and explain the reasons they couldn't deviate from their treasure quest. No one would understand better than an old treasure hunter like Bowden. They dialed him on speakerphone to deliver their regrets together.

Bowden answered on the first ring.

"Tracy, it's John and John. We're calling about the pirate ship and that captain, Bannister."

"Have you guys made a decision?"

"We have."

Numbers flashed on the arrivals screen. The flight to Santo Domingo started to board. Chatterton looked at Mattera. Mattera looked at Chatterton. Each waited for the other to speak.

"Tracy," Mattera said, "that pirate ship of yours is about to get found."

Chapter 2

BANNISTER'S ISLAND

Just before dawn in March 2008, in a tropical paradise on the north coast of the Dominican Republic, a leather-skinned fisherman with a cigarette in his mouth leaned over the side of his wooden rowboat and dropped a net into Samaná Bay, just as his ancestors had done day after day in this spot for centuries. In every direction, he and the waves were all that moved.

Soon, his boat began rocking, gently at first, then with a warning—something big was coming his way. In the distance, he could see the running lights of an onrushing boat and hear the hum of its outboard engines. It must have struck him as odd to see anyone in that kind of a hurry in Samaná Bay. There was nothing to rush to here; that was the beauty of the place.

He stood up and shined a flashlight. At the sight of it, the fast boat bit hard into the water and made a sweeping turn to the right. Only navy boats moved like that around here, but this vessel didn't look built to chase drug smugglers or check cargos. With her long back deck and shallow draft, she looked built to go out and find things.

The rowboat nearly capsized as the thirty-foot fiberglass vessel streaked past, but the fisherman still saw a name etched in red letters on her side—*Deep Explorer*—and two men waving to him from the bow. Chatterton and Mattera didn't normally operate their boat in the dark, especially in areas that were new to them, but they had a Golden Age pirate ship to find, and neither of them could wait on the sun to get started.

Even now, it seemed incredible to the men that they'd undertaken this mission. They'd invested two years of work, preparation, and much of their savings to set themselves up to find a treasure ship, only to abandon it all to search for a pirate ship no one had heard of, on the hunch of an old man who kept treasure in his bathtub and still used visual landmarks to find his way.

Yet, as they watched the glowing reds and blues on their instrument panel count down the distance to the island where the pirate ship sank—3.8 miles . . . 3.7 miles . . . 3.6 miles—neither man had a doubt he'd done the right thing. A pirate ship was the single hardest and rarest thing a person could discover underwater. And while galleons had been largely forgotten, the voices of pirates never stopped calling, to the imaginations of children and anyone else who believed the world could be thrilling if one only dared step off the dock.

As the first fires of a red sun spit over the horizon, Chatterton and Mattera called to their two crewmen to look through binoculars at the outline of the distant island. First out of the cabin was Heiko Kretschmer, a thirty-eight-year-old dive instructor, master handyman, and East Germany native who had risked his life at age eighteen to escape Communism and come west looking for adventure and a better life. Engines, regulators, transmissions, pumps—there was nothing Kretschmer couldn't fix with a roll of duct tape and a pair of pliers, and for that reason, and his relentless work ethic, Mattera considered him the most valuable man he'd ever employed.

Following him out of the cabin was Howard Ehrenberg, also thirty-eight, a Long Island native and computer whiz who had previous lives as a follower of the Grateful Dead, a head shop owner,

Heiko Kretschmer

Howard Ehrenberg

and a sound technician. He'd met Chatterton at a dive charity event and the two hit it off. Captivated by the idea of hunting treasure in a faraway land, he asked if Chatterton might use a technical guy who could dive.

"Ever worked with side-scan sonars, magnetometers, or sub-bottom profilers?" Chatterton asked.

"Never," Ehrenberg replied.

"Okay, you're perfect for us," Chatterton said, and Ehrenberg became crew.

Now the men could see Cayo Levantado, where Bannister's ship had sunk. Chatterton cut back on the throttle, and the men stood on the bow and admired the island's white sands and swaying palm trees. In the years since it had been featured in Bacardi ads, it had become home to a luxury resort, complete with sparkling swimming pools and a dock built for cruise ships.

"It's even more gorgeous than in those old *Playboy* magazine ads," Mattera said.

"You were looking at the ads?" Chatterton asked.

As the boat slowed its approach to the island, the men jumped down to the deck and got ready to search the waters. Until about the 1970s, treasure hunters did their work by putting on a snorkel or peering through glass-bottom buckets or, in the case of famed salvor Teddy Tucker, swaying in a window washer's chair under a hot-air balloon. And they didn't look for shipwrecks so much as for straight lines; nature didn't make anything linear, so when they saw straight edges and right angles, they knew they were seeing something man-made.

Technology changed all that. By the turn of the twenty-first century, salvors were using two primary tools to find shipwrecks. One of them, the side-scan sonar, used sound waves to paint images of the seafloor, but it wasn't the right tool for nonflat, coral-strewn bottoms like the ones in Samaná Bay. The other kind of technology, the magnetometer, was perhaps the most important piece in the treasure hunter's arsenal, and it was what Chatterton and Mattera planned to rely on for finding Bannister's ship.

Built into a streamlined, torpedo-shaped unit, the magneto-meter was designed to be towed by boat. When it passed over a ferrous object, it sensed the change in the earth's magnetic field caused by that object. The best units were exquisitely sensitive, able to detect even a screwdriver underwater. And while they did not react to precious metals like gold and silver (which do not contain iron), they were champions at detecting anchors, cannons, cannonballs, and other magnetic objects that had been part of well-armed colonial-era ships. Deluxe versions could cost more than a new Mercedes-Benz, but without a good one a treasure hunter flew blind. Chatterton and Mattera had chosen one of the best—the Geometrics G-882 cesium-vapor marine magneto-meter with an altimeter, priced at almost seventy thousand dollars, including software and upgrades.

Buying the magnetometer was the easy part. Towing it was art. An operator set up a predetermined grid, then towed the instru-ment slowly and methodically back and forth, a process known as "mowing the lawn." As the magnetometer detected ferrous metal objects below, the locations were recorded by the boat's onboard computers, which would make a chart of the hits. All the while, the captain would work to keep his magnetometer at optimum alti-tude, about ten feet above the seafloor. In that way, surveys often turned into an ongoing waltz with the sea. The finest captains were the ones who could dance.

Chatterton, Mattera, and crew planned to move in lanes seventy-five feet wide, each of which stretched for a mile, then to dive every one of the hits the mag detected, looking for any iron remnant from the wreck of the *Golden Fleece*. If the first grid failed to produce evidence of the shipwreck, the men would set up a new grid, adjacent to the last, and survey that area, and they would continue expanding, mowing more lawns until they'd found their pirate ship.

Ordinarily, that kind of search might have required surveying the waters around the entire island, a massive area. But Bowden had provided the men information from historical records that helped narrow the search. The *Golden Fleece*, he told them:

— had sunk in twenty-four feet of water
— had muskets scattered on her deck
— had been careening when confronted by the Royal
 Navy warships

It was the last clue that was most significant to the men. Wooden ships sailing in tropical waters were plagued by *Teredo* shipworms, barnacles, and other marine life that attached to the underside of a vessel's hull, slowing the ship and eating away at the wood. Left unchecked, these tiny scourges could bring down the mightiest of ships. To prevent the damage, crews cleaned and repaired hulls on a regular basis, and they did this by beaching the ships at high tide, then tilting them onto their sides as the water went out, a process known as careening. Since the *Golden Fleece* had been sunk while careening, it meant she would likely be found near a beach.

That, more than anything, gave the men hope for a quick discovery. By studying aerial photographs, they could see that there were no beaches on the northern coast of the island; it was all rocks, so a ship could not have careened there. The southern coast had beaches, but they'd been built for the resort in the past decade, so the island's southern coast was out, too.

The island's eastern coast had a large beach, but the area was rocky and exposed to wind and weather, making that location impractical and risky for a pirate looking to evade authorities.

That left the western beach, the only one that made sense. It was at the leeward side of the island, so it was protected from wind and waves. And it seemed well hidden from the open Atlantic, so passing ships couldn't see it. If a pirate captain chose to careen at Cayo Levantado, that's where he'd go every time. And that's where Chatterton went now.

He guided the *Deep Explorer* toward the southern tip of the western beach and allowed her to drift to a halt. Once the boat was settled, Kretschmer prepped the magnetometer, while Ehrenberg set up the software program to collect data. Just after dawn, it was already eighty degrees outside, the coolest it would be all day.

Mattera reminded the men that the pirate ship had been lost in twenty-four feet of water. Depths could rise and fall at random near islands like this, so they would start their survey a good distance offshore and work their way in toward the beach. That way, they wouldn't miss any area that included the appropriate depth.

The men were ready to go. Mattera pulled out his Nikon D300, set the delayed shutter, then joined the others for a photo. After the camera snapped, he grabbed four diet sodas from the cooler, passed them out, and raised a toast.

"To Captain Bannister," he said.

"To Captain Bannister," the others echoed.

"One unlucky sonofabitch. First, the Royal Navy hunts him down. Now us."

The men towed for hours. They stopped only to wolf down soggy tuna sandwiches, then continued their survey until the waters turned choppy and the magnetometer began porpoising over the surface. It was frustrating to halt work so early in the day, but the bay stayed calm only until early afternoon in these parts, and without quiet waters their readings might be skewed. To both Chatterton and Mattera, survey work was science; there was no room for imprecision. So they pulled in their gear and turned the *Deep Explorer* around.

Twenty minutes later, they docked their boat in a small channel four miles from the island. By a stroke of good luck, Mattera's soon-to-be father-in-law, a former admiral and chief of staff of the Dominican Navy, owned a little villa on the bay, and it was here that the team would be living temporarily while they searched for the *Golden Fleece*. Overlooking the water, the home was cut into the cliff face and accessible only by a narrow road that wound through a mango orchard. Inside, the building opened into a spacious indoor-outdoor living area. All the bedrooms had private terraces. The view of the sunset was spectacular. Mattera's future in-laws would want it back before long.

The men unloaded their gear, but work wasn't done for the day. Ehrenberg still needed to process the data the team had collected, using custom software programs to make a map of the hits detected by the magnetometer. A day or two later, the team would dive those hits. Even the smallest blip would be investigated.

Chatterton and Mattera stepped onto the veranda and called their significant others; in this remote area, if they stood in just the right spot and tilted slightly toward the moon, they could catch a cell phone signal that might last for an entire five-minute call.

Chatterton reached Carla at their home on the Maine coast, where she was curled up on the couch and watching a movie with their yellow Labrador retriever, Chili. Carla missed John and did not approve when she learned that her husband had eaten Zucaritas—Frosted Flakes—for dinner three nights in a row.

Mattera got Carolina while she was reading in the study of their apartment in Santo Domingo. He laughed when she asked if he'd found "Long John Silver," yet the question jarred him. For all the luck shipwreck hunters had in finding real pirate ships, he and Chatterton might as well have been looking for Noah's Ark.

Even during the Golden Age of Piracy, between 1650 and 1720, pirates were rare. Precise numbers are hard to come by, but according to British historian Peter Earle, in the period around 1700, "it seems unlikely that they ever had much more than twenty ships at any one time and less than two thousand men." By contrast, there might have been as many as eighty thousand sailors and navy men working on legitimate ships in the Atlantic and Caribbean at the time. It's difficult to say how many pirate ships in total might have sailed during the seventy-year Golden Age, but the number, in any case, would have been small, perhaps fewer than a thousand.

Not all of those ships had been lost or sunk. Some were captured by authorities; others were sold or traded by the pirates and put to lawful uses. So the number of lost pirate ships is just a fraction of those that ever sailed. Finding any of them would be a long shot. Identifying one would be virtually impossible. The reason lay in the shadowy nature of crime itself.

Stealth was the lifeblood of a pirate ship. To survive, she had to be invisible, anonymous. Pirate captains didn't publish crew lists or file sailing plans, and they didn't paint names on the hulls of their ships. Whenever possible, they sailed in secrecy. These measures helped them evade the forces that hunted them, but it also meant that when they sank, they didn't merely settle to the bottom; they disappeared from existence. No government went looking for them because they belonged to no country. Witnesses to a sinking couldn't have described the location precisely in any case, as measures of longitude were unreliable during that era. If any pirates survived the ship's demise, they weren't going to report the loss to authorities.

Nature took over from there. It might take just a few years for mud and sand to bury a shipwreck completely.

That didn't mean, however, that a sunken pirate ship was never to be seen again. Over the ages, it was near certain that explorers, fishermen, and even snorkelers had stumbled across the scattered remains of Golden Age pirate ships. Few, however, would have known that the debris was special, or could have identified what they'd found. Much of what a pirate ship carried—dishes, rigging, tools, ballast stones, coins, weapons, even cannons—was carried by merchant ships, too, which meant that even if a finder dared to dream he'd discovered a pirate ship, proving it would be near impossible.

Except for one man.

As a boy, American Barry Clifford had heard stories about the pirate captain "Black Sam" Bellamy, whose ship had been lost in 1717 off Cape Cod. As an adult, Clifford went out and found Bellamy's ship, the *Whydah*, not far from Clifford's own childhood home. News of the 1984 discovery reverberated worldwide, but it wasn't just the artifacts or piles of silver or even the story of the crew's dramatic end in a storm that fired people's imaginations. It was a bell Clifford had pulled from the wreckage, inscribed "The Whydah Gally 1716." It made identification of the wreck ironclad, and the *Whydah* the first pirate ship ever confirmed to be found. No one else had ever gotten so lucky.

But that didn't keep capable people from trying.

In the years after Clifford's discovery, research teams claimed to have found the ships of two of history's most famous pirates. Neither team, however, seemed able to prove the identity of its wreck.

The first of the two discoveries had come in 1996 at Beaufort Inlet, just off the North Carolina coast. There, a shipwreck exploration firm discovered what appeared to be the wreck of Blackbeard's flagship, *Queen Anne's Revenge*, which had run aground and sunk in 1718.

Almost immediately, the governor of North Carolina publicly announced that the notorious pirate's ship had been found. Just as fast, some experts cast doubt on the wreck's identity. Among their objections: The artifacts could have come from any merchant ship of the time; the *Adventure*, a ship that sank with Blackbeard's, was nowhere to be found; and one of the cannons discovered seemed marked with a date of 1730 or 1737, at least twelve years after the loss of *Queen Anne's Revenge*. Debate raged, a technical back-and-forth that never settled the matter. In 2005, experts wrote in *The International Journal of Nautical Archaeology*, "The incontrovertible fact remains that no single piece of evidence, or trend of circumstantial evidence, indicates that this wrecked vessel is actually the *Queen Anne's Revenge*." They also addressed the issue of money, noting that the project had received nearly one million dollars in grant funding to date, and was seeking almost four million dollars more. "One may speculate," the authors wrote, "that the investments already made, plus the possibility of future financial gains, may indeed be the reason for a continued emphasis on the identification of the wreck, and a refusal to consider that the identification could be flawed."

None of that deterred North Carolina officials and entrepreneurs from opening exhibits, walking tours, historical reenactments—even Blackbeard's Miniature Golf—and tourists flocked to the area.

A second possible pirate ship was found in the Dominican Republic in 2007, when a team from Indiana University was led to a site they thought to be the *Quedagh Merchant*, the 1699 wreck of infamous pirate captain William Kidd. Media such as NPR, CNN, and *The Times* of London swarmed to the story, telling how the researchers had found the ship, exploring theories about Kidd's possible innocence, and recounting how Kidd had been hanged by the British (the rope had broken on the first attempt; after the second did the job, his body was hung over the River Thames for three years as a warning to those who fancied the pirate life).

Yet, even as plans were made with the Dominican government to turn the wreck site into an underwater national park, the Indiana University team didn't seem willing to say it had definitive proof of the wreck's identity. Charles Beeker, who led the expedition, said, "As an archaeologist, I cannot say conclusively that it's Captain Kidd's ship, but as a betting man, I am betting on the ship."

Four years later, Indiana University officials would be speaking in stronger terms about the identity of the wreck, though a smoking gun—proof-positive evidence—still hadn't been found. Nonetheless, the discovery generated more than two million dollars in grants, a push by the Dominican government to promote the site for tourism, and a permanent exhibit, "*National Geographic* Treasures of the Earth," at the Children's Museum of Indianapolis.

A few other pirate ship claims had been made over the years, all based on circumstantial evidence, not a smoking gun among them.

But grants and exhibits and circumstantial evidence and miniature golf didn't cut it for Chatterton and Mattera. Neither could imagine going through life thinking he'd probably found a pirate ship. Neither could imagine going to sleep at night wondering if he'd really done what he'd dreamed.

But that was the rub with a pirate ship. No matter what anyone did, it was near certain he wouldn't find proof of identity. Even if Chatterton and Mattera did find the *Golden Fleece*, even if historians wrote about them in books and curators gave them a museum exhibit of their own, without definitive proof there would always be doubt. And that was an outcome neither man could abide.

As Chatterton and Mattera hung up the phone with their significant others, Ehrenberg walked onto the veranda at the villa holding his laptop high. The screen showed a Rorschach-like pattern, the hits detected by the magnetometer that day. The men had to look twice at what they were seeing. Several of the hits were clustered in an area the size of a large wooden sailing ship. Chatterton and Mattera had been around long enough to know things didn't happen so perfectly with shipwrecks—no one found what they were looking for on the very first day. Still, staring at that beautiful blotch, they couldn't help but think they'd done it, that they'd already discovered the *Golden Fleece*. Now they just had to go out the next morning and find her.

Chapter 3

NONE OF THIS MAKES SENSE

The men didn't talk much during sunrise as they loaded the *Deep Explorer* and set out for the island, but inside, each was hoping he would be the first to pull up a hook or a cannon from the *Golden Fleece*. Even a handful of beads—the colorful and vivid trinkets that Golden Age pirates wove into their clothing, hair, and beards, and which terrified the pirates' prey—would do.

No one expected to find the pirate ship as she'd sunk, skeletons frozen in fighting positions, a skull-and-crossbones flag crumpled beneath shattered beams. If they got lucky, they would see a part of the shipwreck lying exposed—the fluke of an anchor, a cannon's muzzle, broken wood from the hull. More likely, they would see small pieces, or even shadows, of the objects that had made their magnetometer react. But all they needed was one artifact, and that would lead to the rest.

Not everyone would dive at once. Two of the men would remain on board the boat, securing it against drift and guarding against bandits who might steal electronics and guns. Firearms were necessary in these wilds; you didn't leave home, or shore, without them.

Arriving on site, Chatterton and Ehrenberg geared up and splashed. Carrying handheld metal detectors, they descended to a depth of twenty feet, to the first of the hits on their chart. In the sand, Chatterton saw a silver shape. Swimming toward the object, he could see it was box shaped—treasure chest shaped—which only made him swim faster, until he reached the container and discovered not pieces of eight or emeralds inside, but a parrot fish. He surfaced and shouted back to the boat.

"Fish trap."

Mattera made the notation, but when he turned back Chatterton was gone, already onto the next hit. Chatterton and Ehrenberg floated above a straightened section of iron that rose from a coral mass on the bottom. Straight lines were the stuff of shipwreck hunters' dreams. Chatterton moved closer, then pulled out a slate and wrote:

ANCHOR

Ehrenberg's eyes lit up. Chatterton looked even closer. Slowly, he erased the word and wrote a new one:

WORKING

A working anchor was one that had been lowered by a ship in the routine course of its business, but which had become stuck in the coral or otherwise lost on the bottom. Chatterton and Mattera had found many such working anchors in the Dominican Republic while learning to use their gear, and though it was interesting to see these pieces, they were rarely associated with a wreck. The kind of anchor Chatterton and Mattera wanted likely would be lying flat on the bottom, meaning it had gone down with the ship.

Ehrenberg went after the third hit. He, too, found a working anchor. Back on board the *Deep Explorer*, the men drove the boat to the next set of numbers, which Mattera and Kretschmer would dive.

Their exploration proved equally fruitless: some telephone cable and a hammer. Still, cruising back to the villa, the team couldn't hide its excitement. The magnetometer had worked.

And there were more hits to explore the next morning. No one wanted to say it, but each of them believed it would be just a matter of days before the *Golden Fleece* was theirs.

Too jazzed to stay home that evening, the team went to Fabio's, a pizza parlor they'd nicknamed for its owner, who had hair (but little else) like the Italian male model. They ordered meat-lovers pies and Presidente Lights, and took turns listing how they would spend whatever treasure they might find aboard the *Golden Fleece*. This is what each man vowed to do with his haul:

Mattera

- Buy a five-hundred-acre ranch in Pennsylvania
- Buy a Beechcraft King Air B200 (capable of flying from Miami to the Dominican Republic)
- Buy the Binghamton Mets, the New York Mets' minor-league team (a pirate ship, if it had treasure on board, wouldn't carry enough to buy a major-league franchise)

Chatterton

- Buy the blue Maserati in the window of the Fort Lauderdale dealership (using his Mini Cooper and a bag of gold coins as trade-ins)
- Take a three-month tour of Machu Picchu and the Galápagos Islands
- Hire a chauffeur (must wear traditional chauffeur's hat)
- Buy a solid gold dive helmet

Ehrenberg

- Stage a private concert by the remaining members of the Grateful Dead (the band he followed for three years in the late 1980s)

— Buy an Aston Martin DB5, the fabled James Bond car
equipped with ejector seat, machine guns, bulletproof
plates, and tire spikes
— Buy the best drum set in the world, along with a house far
enough from neighbors so they wouldn't complain about
the noise when he played it

Kretschmer
— Move his wife, daughter, and stepson from the
Dominican Republic to the United States

At closing, the men paid the bill and walked into the steamy night.
They felt lucky to be staying at the villa, with its dependable
plumbing and view of the bay. They had no doubt, however, that
Mattera's future father-in-law would soon want his place back for
family getaways and weekend entertaining, just another reason to
find the pirate ship fast.

The men were back at the island and diving hits the next
morning. This time, they found a toolbox, a radio antenna, and
three fish traps. Mattera logged the results and called the others
to the wheelhouse.

"I know this is frustrating. But we gotta keep mowing the lawn
and diving the hits; it's part of the game. So back at it tomorrow
morning."

Chatterton fired up the engines and put the *Deep Explorer* into
a sweeping turn that brought the men to within fifty yards of the
beach at Cayo Levantado. They watched sunbathers stretch under
the rays of a giant sun.

"Every woman is in a bikini," Chatterton said. "Poor Bannister
never got a view like this."

The team began a new survey the next day. Chatterton moved

the *Deep Explorer* east and west, shortening the towline around jagged reefs, speeding up when waters turned shallow. And the men did it again the next day, and the next after that, until they'd compiled a new set of targets to dive. Some of the hits looked certain to be duds—tiny specks off by themselves in areas too deep or too shallow. But Chatterton insisted they dive every one. The first time they skipped something, that would be the musket ball that led to the ship's rigging that led to the cannon that led to the *Golden Fleece*.

The next time they got in the water, the men found a modern ax, a paint can, and some drainpipe.

And that's how it went for the next week: more surveys, a few rainouts, and dozens of hits, but no trace of Bannister's ship. Despite it, the men stayed in high spirits, knowing the wreck couldn't hide from them. It had been folly, in any case, to think they might find a Golden Age pirate ship in the first days of exploring. Things only worked like that in the movies.

For the next three weeks, the men expanded their survey westward, but found nothing important. One afternoon, Chatterton gunned the boat's engines and headed east into the open Atlantic. At the entrance to Samaná Bay, he shifted to idle and brought the craft to a halt. Standing on the bow, he and Mattera looked back toward the island, and they kept looking until the sun disappeared.

At Fabio's that night, they laid things out for their crew.

"There are problems with the island," Mattera said.

In Bannister's time, a ship could have careened only on the island's western beach. But that beach could be seen from the open Atlantic; they'd proved it themselves that day. Bannister was a capable man on the run from the Royal Navy. It seemed unlikely he would have made himself so visible, and so vulnerable, by beaching the *Golden Fleece* in view of passing ships.

And that wasn't the only problem with Cayo Levantado. The surrounding waters were full of shallow reefs capable of tearing open the hull of a large sailing ship. There was no way a captain smart enough to defeat British warships in battle would risk bringing his ship into a minefield like that.

And then there was the issue of depth. According to Bowden, the *Golden Fleece* had sunk in twenty-four feet of water. It was true that the depths of seafloors could change over time, but the men had to move the *Deep Explorer* nearly a half mile offshore to reach waters twenty-four feet deep—too far from shore to careen a ship.

Pizzas arrived and everyone dug in.

"Maybe it's us," Mattera said. "What do we know about seventeenth-century naval strategy? I'm a bodyguard. Chatterton's a commercial diver. Heiko, you're a mechanic, and Howard, no offense, you're a geek."

"Maybe," Chatterton said. "But the *Golden Fleece* is out there. If we can find fish traps and hammers, we can damn well find a pirate ship at some tiny bullshit island."

Standing on the bow of the *Deep Explorer* the next morning, Mattera caught sight of a twenty-foot boat about a mile away, bobbing on the waves but not moving. Probably sightseers or a fishing charter, he figured, but not locals; the boat looked too expensive for that. Later in the day, the boat was still there. Mattera showed it to Chatterton, who watched it through binoculars.

"They haven't moved in hours," Mattera said. "Drive toward them, real slow. I want to see what they do."

Chatterton took the wheel and set course for the target. The distant boat began moving away, leaving white foam in its wake.

"Think they were watching us?" Mattera asked.

"I don't know," Chatterton said. "But now I'm watching them."

The crew collected strong magnetometer hits over the next two weeks but found nothing old when they dove them. Every miss frustrated them more, especially Chatterton, who found himself tossing and turning at night, trying to figure out what he and the others were doing wrong. "Think creatively," he told himself. "Think like John Chatterton." But the answers never came.

One evening, while the men were studying aerial photography of the island, the power went out at the villa, as it did almost daily.

"Goddamn it!" Chatterton yelled, slamming down a stack of photographs. Again, he would need to sleep without covers, windows open, a mosquito net his only protection against the swarms. In minutes, he was dripping sweat and stringing together expletives that would have made the pirates blush.

The move to Samaná hadn't been easy for the team. The sudden decision to swerve from treasure to pirates had required all four men to uproot their already-uprooted lives. They'd planned to search for treasure near Santo Domingo, population nearly three million, a place of modern conveniences and a dazzling nightlife. Samaná, on the other hand, was a portal into the past. A treacherous six-hour drive to the north of Santo Domingo, its roads had pumpkin-sized potholes, chickens ran wild in town, and ice was a luxury.

Just reaching the place required an explorer's heart. To get there, the men had loaded their belongings into a truck, then picked up a makeshift road that took them past abandoned towns, feral dogs, and cliffs so muddy a small tire slide would have plunged them into an unfindable grave. For miles at a stretch they saw no living thing. Halfway to Samaná, Mattera ran over a wild pig that had darted in front of the truck. An hour later, he reached for his gun when a gang of men with machetes refused to move off the road. (He steered around them and never looked back.) On the outskirts of Samaná, a bull wandered into the street and lowered its horns to fight them. If Samaná Bay hadn't been the most beautiful place the men had ever seen, with its jumping dolphins, elderly fishermen, and crystalline waters, the mosquitos alone might have driven them mad.

Mattera knocked on the door and invited Chatterton to sleep with him in the pickup truck.

"There's no room in that Mitsubishi," Chatterton said. "The seats don't recline. How are two grown men going to sleep in that?"

Mattera shrugged and walked away. In the driveway, he got into the truck and put his Glock under his right thigh—a running vehicle made a tempting target in this part of the country. Cranking the air conditioning, he was asleep in minutes, and he stayed that way until a strange figure began pounding on the passenger window. Mattera reached for his gun, but then saw it was Chatterton, standing in the driveway wearing nothing but his underwear and a mosquito net.

"Jesus, John, do you want to get shot?" Mattera said, rolling down the window.

"It would've put me out of my misery. Can I sleep here?"

"Sure. But only if we can cuddle."

"Don't make me laugh, Mattera. Laughing makes me sweat."

Chatterton climbed in the truck and the men sat staring up at the stars.

"We're looking in the wrong place," Chatterton said. "I've been around a long time, and I'm telling you—none of this makes sense."

Rain pounded Samaná the next morning, so for the first time in a month, the men took a day off. Chatterton needed to open a bank account anyway, and Mattera had errands in town.

After the usual cold shower, Chatterton went to call Carla. His cell phone was out of power. He opened his laptop to send her an email. Dead.

The men went to the local bank. Inside, they waited in line for nearly an hour before a manager explained that Chatterton would need more documents in order to open an account, and in any case would need to wait several weeks before paperwork could be processed. Mattera could see veins bulging from Chatterton's neck.

"You gotta go with it, John," Mattera said. "This isn't the States. We're in the wild up here. Third world."

Chatterton thanked the manager, and he and Mattera went outside.

"It takes three weeks to open a goddamn bank account?" Chatterton asked. "I have to break my ass to give them my money?"

The men were back on the water the next morning. Only the outer edges of the western beach remained to be surveyed. Chatterton landed the boat near the northern edge and set up a grid, and by sunrise the men were mowing the lawn. By now, the team had become so sensitive to the magnetometer's blips and spikes that they could tell the fish traps from the anchors just by scanning the data readouts. But they dove every hit, fearful that the first one they skipped would be the key that led to the pirate ship.

And then, in late April, nearly two months after the team had launched its search, their magnetometer registered an especially strong reading. Mattera had a feeling about this one. He and Kretschmer got in the water. Not far down, they saw an unmistakable shape rising four feet out of the sand. Mattera wrote on his slate:

CAREFUL!

It was a grappling hook, an anchor-like device with sharpened claws. Ominous, even frightening, in appearance, they were often used by salvors—and opportunistic pirates—to pull up objects from sunken ships.

Mattera drifted slowly toward the hook and pulled it from the mud. Four claws bloomed from the shaft, each still razor sharp. The base, overgrown in gravel-colored coral, made Mattera's heart race; by his estimation, it was at least three hundred years old. He glanced at his depth gauge. Twenty-four feet.

He motioned to Kretschmer to summon the others, and soon the four-man team was in the water and gathered around. One by one, they examined the hook's hand-forged black iron and timeless design. But mostly, they were impressed by its age. The grappling hook was period. It had come from Bannister's time.

They would have given anything to salvage the hook, but no one dared expose it to air for fear it would oxidize and fall apart in their hands. Instead, they photographed it and buried it back on the bottom. Topside, they made sober notes in their books, but couldn't hide their excitement. Beneath them, at just the right depth, was the first solid piece of evidence that a late-seventeenth-century ship had sunk at the island. No one said it aloud, but everyone was thinking the same: They'd found a piece of the *Golden Fleece*.

The men stayed out late that night, raising toasts to Bannister and his pirate crew. Back at the villa, after stripping for bed, Mattera found a book about anchors in the villa's small library. The power went out, but by flashlight he found a page that showed a grappling hook almost identical to the one he'd discovered that morning. Carrying the flashlight in one hand and the book in the other, he made his way to Chatterton's bedroom and knocked on the door. Receiving no answer, he let himself in. Chatterton awoke with a start.

"Jesus, Mattera, you look like Jacob Marley!"

"Look at this book."

Chatterton pressed his face to the page and saw a photograph of the very same grappling hook they'd found that day. The author dated it to the late seventeenth century.

Chatterton fist-bumped Mattera.

"You know what, partner?" he said. "I think we just found our pirate wreck."

The men set out early the next morning for Cayo Levantado, setting up a new grid centered over the grappling hook, this one with narrower lanes—a hard-target search. If the hook belonged to the *Golden Fleece*, there would be more pieces of the wreck nearby.

They surveyed for days. This time, they didn't even find fish traps. Whatever ship had used the grappling hook was long gone. Chatterton got out of his dive gear and sat on the stern, talking to no one in particular.

"I've found wrecks in the open Atlantic, in hundreds of square miles of water. Why can't I find a pirate ship in an area no bigger than Central Park?"

Chatterton was in no mood to drive the boat, so Kretschmer took the wheel and set course for the villa. When the water turned choppy, Kretschmer eased back on the throttle, but water still broke over the vessel. Chatterton charged into the wheelhouse.

"What the hell are you doing, Heiko? We have water over the bow! We have a hundred thousand dollars of electronics in here! What's wrong with you?"

Mattera put up his hands.

"Whoa, John. It's Mother Nature; it's nobody's fault. He's driving fine."

"He is not driving fine. Salt water on electronics means we're out of business. If you can't drive, Heiko, don't take the goddamn wheel."

Mattera motioned for Kretschmer to leave the wheelhouse, then closed the door behind him.

"John, you gotta calm down. You're going to give yourself an aneurysm here, and I'm going to be the one feeding you oatmeal while you drool on yourself, and I don't want to do that."

Chatterton told Mattera he just wanted things done right—anything less than perfect wouldn't be enough to find something as elusive, as impossible, as a pirate ship. In the past, it had been his commitment to excellence—his insistence that things be done beautifully, not just correctly—that had delivered him into places others couldn't reach.

Chatterton let a few minutes pass, then took a deep breath and walked out of the wheelhouse. At the stern, he found Kretschmer smoking a Marlboro.

"Heiko, I'm sorry for yelling," he said.

"No problem, John. Don't worry about it."

"No, really, I'm sorry."

"It's forgotten."

"Thanks. I think I yelled because I have a rash."

Kretschmer looked confused.

"I'm sorry?" he said.

Slowly, Chatterton turned around and lowered his shorts, exposing his buttocks. A grin spread across his face.

"Heiko, do I have a rash?"

Kretschmer looked shocked, then horrified. The others started laughing. This was trademark Chatterton humor—a sudden shift from tension into farce.

"Heiko!" Chatterton called, his butt still showing, "Give me a hug!"

With that Chatterton reached for Kretschmer, who ran as fast as he could. Chatterton began chasing him, bottomless and hot on his heels.

"Run, Heiko!" the others called out.

"I have a gun!" Kretschmer warned, and now he was laughing, too, but Chatterton would not stop chasing him. His only means of escape was into the water, and that's where he leaped.

Chatterton called out over the side.

"Heiko! Give me a hug!"

It had been two months since the team started work at the island. As much as either man hated to do it, Chatterton and Mattera agreed it was time to bring Bowden up to date. It would be easy, since Bowden was in the area doing work on his dive boat.

They met him the next evening at Tony's, a restaurant on Samaná's main street fancy enough to serve ice with its sodas. Bowden looked like a kid about to open a birthday present, which made the disappointing report even harder to deliver. But deliver it they did. If the *Golden Fleece* had sunk anywhere near the western beach at Cayo Levantado, they assured Bowden, they would have found her by now.

Bowden asked about the other parts of the island. Chatterton explained the team's thinking—that no other area at the island had been suitable for careening in the seventeenth century, and in any case, no pirate captain, no good one, at least, would have left himself exposed in those parts.

Bowden ordered a glass of wine. He seemed, in the most gentlemanly of ways, to be annoyed.

"Are you sure you guys didn't miss something? Would it help to go try again?"

Mattera could see Chatterton's face reddening. He jumped in before his partner could answer.

"Absolutely, Tracy. Don't worry. We'll get it."

The rest of the dinner was spent telling old war stories about the early days of East Coast wreck diving. Between laughs and refills on drinks, Bowden spoke about the importance of patience in hunting shipwrecks. During these moments, it was all Chatterton could do to hold his tongue.

Driving home that evening, Chatterton and Mattera talked about how much they liked Bowden. He was warm and engaging, and his stories were often speckled with pearls of wisdom about salvage, instinct, and life. Still, there was no point in redoing their search at the island, as Bowden had suggested. Mattera said he didn't think they had to. He'd been thinking, and it had occurred to him that neither he nor Chatterton knew anything about Joseph Bannister. Perhaps there was something in the pirate captain's story that might help. They were getting nowhere in their search for the *Golden Fleece*, so maybe it was better to search for the man than the ship.

Chatterton loved that kind of thinking. He asked what Mattera needed to make it happen.

"Just time to hit the books," Mattera said.

The men pulled into the entrance of the villa's zigzag driveway.

"I can't wait to see what you find out about our pirate," Chatterton said.

"Me, too," Mattera replied. "Because you know what, John? I've had good street instincts all my life. And I've got a feeling about this guy."

Chapter 4

A WELL-RESPECTED ENGLISHMAN

Santo Domingo, the capital city of the Dominican Republic, looked like Manhattan, London, and Hong Kong rolled into one when Mattera arrived to start his research. After living in Samaná for the previous two months, he needed a while to adjust to the sights and sounds of modernity.

He stopped first at home, where he picked up Carolina for a breakfast date. He could not have hoped for a more supportive fiancée. Rather than hurry him to finish his pirate hunt, she had been sending home-cooked barbecued chicken and macaroni salad to the villa, and promising to help with research when needed. Today, he would take her up on that offer. Carolina had earned a master's degree in economics from the Sorbonne in Paris, spoke fluent English, Spanish, and French, and was proficient in Italian and Mandarin. She was also a beauty, elegant and curvaceous, with long black hair and wide dark eyes. Best of all, she liked shipwrecks.

After breakfast, the couple headed to the Museo de las Casas Reales, one of the country's finest museums and archives, located in Santo Domingo's historic Colonial Zone. Mattera and Carolina checked hundreds of sources there for references to the pirate Joseph Bannister. But for a few scant mentions, they could find nothing more about him than what Mattera already knew. If he were to learn more, he would have to expand his search.

A few days later, Mattera was on a plane by himself to New York. He didn't bother checking into his hotel when he arrived.

Instead, he took a taxi to one of his favorite places: the main branch of the New York Public Library on Forty-Second Street. Since boyhood, he'd loved the iconic Beaux Arts building and its massive, seemingly endless collection of resources, manuscripts, and even old baseball cards. Like many, Mattera considered it to be the world's greatest library.

He began in the maritime section, as he always had during high school. He hadn't been to this place for years, but the smell was the same—a perfume atomized from the must of old books, oils from wooden bookshelves, and bleach from freshly scrubbed floors. Even in the 1970s, when New York City seemed to many to be dirty and neglected, this place remained spotless, a repository of history impervious to time.

Standing on tiptoe, Mattera began pulling volumes from the stacks, and he spent the rest of the day, and the next, pushing into the farthest colonies of the library, making copies of whatever documents made the slightest mention of Bannister.

The next morning, he was first in line at the Strand, a famed bookstore at Twelfth Street and Broadway. It had opened in 1927 and advertised eighteen miles of new, used, and rare titles, and Mattera came ready to look through them all. He estimated that he'd spent a month of his life at the Strand already, going back to his purchase of Robert Marx's *Shipwrecks of the Western Hemisphere* when he was twelve. For the next several hours, he scoured every section that related to pirates, maritime history, Hispaniola, the Caribbean, shipwrecks, and the Royal Navy. He found only one or two volumes that made reference to Bannister, but they added more to the narrative he was building.

That night, Mattera met a childhood friend for dinner at a Staten Island diner. They talked of old times and reminisced about the pirates they'd known growing up. Only at dawn, when the friends needed to return to work, did they hug each other good-bye.

Mattera spent that day visiting rare map dealers, then he rented a car and began driving south and west, dropping in at libraries and used bookstores. A few days later, he was at the archives in Colonial Williamsburg in Virginia, where he found letters from English officials describing their pursuit of the pirates. Then it was on to London to visit various archives, where he discovered important papers and correspondence that dated to the seventeenth century. None of it provided more than a glimpse of Bannister, but taken together, the information he gathered over his journey told a singular story.

Joseph Bannister began his career not as a pirate but as its opposite: a well-respected English merchant sea captain responsible for carrying valuable cargo like animal hides, logwood, indigo, and sugar, and sometimes well-to-do passengers, on the profitable trade route between London and Jamaica. By 1680, he was making the transatlantic trip perhaps twice a year at the helm of a ship called the *Golden Fleece*, an expensive and heavily armed vessel owned by wealthy merchants who were likely based in London. These owners must have had great faith in Bannister—every cargo was worth a fortune, the *Golden Fleece* many times more.

Their trust seemed well placed. Before a man became a merchant captain, he spent years proving himself, starting perhaps as a ship's boy and, if capable and reliable, working his way up to officer of the watch or even first mate. If he were truly exceptional, he might make captain. By then, he likely would have been in his thirties, and would have shown himself time and again to be loyal to the masters of his ship.

Only the best captains were entrusted with a transatlantic route. The trip could take between three weeks and three months, depending on weather and how accurately one made landfall. In charge of a crew of perhaps sixty or seventy, a captain like Bannister needed to be a leader of men as much as a first-rate sailor. Often, a ship like the *Golden Fleece* found herself in peril, at the mercy of hurricanes or reef systems that could smash the sturdiest vessels, or vulnerable to pirates, who prowled the oceans looking for prey. To avoid being ruined by nature, a captain like Bannister would draw on years of experience with weather and cartographic charts. To evade pirates, he'd best learn to think like one, in order to stay one step ahead.

Given Bannister's trade, it is likely he hailed from near London or another of the English ports, perhaps Bristol or Liverpool. The ship he captained was impressively large, near one hundred feet long and carrying as many as twenty-eight cannons, roughly equal in size and power to a small Royal Navy warship. A pirate who chose to attack her did so at his peril.

The ship's name, the *Golden Fleece*, would have been understood by many in the late 1600s. The classic Greek story, in which Jason and his band of heroes, the Argonauts, set sail in search of a magical ram's golden coat, was familiar to educated people in the seventeenth century. Such names were common, too, in Jamaica and other parts of the West Indies, where slaves often received classical names such as Cassius or Hercules or Brutus.

By 1680, Bannister was running the London–Jamaica route and, as a prominent captain, making a handsome salary. He even might have shared in the ship's profits. If he managed to stay healthy and continue sailing without falling to nature or pirates, he could expect to work into his fifties or sixties, perhaps retiring to a small house in England, where he could live out his days looking out over the sea.

Bannister seemed well on his way to that sort of soft landing when he anchored in Port Royal, Jamaica, in March 1680. There, while being scrubbed by her crew, the *Golden Fleece* rolled out of control, her masts crashing into the water. Bannister, aloft in the sails, managed to save himself, but eight other men drowned. Crew from the *Hunter*, a small Royal Navy warship, moved to the scene and helped Bannister refloat and repair the *Golden Fleece*.

Soon, the ship had been restored and, for the next four years, Bannister continued making the London–Jamaica run. The westward trip terminated at Port Royal, the epicenter of trade and shipping in the Caribbean, where captains often waited weeks, or months, for enough sugar and other cargo to carry back to England. Few complained, however, about laying over in Port Royal. In the late seventeenth century, there might not have been a more lively and lusty place in all the world. And it would be the place where Bannister's life changed.

In 1655, England invaded Jamaica and captured it from the Spanish. The conquest planted the English into the heart of the Caribbean, well positioned to disrupt Spanish shipping and attack her colonies.

But just a year later, many of the warships that had captured the island had been retired or returned to England. Left vulnerable, the English governor of Jamaica needed to figure out another way to defend the island. And he had to do it fast.

So he turned his attention three hundred miles northeast to Tortuga, a wild island inhabited by English, French, and Dutch cutthroats who made their livings by attacking Spanish ships. People called these bandits buccaneers, from the French word *boucan*, for the wooden cooking frame used by area hunters to smoke meats.

CITY OF PORT ROYAL, JAMAICA
as it may have appeared in about the year 1690

The governor made the buccaneers an offer: Protect English interests in Jamaica with your heavily armed ships and you can use Port Royal's harbor as a base for your pirating operations.

Tough men, from Tortuga and elsewhere, lined up to accept. Some secured official commissions from the English Crown and were known as privateers. Others worked independently, answering to no one but themselves; they were called pirates. No matter the title, these men lit into their jobs, harassing and plundering Spanish shipping, launching operations against Spanish settlements, and keeping Jamaica safe for the English. Many got rich. The best of them, including the legendary pirate Henry Morgan, became wealthy beyond imagination.

All seemed to spread their good fortune across Port Royal, and, in turn, many people in the town became rich. Merchants, government officials, and townsfolk profited by dealing in vast quantities of stolen goods. The town expanded, its crooked wharf-side streets filling with markets that offered anything, legitimate or lurid, that a person desired. Weekly, it seemed, new pirates and privateers arrived with prizes in hand. Every one of them needed a place to spend his money, and Port Royal obliged them on this account, too.

Brothels, taverns, and gambling joints sprang up everywhere. Of Port Royal, one visiting Englishman wrote: "The port indeed is very loose in itself, and by reason of privateers and debauched wild blades . . . 'tis now more rude and antique than was Sodom, filled with all manner of debauchery. . . . It is infected with such a crew of vile strumpets and common prostitutes that 'tis almost impossible to civilize it."

Some of the prostitutes at Port Royal became known across oceans. Mary Carleton, perhaps the most famous, was said to be "as common as a barber's chair: no sooner was one out but another was in." In a town of fewer than three thousand inhabitants, one brothel alone, run by a man named John Starr, employed twenty-three prostitutes.

The pirates couldn't get enough of it all. Leading lives dangerous and often measured in months, they spent money with abandon. Said one contemporary historian of the pirates of Port Royal: "Wine and women drained their wealth to such a degree that, in a little time, some of them became reduced to beggary. They have been known to spend 2 or 3,000 pieces of eight in one night and one gave a strumpet 500 to see her naked. They used to buy a pipe [105 gallons] of wine, place it in the street, and oblige everyone that passed to drink."

Even the birds at Port Royal imbibed. Dutch explorer Jan van Riebeeck is said to have described a scene in which the parrots of the island "gather to drink from the large stocks of ale with just as much alacrity as the drunks that frequent the taverns that serve it."

Alcohol was everywhere. One kind of island-made rum called Kill Devil was known to contain gunpowder, and was drunk from massive steins. "The Spaniards," wrote Jamaica's governor, "wondered much at the sickness of our people, until they knew the strength of our drinks, but then wondered more that they were not all dead."

Far from dying, the town and its people, strengthened by plunder, continued to thrive. Before long, one of every four buildings in Port Royal was either a whorehouse or a drinking establishment. Throwing his hands up, one clergyman wrote: "This town is the Sodom of the New World and since the majority of its population consists of pirates, cut-throats, whores and some of the vilest persons in the whole of the world, I felt my permanence there was of no use."

For all its wickedness, however, Port Royal seemed to tolerate everyone. Quakers, Catholics, atheists, Jews—all were free to worship and believe as they pleased, and they lived peacefully alongside one another as Port Royal became the richest town in the New World. Pirates and buccaneers continued to arrive, welcomed by a public that understood the wellspring of its good fortune, and who ate, drank, and lived among these fast-living men.

For years, there were few better places for pirates or privateers than Port Royal. But in the early 1670s, as trade between Jamaica and the rest of the world grew, pockets of opposition formed against these bandits of the sea. Jamaica was becoming a major producer of sugar; anything that caused mayhem or interfered with trade came to be seen as a threat by powerful merchants and government officials. A peace treaty between England and Spain made the island less vulnerable. Antipiracy laws were enacted; those who didn't abandon the trade could be prosecuted and hanged.

The pirates did not go gently. But as London sent warships and sailors to Port Royal, the statistical life expectancy of a pirate dropped further. By 1680, the year Bannister nearly lost the *Golden Fleece* in Port Royal harbor, many pirates and privateers had been driven from the island. Those who continued to operate there did so at great peril.

Still, opportunity beckoned. As transoceanic trade increased, ships crossed the Atlantic and Caribbean in greater numbers than ever, many loaded with valuable cargos, some with treasure. A man of a certain daring, able to secure a powerful ship and inspire a crew, could still make a fortune by hijacking these vessels on the open seas. The question, as the 1680s wore on, was whether such a man existed anymore.

By 1684, Bannister had been making the London–Jamaica run for at least four years, delivering his cargos and building his reputation. In June of that year, however, the lord president of the Council of Jamaica received a disturbing letter from the island's governor, Thomas Lynch: "One Bannister ran away with a ship, the *Golden Fleece*, of thirty or forty guns, picked up over a hundred men from sloops and from leeward [at Port Royal], and has got a French commission."

Bannister, in fact, had no commission, but he most certainly had stolen the *Golden Fleece*, and he'd done so with a single purpose—to turn pirate. His actions hardly could have been bolder. It was near unheard of for a transatlantic captain, especially one as well regarded and trusted as Bannister, to "go on the account," as it was said of pirating. Even in Port Royal, where everything happened, few had seen anything like this.

Lynch didn't sit around and wait for Bannister to return to his senses. Instead, he ordered the *Ruby*, the biggest and deadliest warship in the Jamaica fleet, to go after the *Golden Fleece*. A monster rated at 540 tons, with forty-eight cannons and a crew of 150, the *Ruby* was a pirate killer down to her timbers.

Bannister did not intend to make it easy for Lynch's enforcers. Since stealing the *Golden Fleece*, he had picked up additional crew, robbed a Spanish vessel, and made his way to the Cayman Islands to take turtles and gather wood. But the *Ruby* surprised him there, and her captain, David Mitchell, and his crew captured Bannister and put an end to his six-week pirate career.

Lynch was delighted.

"Last night," he wrote, "the *Ruby* brought in Bannister. He took him at Caymanos; he has about 115 men on board, most of the veriest rogues in these Indies. I have ordered the ship and the men to be delivered into the Admiralty and commanded the judge immediately to proceed against them, because we do not know how to secure or keep such a number. We conclude they'll be found guilty of piracy."

The case against Bannister was airtight. Not only had he stolen the *Golden Fleece*, he had taken two Spaniards captive after attacking their boat. The testimony of those two men alone would secure a conviction. By now, Bannister could only hope for leniency, but if he expected it, he'd chosen the wrong governor under which to become pirate.

"I intend if it proves so to make a terrible example of the captain, his lieutenant, officers, and all the men that have committed other crimes as many of them have," Lynch wrote, "and hope the severity may have some influence on the other rogues that swarm in these Indies."

By that, Lynch meant Bannister would hang. His crew, if lucky, might be whipped, jailed, or put into irons or stockades. If unlucky, they might follow Bannister to the gallows.

The pirates were returned to Port Royal and held aboard the *Ruby* pending trial. One might have expected Bannister to use the time to pen letters of good-bye or to contemplate eternity; instead, he waited for a break in his captors' attention, then managed to get word to onshore associates to bribe the two Spanish witnesses against him. It was an audacious plan and one that, even if the connections were made, seemed doomed given that the Spaniards had been rescued by the Royal Navy.

At trial, a strong case was made against the pirates. But when it came time for the Spaniards to testify, they swore "backward and forward" that they had sold their boat and cargo to Bannister, and that he had paid them to serve as crew aboard the *Golden Fleece*.

If that testimony shocked the prosecution, at least the

governor could still rely on the jury, who were certain to see through the ruse. But this was Port Royal, where ordinary folk, remembering who'd made their town rich and had infused it with spirit, still counted pirates as neighbors and friends. They returned with a verdict: not guilty. Bannister had cheated the hangman.

Already a sick man, Lynch suffered "such disturbance of mind" from the verdict that, according to accounts, he died of it a week later. By all rights, his replacement should have set Bannister free. Instead, Hender Molesworth tried to convince the jury to reverse itself, but the jurors wouldn't budge. Worse, Bannister threatened to sue the captain of the *Ruby*, "as though [Bannister] were the honestest man in the world." That was more than Molesworth could take. Stretching the boundaries of the law—if not breaking them—he had Bannister rearrested and charged. Bail was set at three hundred pounds, a staggering amount in an age when the annual wage for a seaman might be twenty pounds.

Somehow, Bannister raised the money and, at least for the moment, remained free. He was not, however, permitted to leave Port Royal, and in any case was likely too broke to do it. To make certain he entertained no thoughts of fleeing, officials cut down the sails of the *Golden Fleece*. By January 1685, five months after the original charges against him were thrown out, Bannister was still languishing in Port Royal, waiting to be retried.

He was still waiting when, on a dark night in late January, he began to make his way through the narrow streets of Port Royal. As he crept past taverns and brothels and sleeping families, fifty men were already at work aboard the *Golden Fleece*, moving furiously but making no sound. Before long, Bannister reached Thames Street, which ran along the wharf on the northern side of town. There, he rushed for the *Golden Fleece*, tied up at the docks, and stole aboard his former ship. Sails were hoisted and lines cut, and soon the vessel picked up the breeze and moved out into the harbor.

Landlocked to the east, the harbor offered only one way out, to the south, and that is where Bannister steered. To make it into the open Caribbean, he had to hope that no one in town noticed the *Golden Fleece* missing, or sounded the alarm at the sight of a ship moving in the dead of night. Even then, he would have to pass the twenty-six cannons at Fort James and, in the unlikely event he were still living after that, turn south and get by the thirty-eight cannons, and hundreds of men, at Fort Charles. At any point along the way, he might be spotted by Royal Navy ships anchored just a mile to the west, or by men at work in nearby Chocolata Hole. If such a thing as a suicide mission existed in seventeenth-century Port Royal, Joseph Bannister had just embarked on it.

Generally, winds were calm at night in Port Royal, but on this evening Bannister picked up a fresh breeze off the land and began moving west along the town's docks, maybe as fast as five knots, or about six miles per hour. Before long, he reached Fort James. Perhaps because of the hour, or because the garrisons there never expected such an unlikely event, it seems no one fired on the *Golden Fleece*, or even took notice of her. For the moment, Bannister and his crew remained safe.

Now rounding Port Royal's western shore, Bannister headed south toward Fort Charles, about a half mile in the distance. By now, he might have been fifteen minutes into his rush toward freedom, but he had at least another fifteen minutes to go—critical moments that would determine whether he and his crew lived or died.

Soon, he could see the guns at Fort Charles, the most heavily fortified place in all of Jamaica. Staying within a few hundred yards of the shore, he ordered his men to ready their "plugs," chunks of mattress or wood they'd brought to fill holes in the ship they knew would be made when the cannons at Fort Charles began firing.

A moment later he was at the northern end of the fort and sailing the *Golden Fleece* for all she was worth, waiting for the explosion of cannons but hearing nothing more than the wind in his sails and the crashing of waves against his ship. He was perhaps ten minutes from freedom, but they would be the most dangerous minutes of his life.

Passing the first of the cannons, he braced for destruction. Any one of the guns at Fort Charles could be deadly from a half mile. Thirty-eight of them together, aimed at a single enemy just a few hundred yards away, couldn't miss.

Bannister kept sailing, passing more of the guns, waiting for explosions, drawing nearer to the open Caribbean. Now abreast of Fort Charles, he might have begun to have hope of slipping by undetected, but as he passed the fourteenth cannon, someone at Fort Charles caught sight of him and notified Major Beckford, the fort's commander. Moments later, Beckford sounded the alarm and ordered his cannoneers into action.

Never before fired in anger, the guns at Fort Charles rang furiously now, a series of concussions that shook all of Port Royal and must have caused townsfolk to think a foreign force was invading. At the sound, local militiamen would have been roused by their duty officer and run toward Fort Charles with their muskets. Now that the town was alert, Bannister's only hope was that darkness would conceal him.

He would not be so lucky.

Cannonballs slammed into the *Golden Fleece*, first one, then another, then a third, but Bannister's men stuffed the splintered holes with plugs, and the ship kept sailing, and even though the cannons continued to roar the rounds began to fall short, and in a few minutes the *Golden Fleece* had reached the open seas, and in another few she disappeared into the mist. By now, the navy ships would have been roused to action, but they were almost certainly anchored and could not hope to get going so suddenly, and soon the *Golden Fleece* and her captain were gone.

Bannister's escape blindsided Governor Molesworth. Still, he couldn't hide a grudging respect for the captain. Writing to an English colonial official, he said of the getaway: "[It came as] a great surprise to me, for I thought Bannister's want of credit would prevent him from ever getting the ship to sea again . . . yet now he has obtained credit from some persons underhand, and has his ship well fitted in every respect. It was done so artfully that no one suspected it, or I should have found some pretext for securing him."

Impressed though he might be, Molesworth wasted little time in going after Bannister, sending Captain Edward Stanley in the four-gun sloop *Boneta* to hunt down the *Golden Fleece*. A light ship with a crew of perhaps ten, the ship was likely the smallest in the Jamaica fleet, but Bannister had surrendered to the navy with little struggle months earlier, and Molesworth surely expected more of the same.

For all she lacked in size, the *Boneta* was fast, and it didn't take her long to catch up to the *Golden Fleece*. When she did, however, Captain Stanley thought better of engaging the more powerful ship and her thirty guns. Instead, he sent a note to Bannister warning that he would face new charges for piracy unless he returned to Port Royal with the *Golden Fleece*. Bannister denied being a pirate, telling Stanley he was simply headed to the bay of Honduras for logwood. Helpless to do more, Stanley sailed back to Port Royal empty-handed.

Bannister wasted little time adding to his pirate crew, recruiting tough guys looking for adventure and a fast path to riches—brave men who understood, with Bannister's new reputation, that the Royal Navy was coming, and that they would be pursued by merciless hunters charged with bringing them down.

By now, Molesworth must have realized that Bannister did not intend to go gently. He sent warships to chase every report of Bannister's plunders, but when the frigates arrived they were always too late. This continued for months as Bannister took prizes across the Caribbean and Atlantic.

In April, however, Molesworth caught a break. The *Ruby* had tracked Bannister to the Île-à-Vache, a small island off the southwestern tip of Hispaniola (now Haiti), a notorious pirate hangout, and a place once used by Henry Morgan as an operating base. But as Captain Mitchell closed in, he found not one pirate ship but five, each nearly the size of his own. The *Golden Fleece* was among them, and Bannister was in the company of four French privateers, including the infamous Michel de Grammont.

Against any one of these pirates the *Ruby* held an advantage. Against them all, she couldn't hope to survive. So Mitchell demanded of Grammont, likely by pulling up alongside his ship and shouting, that Bannister be arrested and turned over for serving under a foreign commission. It shouldn't have surprised him that Grammont and the other French pirates refused to give over Bannister to the *Ruby*. That kind of flouting of English authority must have rankled an accomplished navy captain like Mitchell, but he deemed it prudent "not to insist further."

Three months later, in July 1685, Grammont helped lead a historic pirate raid on the Mexican port city of Campeche, in which a landing force of seven hundred pirates sacked the town, took prisoners, and burned the city before leaving with their plunder. It is possible, perhaps even likely, that Bannister and his crew were among those invading pirates, as he was in Grammont's company in the months leading up to the raid. But no one knows for sure.

Later that year, the *Golden Fleece* was spotted sailing alone off the western coast of Jamaica. This time, Molesworth sent two ships after Bannister, but neither could find him. Every month, Bannister took more prizes and, with quick footwork and deft escapes, continued to blacken the eyes of Molesworth, the Royal Navy, and England. By January 1686, Molesworth seemed to be losing hope. "Captain Mitchell will receive orders . . . for the arrest of Bannister," he wrote to an official in London, "whom he is as likely to encounter on this voyage as on any other." Meaning he was not likely to find him at all.

Still, Molesworth continued to plan for the day, however unlikely, that he would lay his hands on Bannister. Rather than allow him to bribe another witness or go free on bond, he would bring him to trial "very suddenly," and not at Port Royal but at a court outside the town, with a jury "more sensible of the damage we suffer by privateering than are the generality of people in Port Royal."

By May, Molesworth might have abandoned all hope of capturing Bannister, but it was in that month that two vessels arrived at Port Royal from Dublin with a report from their captains that Bannister had plundered their cargos. That news should have hardly surprised Molesworth, but a last bit of information stood him up in his seat. Bannister, the men said, was headed to Samaná Bay to careen—a process that could take weeks and would immobilize his ship. Molesworth issued an order to two of the navy's powerful warships, the *Falcon* and the *Drake*. Their mission: find and destroy Bannister.

The Royal Navy ship Falcon, *drawn by Dutch marine artist Willem Van de Velde the Elder, about 1677. The artist filled all the gun ports with cannon, but in practice several would have been left empty so that some weapons could be shifted from side to side as needed.*

The Drake, *drawn by Willem Van de Velde the Younger, about 1681.*

At Molesworth's order, the two frigates sailed for Samaná Bay. The *Falcon*, commanded by Captain Charles Talbot, could carry up to forty-two guns; the *Drake*, helmed by Captain Thomas Spragge, sixteen.

They arrived several days later and found Bannister and the *Golden Fleece*, along with a smaller vessel, identity unknown, "fit to go on the careen." Here was the chance Molesworth had been waiting for. A ship on the careen, even one as strong and well commanded as the *Golden Fleece*, remained highly vulnerable to attack. The warships began to close in.

For an ordinary pirate captain, this meant the end. But Bannister had taken precautions, having ordered several of his cannons onto land in two separate batteries, hidden in trees and aimed into the bay. Whether he would attempt to use them against two Royal Navy frigates, armed with as many as fifty-eight guns and manned by superior personnel, was another matter entirely.

By surrendering now, Bannister would have hope. He would have his day in court, where he could deny being a pirate, or claim he'd been forced into it by the French, or beg Molesworth for leniency, or bribe another witness or jury. If he chose to fight now, he could never know if his crew, outmanned, outclassed, and pinned down, would follow him into battle and engage a world-class force like the Royal Navy. Far better, it would have seemed to ordinary pirates, to suffer the lashes in Port Royal than go to their dooms like that.

The warships drew closer. It was now midafternoon, and the navy captains should have seen signs of surrender. Instead, they heard the sounds of a trumpet.

Bannister's cannons roared to life from behind the trees, and after that the muskets rang out—a barrage by the pirates that rained down on the navy ships. The frigates returned fire, maneuvering into position and trading salvos into the evening, each side pounding the other, men dying and suffering, the *Golden Fleece* and the smaller vessel alongside her being torn into by navy cannonballs and musket fire. By all rights, the battle should have lasted an hour or two. Yet the next morning, it was still going strong.

And it continued, bloody and violent, into a second day, until both the *Falcon* and the *Drake* found themselves out of gunpowder and ammunition. By this time, the pirates had killed or wounded twenty-three navy crewmen, and stood poised to kill more. Unable to mount any further offensive, the frigates sailed away—a stunning, almost unbelievable victory for the pirates.

At least for the moment.

The navy ships, Bannister knew, would return as soon as they could be rearmed and refitted. That meant he and his remaining crew needed to leave Samaná Bay in a hurry. But the *Golden Fleece* had been badly damaged and lay nearly sunk. The smaller vessel, however, must have remained seaworthy, as Bannister and most of his men seemed to have made their escape on her.

On returning to Port Royal, the navy captains were "much censured" for failing to capture or kill Bannister. Censure was a serious business, and penalties could range from a reduction in pay to banishment or even execution. Officials, however, must have appreciated that Talbot and Spragge had expended all their gunpowder and ammunition—and that they had gone up against a pirate of exceptional talents. Rather than inflict a severe punishment, Molesworth instead ordered the frigates refitted and resupplied, then sent the captains back to Hispaniola to "seek out and destroy the pirate Bannister."

The *Drake* was the first to reach Samaná Bay. By now, most of the pirates had fled the island. At the battle scene, Captain Spragge found the *Golden Fleece* burned to her decks and sunk. He did not report finding treasure (the wreck's cargo hold might have been too deep for breath-hold divers to reach) but his men recovered many of the ship's cannons. Bannister himself, as always, was gone.

Governor Molesworth, however, was not finished. Bannister had stolen his own ship (and an English one, at that), escaped retrial and likely execution, vexed Governor Lynch into an early grave, threatened to sue government officials, consorted with notorious pirates, took prizes across the high seas, and defeated the Royal Navy in battle. If it took Molesworth the rest of his life, he would get the pirate captain.

It would not take him nearly that long.

Late that year, the *Drake* tracked Bannister to the Mosquito Coast, a no-man's-land of tropical forest and swamp along the eastern coast of present-day Nicaragua and Honduras. In January 1687, Spragge and his men captured Bannister and a handful of his men, led them aboard the *Drake*, and set sail back to Port Royal.

During the journey, it was likely that Bannister was planning for the trial to which he was legally entitled. But Molesworth wasn't willing to risk any such thing. Instead, he issued orders to Spragge to execute Bannister on board the ship as the *Drake* pulled into Port Royal—no charges, no trial, no verdict. Such an action against an English citizen by English officials was highly unusual and absolutely illegal. The only question was whether Captain Spragge would go through with it.

On January 28, 1687, as the *Drake* pulled into Port Royal harbor, nooses were affixed to the ship's yardarm, the horizontal beam that held up the sail, and Bannister's arms were bound. Then, in view of the town and its residents, Bannister and three of his cohorts were hauled up and hanged by the neck until dead. Their bodies were then cut down and thrown into the sea.

Delighted, Molesworth issued a report to London. The hanging, he said, was: "a spectacle of great satisfaction to all good people and of terror to the favorers of pirates, the manner of his punishment being that which will most discourage others, which was the reason why I empowered Captain Spragge to inflict it."

No matter the legality of his actions, Molesworth had been unwilling to try Bannister again in the courts. "I find from letters that [Bannister] wrote . . . that he intended to plead that he had been forced into all that he had done by the French. How far this would have prevailed with a Port Royal jury I know not, but I am glad that the case did not come before one."

John Mattera could find no further information on Bannister. So, nearly a month after he'd begun research, he packed his bags and booked a flight from London back to the Dominican Republic. In a taxi on the way to the airport, he sent Chatterton an email.

"Partner," he wrote, "have I got a story for you."

Chapter 5

THE WISDOM OF OLD FISHERMEN

Chatterton couldn't wait to hear what Mattera had learned about the pirate Bannister, so he drove six hours from Samaná and picked him up at the Santo Domingo airport. But before they could start talking, Mattera's phone rang. It was Victor Francisco Garcia-Alecont, Mattera's soon-to-be father-in-law, calling to ask the men to meet him downtown. The urgency of the request startled Mattera, but at least he knew Carolina must be okay, or he would have been asked to come alone.

The partners arrived a short time later at a small restaurant across the street from the Caribbean Sea. Garcia-Alecont was already there, the only customer inside.

Few men in the country commanded as much respect as Garcia-Alecont. He had been vice admiral and chief of staff of the Dominican Navy, a director of immigration, a cultural attaché in Washington, D.C., and the author of several books on Dominican naval protocol and tactics. Garcia-Alecont was a serious man; this meeting hadn't been arranged to discuss table settings for Mattera's upcoming wedding to Carolina.

The admiral got straight to business. Through high-ranking political and military sources, he'd learned that the Dominican government was amenable to signing on to the UNESCO international treaty that would kill private shipwreck hunting in the country. The deal hadn't been finalized, and the timing still was uncertain, but the political winds were blowing unmistakably.

Soon, the days when ordinary guys like Chatterton and Mattera could hunt galleons in the Dominican Republic would be over.

The news blindsided the men. They'd intended to return to treasure hunting after finding the *Golden Fleece*. And while they'd been sober about the threat posed by UNESCO, they never expected the hammer to drop so soon. Yet, here was Garcia-Alecont, a man with ties to the government, telling them to choose between pirates and treasure—there didn't seem to be time to do both.

For several moments, no one spoke. Then Mattera pulled a notebook, drawings, and a map from his messenger bag, and spread them across the table.

He laid out Bannister's history, even acting out some of the parts, barking orders aboard the *Falcon* to fire on the *Golden Fleece*, and firing at navy warships from salt and pepper shakers he set up on the table to look like cannons. By the time Mattera finished, the waiter had replaced lunch menus with dinner menus, but none of the men seemed interested in food. They just wanted to talk about Bannister.

"This guy was already made," Chatterton said. "He's got money, he's got respect, he's got the admiration of society. All he has to do is cruise to the finish line and call it a good life. But he can't do that. Something is calling to him. He has the chance to do something great—something beyond what he ever imagined for himself; he just has to figure out what it is. And in the seventeenth century, the hardest and greatest thing you can do is turn pirate. The whole world is chasing you. Countries have signed treaties against you. You know you're going to hang if they catch you. But think of the life you're going to live if they don't."

"Here's how I see it," Mattera said. "You've got a guy who's played it safe since he's a kid—they don't give you a transatlantic merchant route unless you're really responsible. Then his ship

66

Carolina Garcia (Mattera's fiancée) and Victor Francisco
Garcia-Alecont (her father, and former vice admiral and chief of staff
of the Dominican Navy).

turns over in Port Royal and some of his guys get killed, and he sees how short life can be. At the same time, he's watching all these pirates in Port Royal making history. They're writing their names in the history books in real time. And he sees he's got a chance to do the same thing. He's got a chance to do something people will remember, and maybe even read about, centuries later."

The men waited for Garcia-Alecont to steer the conversation back to the dangers of UNESCO. The retired admiral gazed out the window toward the Caribbean.

"Bannister was a born leader," Garcia-Alecont said. "He had an instinct to lead men to greatness. If you have that quality you must act on it. But you can't do it carrying sugar and animal hides across the Atlantic. And if you're thirty-five or forty years old, as I'm guessing Bannister was, it's too late to go do it in the navy. But you can do it on a pirate ship. And you can keep doing it as long as men believe in you. If men believe in you, you can even defeat the Royal Navy."

The men finally called over the waiter. But even as they enjoyed grilled octopus and spoke of baseball and the upcoming elections, each was thinking of Bannister. In the parking lot after dinner, Chatterton and Mattera began to apologize for staying so long at the villa, but Garcia-Alecont put up his hand.

"*Mi casa su casa*," he said. "Go and find your pirate."

No matter how fascinating Bannister's life, it was all academic if the information didn't help lead Chatterton and Mattera to the *Golden Fleece*. On the hours-long journey back to Samaná that night, the men spread out a chart of Samaná Bay between them in the front seat, and set out to connect the dots.

It was clear to them now that Bannister was too skilled a captain to have careened his ship at a place so exposed and vulnerable as Cayo Levantado. But that didn't mean the *Golden Fleece* wasn't near the island. Located just a mile north, on the mainland, were several stretches of beach where the pirate captain might have careened. Chatterton marked each of the places that looked large enough to hide a great sailing ship. If the *Golden Fleece* had sunk at any of them, she could still be said to have been lost at Cayo Levantado, as Bowden had urged from the start. The men would begin a new search at sunrise, and they wouldn't stop until they had Bannister's ship.

The next morning, as the team loaded its boat, Mattera's security man, Claudio, brought a local fisherman to the villa. The man reported seeing an expensive dive boat off the western beach at Cayo Levantado a few days earlier. He hadn't spotted divers, but watched crew members pull electronics from the water.

To Chatterton and Mattera, there were two possible expla-
nations for the sighting. The boat might have been chartered by
weekend divers using department store metal detectors to look
for sunken treasure—a common tourist fantasy in these parts.
Or it might have belonged to a rival salvage company that heard
Bowden was closing in on the *Golden Fleece* and wanted to jump
his claim. Neither man was bothered by the first possibility. The
second was a dagger.

For more than thirty years, Bowden had maintained a lease
with the Dominican government that granted him exclusive salvage rights to any shipwrecks sunk in a massive area that included
Samaná Bay. On paper, that meant no other person or entity was
permitted to search for wrecks in those areas. In reality, it was
almost impossible to stop them from trying. There was simply too
much water to patrol, and in any case, the few navy boats stationed
in the area did not have enough fuel or resources to protect the
claims of treasure hunters.

But that's just where the trouble started.

If an outsider happened to find a wreck in a leaseholder's area,
or even could make a good claim it was close, it could petition
the Ministerio de Cultura, the government agency in charge of
the country's cultural heritage, to award it rights to that wreck.
Ordinarily, Cultura rejected such requests in favor of the leaseholder. But if the outsider had good credentials—perhaps as an
established salvage company or as university researchers—and
could show that the wreck might remain unfound without its continued efforts, it could prevail. And that's the part that worried
Chatterton and Mattera most. Bowden had spent the past several
years working the great galleon *Concepción* in the Silver Bank, more
than one hundred miles from Samaná Bay. It would be easy for an
interloper to argue that Bowden had long since abandoned his

search for the *Golden Fleece*. If Cultura agreed and awarded rights to the wreck to the interloper, that would be the end of Chatterton and Mattera's pirate ship dreams.

Still, the presence of a dive boat around the island, even one loaded with high-end electronics, shouldn't have worried the men by itself. Academics and researchers often parked their vessels in the area to study whales or marine biology. But the memory of an incident that had occurred a year earlier still weighed heavy on their minds.

It had happened on the eve of a dive workshop Mattera was sponsoring in the town of Juan Dolio, near Santo Domingo. A young man had shown up unannounced, pulled Mattera and Chatterton aside, and told them that complaints had been filed at Cultura against Carolina, Mattera's fiancée. She'd been accused of taking gold coins that had washed up on shore near the dive center without reporting it to the government—cultural theft. Some at Cultura were even calling her "the Pirate Princess of Juan Dolio." The news infuriated Mattera—Carolina hadn't found any coins, and she wouldn't have stolen so much as a seashell—and he demanded to know who'd made the charge. The informant, however, had no further information. So Mattera went to Garcia-Alecont, who was enjoying a drink at the bar.

If anything, Garcia-Alecont was even angrier than Mattera. Moments later, he was pacing the beach and barking into his cell phone. Garcia-Alecont's network of contacts ran deep, and there was little doubt he was calling on them now. When he returned, he told Chatterton and Mattera that the complaints against Carolina had been anonymous, which led him to believe they'd come from rival treasure hunters who didn't appreciate new competition from the Americans. He'd straightened things out and warned Cultura to never again sully his daughter's name. But he told Chatterton and Mattera that two things should be clear to them from that moment forward. First, things could turn on a person—and especially gringos—very fast in the Dominican Republic. And second, someone was already gunning for them in the country.

It was that memory that now caused Mattera to pull out a wad of cash and hand it to the fisherman who'd brought news of the dive boat at Cayo Levantado. In his makeshift Spanish, Mattera asked the man and his friends to keep an eye out for more boats, and the man promised he would.

The team resumed loading the *Deep Explorer* with dive gear and computers, then set out for their new target area, just a few thousand feet to the north of Cayo Levantado. There were miles of shoreline to search, but the men would cover only those areas that:

1. included a beach suitable for careening
2. were well hidden from passing ships
3. had good areas for cannon defenses
4. included waters roughly twenty-four feet deep (the depth at which the *Golden Fleece* had sunk)

The group arrived at a U-shaped stretch of beach about a quarter mile long. It had been weeks since they'd last dragged the magnetometer, but everyone moved instinctively now, flipping switches and connecting cables in a shipwreck hunter's ballet.

Mag hits piled up from the start, and the team returned to dive them the next morning. In the water, Mattera followed the blips of his handheld metal detector until he came upon a pile of sandstone slabs near the shore. Lifting one toward his mask, he could see the shape of an angel engraved on the stone, along with faint lettering in a language he couldn't make out. He picked up another, this one shaped like a cross, and ran his fingers along the edges of the letters etched onto its surface. Again, he could not decipher the words, but now he knew where he stood. This had been a cemetery, built centuries ago on an edge of the earth that had since fallen into the sea.

The discovery fascinated the men but didn't further the cause. Chatterton and Ehrenberg fared little better underwater nearby. Still, they dove every hit from the survey. No one pulled up anything but junk.

That meant the team would need to move farther west, to the next viable stretch of shoreline. Studying charts at the villa that night, they zeroed in on a location, but when they tried to examine it closely, the lights in the house went out.

"Sonofabitch!" Chatterton said.

A minute later, Claudio, the security man, walked into the room, holding a flashlight and a bottle of suntan lotion.

"They still have power at the Gran Bahia, boss."

A short time later, the men pulled up to a resort located just across the channel from the villa. Only registered guests were permitted on the grounds, but the team had taken precautions by dressing in Bermuda shorts and carrying cameras and the bottle of lotion, their tourist disguise. Security waved them through. In a corner of the lobby, they laid out their maps and charts across a table, focusing on a stretch of beach about a mile and a half to the west of the ancient cemetery they'd found. This place was hidden behind a small island and looked to be surrounded by water of just the right depth. Best of all, on one of Mattera's old charts, the area had a name: Carenero Samaná. Mattera made the translation—*carenero* meant careening place. The *Golden Fleece* had been careening when she was sunk by the Royal Navy.

"I would've fought the British there," Mattera said.

"This could be it," Chatterton said. "We go there in the morning."

The electricity was still out when the men returned to the villa, so Chatterton and Mattera slept in the Mitsubishi. They set out at sunrise and spent that day, and several more, surveying and diving Carenero Samaná. They found nothing.

Chatterton was scheduled to fly back to the States to give a talk, and it was just as well, since no one could find another area on their charts near Cayo Levantado that fit even half their criteria. Mattera gave Ehrenberg and Kretschmer a few days off, then did the only thing he could think to do by himself in Samaná—he went to talk to old fishermen.

He started near the old cemetery he'd found, carrying a bottle of Brugal rum and a rusty can full of gasoline. At the shore, he approached two elderly Dominicans who were baiting their hooks. He admired men like this, hard workers who ran fishing line from plastic bottles and who rigged sails from blue tarp when they ran out of gas. Some, even into their seventies, used spear guns to shoot parrot fish or snapper while holding their breath underwater.

He handed the men the rum and the gas and took a shot with his Spanish.

"Dónde están los barcos perdidos?" Where are the lost ships?

The men asked what kind of ship he was looking for.

"Pirata."

The men smiled, but they had no answer.

Mattera moved on to the next group of fishermen, and the next, handing out rum and gas. One after another, they said, *"Lo siento"*—I'm sorry—but not far from the villa, he found an elderly man who began talking and waving his hands, and this is what Mattera took him to say: "I have a cousin in Rincón whose grandfather knew of a pirate ship in Samaná Bay. My cousin is old now but he will help you." The fisherman wrote a phone number on a piece of paper and handed it to Mattera, but would not accept any money in return.

Mattera didn't wait to get back to the villa. From his truck, he dialed the phone number and reached another elderly man, this one who spoke passable English. Yes, the man said, he might know something about a pirate ship sunk in Samaná Bay. He could talk about it that evening, and gave Mattera instructions for a beach-side meeting place at Rincón Bay, a forty-five-minute drive north.

Mattera knew Rincón Bay. Galleons were said to have sunk there, and he and Chatterton had considered working the area when launching their plan to find treasure. Rincón was equally beautiful and dangerous, a spot at the end of the peninsula and at the end of the earth, where smugglers and killers did business in tiny inlets too remote and too dangerous for authorities to patrol. Mattera was willing to go there, but not without the Glock 19 pistol he'd carried for years.

His Mitsubishi, however, would not start, so he grabbed the keys to Garcia-Alecont's Mercedes C230. Anything more than a jalopy was too valuable to take to a place like Rincón, but what choice did he have? If he postponed his appointment, the fisherman might change his mind. "Sorry, Victor," Mattera said to himself. "I'll do my best with her."

An hour later, he pulled off the main road near Rincón and turned onto a gravel side street that led to the beach. In the distance, a young man stepped onto the road and waved for Mattera to come through. In all likelihood, he'd been sent by the fisherman, but Mattera slowed the Mercedes to a crawl to make sure. Shining his brights, he could see the man take a long drag from a cigarette, then flick the butt into the air. When it landed, the street burst into flame, a wall of fire that blocked Mattera's path. By instinct, Mattera slammed his car into reverse—he knew he was being ambushed—and as his tires dug into the gravel, six more men jumped into the street and began running toward him, waving clubs and knives, and throwing flaming bottles. Mattera screeched backward about forty yards and then spun his vehicle around, but when he shifted back into drive to get out, the transmission grinded and the Mercedes died on the spot. This was a place where men killed for ten dollars, so Mattera had a decision to make. He could try to restart the car. Or he could reason with the men in the best way he knew how.

He pulled the emergency brake and opened his door halfway. Placing one foot out onto the road, he stood up into a crouch, lifted his T-shirt, and drew his pistol, then began firing rounds into the pavement in front of the onrushing gang. At the sound of the gunfire, the attackers skidded to a halt and rushed back toward the flames. Mattera looked for muzzle flashes—signs of return fire—but none came, and in just seconds the street was silent but for the barking of wild dogs. Breathing hard, he changed the magazine on his weapon, then got back in the car and got it started. If he left now, he could make it home before anyone came looking for revenge.

And he would have done just that if he didn't have a pirate ship meeting to attend.

He drove his car out the way he came in, found the next road in to the beach and, sweat dripping down his face, made his way to the makeshift bar where the old fisherman had told him to go. He found the man, dark-skinned and about seventy years old, already nursing a beer, and the two men shook hands. When the fisherman asked if Mattera had trouble finding the place, Mattera said, "Just a few pirates along the way."

The men settled in and got to talking. The fisherman said his grandfather had been a great storyteller. One of his best was about a pirate ship in Samaná Bay.

"How did he know it was a pirate ship?" Mattera asked.

"That's what his grandfather told him."

That's what Mattera had hoped to hear. Stories were heirlooms in these parts of the Dominican Republic. That's how the best wrecks were found.

"What did your grandfather tell you?"

The fisherman laughed. He said the story changed every time his grandfather told it, but a few of the details remained the same. A great pirate captain fought a battle against his sworn enemy. Many men died. The captain got away. But the pirate ship sank to the bottom of the bay.

"Where in Samaná Bay?" Mattera asked. He held his breath for the answer. Samaná Bay was massive, reaching nearly thirty miles in from the Atlantic Ocean, and stretching more than five miles from north to south along its shores. If the fisherman couldn't specify an area, his story would be useless.

"Near Cayo Levantado."

Bingo. Now Mattera needed the exact location. Which meant it was time to talk business. If the fisherman asked for a large sum of money up front, his information was probably no good. In the two years since Chatterton and Mattera had joined forces, they'd been approached by several locals offering to steer them to lost shipwrecks—almost always for a price. One had even promised to show them to the *San Miguel*, perhaps the most valuable Spanish galleon ever lost, for two million dollars cash. They always passed on such offers. To them, if a guy had real information, he didn't need the money up front; he'd be content to make a deal in exchange for a piece of the wreck. Everything else, like so much in the wilds of this country, was just a cash grab.

"What can I offer you?" Mattera asked.

"Give me what you think is fair after you find the ship," the old man said.

The men shook hands and Mattera pulled out a small black leather notebook. A few minutes later, he had a description of the area, a place less than a mile from the villa on the northern shore of the bay. Nearly four miles from Cayo Levantado, it stretched the limits of the team's search parameters, but the water depths seemed right, it had a good beach for careening, and there was ample cover for pirates to fire on English warships.

After thanking the fisherman and saying good night, Mattera returned to his car, where he checked the magazine in the pistol to make sure it was full, and that there was a round in the chamber. Driving down the side road, he steered with his knees, keeping one hand on the gun and the other on the directions to the pirate ship. He wasn't about to let go of either of them.

Chapter 6

NOWHERE LEFT TO GO

When Chatterton returned from the States, the team loaded their boat and headed out to the place where the fisherman's grandfather said a pirate ship had sunk.

The men began their survey about two hundred yards offshore, in waters thirty feet deep. Ehrenberg could hardly keep up with the magnetometer's readings. There was something large and metallic in the water here; that much was certain. He called over to the others to take a look.

Ordinarily, the men would have waited a day or two to complete the survey. But Chatterton and Mattera stripped off their T-shirts and shorts and pulled on their dive gear, and before Ehrenberg or Kretschmer could wish them good luck, they'd gone over the side to find the massive object sunk beneath them.

Landing on the soft muddy bottom, the men checked their depth gauges—twenty-eight feet—a near match for the depth at which they expected the *Golden Fleece* to lie.

Now their job was to zero in on the source of the mag hits. They'd brought along a handheld magnetometer, and as they moved it back and forth, the instrument began whistling into Chatterton's earpiece; Mattera could hear it through the water from three feet away. The men followed the sound until a shape materialized in the distance, a wall rising out of the mud and reaching up twenty feet from the bottom, something huge and, with its stark right angles, man-made. As they drew closer, the shape of the wall came into focus. To both of them, it looked like the gun-wale or upper edge of a large boat, and when they got there they knew they were right, and it deflated them, because the gunwale was made of steel, and steel hadn't been mass-produced until the mid-nineteenth century, more than 150 years after the *Golden Fleece* had sailed.

Still, the men drifted over the top of the wall to investigate. Looking down, they could see rows of benches, each with room for five or six passengers. Both Chatterton and Mattera had grown up in New York; they knew what a ferryboat looked like. They could only hope this one had been empty, or at least that the passengers had escaped, before the boat went under.

Both men had seen human remains on shipwrecks through the years, and now they steeled themselves to see more. Near one edge, Mattera saw what appeared to be a human femur. He reached to move debris from the area, but when he got near the object, a cloud of sand and mud exploded near his hand, and a row of razor-sharp teeth lunged toward his face, knocking him backward and sending him sprawling. He regained his footing just in time to see his attacker, a four-foot barracuda, and that the fish had turned back to come at him again. Local legend had it that the barracuda in these parts were crazy, that they lost their minds by eating parrot fish infected with toxins— a disease called ciguatera—and that they would tear off a man's face if given the chance. Mattera did not wish to test the legend now. Swinging the giant lens from his camera, he hit the barracuda in the nose and sent it torpedoing out of the wreck.

"Sorry, buddy," he said. "We were just looking for pirates."

Neither diver found human remains. Still, they searched the surrounding area for another two days in case the *Golden Fleece* lay nearby, but every mag hit they collected belonged to the ferryboat.

By making a few phone calls, they learned that a ferry had sunk in the area in the 1970s. Samaná officials were thankful to know of the discovery, as they'd never been able to find her. But it left the men nowhere to look. And no one knew what to do next.

It made little sense to continue searching Samaná Bay to the west—they'd already strayed too far from Cayo Levantado. There was a mile or two of coastline to the east of the island, but it seemed impossible that Bannister would have gone there, so close to the battering weather of the open Atlantic and so easily seen by passing ships. Mattera had wished to avoid this moment, but he could put it off no longer. At the villa, he pulled Chatterton aside for a talk.

He needed a break, he told his partner, not for a vacation or for clearing his head, but to take paying customers diving. The salvage business had become more expensive than either of them had imagined, draining thousands of dollars from their bank accounts every week. Boats, generators, electronics, fuel tanks, stomachs—all of it needed fixing or filling constantly, and it all cost a fortune here. Already, they'd had to replace the magnetometer cable three times, at a price of nearly four thousand dollars each. It cost more than seven hundred dollars a month just for the crew's cell phone service and Internet access. Salt water was eating everything. It had been more than two years since Chatterton and Mattera had gone into business together. Combined, they'd spent nearly a million dollars between them. Neither had seen a dime in return.

"Are you quitting?" Chatterton asked.

"No," Mattera said. "But we have to earn when we can. I've got clients who will pay good money to come here and dive with us. With you, I mean. You're the attraction. You're the brochure."

Chatterton shook his head.

"We're in a fight for our lives here. They can take Tracy's lease any time. UNESCO is breathing down our asses. And we might have thieves trying to jump our claim as we speak. And you want to take tourists out to look at the pretty coral reefs?"

"I don't want to. I have to," Mattera said. "It's just a week, John. Smile, sign some books, tell stories. We need to do what we can."

Samaná Bay was breathtaking when one didn't need to find a pirate ship there. For a week, Chatterton and Mattera took a group of well-heeled Americans to dive the ferryboat they'd found, some sunken cannons in nearby Barco Perdido Shoals, even the *Tolosa*, one of the galleons Bowden had worked. Both men smiled and laughed, and Chatterton told thrilling stories about exploring the U-boat and *Titanic*. But whenever the partners could steal a moment away, they talked about where they might search next for the *Golden Fleece*. Neither could come up with an answer.

When tourist week ended, the partners took their guests to dinner at Tony's. The power went out, so the group ate in the dark, making sure to drink their Presidente Lights before the beer turned warm. Talk turned to a recent news event, one making international headlines.

In 2007, Odyssey Marine Exploration, a publicly traded salvage company, made one of the richest treasure scores of all time when it pulled half a billion dollars' worth of silver coins from an early-nineteenth-century shipwreck off Gibraltar. Now, more than a year later, Spain was claiming the wreck, and demanding that the treasure be returned to the government. Odyssey contested, and the two parties were slugging it out in court. The case likely would determine the future of private treasure hunting.

One of the guests asked if Chatterton and Mattera were afraid a government might claim the *Golden Fleece*. Chatterton shook his head. That was the beauty of a pirate ship, he explained. She didn't belong to any country. No government could claim her.

"So the treasure's all yours?" one of the guests said.

"Might not be any treasure," Mattera replied. "And besides, treasure's not the point."

Now the man looked confused.

"Treasure gets found all the time," Mattera said. "But a Golden Age pirate ship? That's once in a lifetime. That's forever."

The men couldn't wait to get back to the pirate search, but when they went to draw up a plan there was nowhere left to go. They'd surveyed every viable area near Cayo Levantado, dived every last magnetometer hit. For the first time since arriving in Samaná five months ago, the team was out of ideas.

For a week, no one did much more than clean the boat or organize the supply shed beneath the villa where they kept their equipment. In between chores, they wondered who among them might be the first to quit. They missed their homes, no one was making money, and they were being eaten alive by mosquitos while living on pizza and Frosted Flakes in the middle of nowhere. Chatterton's wife, Carla, and Mattera's fiancée, Carolina, began asking if the men might come home more often.

Chatterton and Mattera met at Fabio's to discuss their next move. It had occurred to each of them, more than once, that things would be easier if they abandoned this pirate quest and went back to hunting treasure before UNESCO pulled the plug on salvors. Or, and they both hated to think this, they could even go back to their original lives, pre-partnership, while they still had enough money left to get a proper business started.

They ordered pizzas and ate mostly in silence, a Shakira video blaring on a crooked TV above them the only sound in the joint. But after a while they got to talking. What was the evidence that the pirate ship had sunk in twenty-four feet of water? And what was the evidence that it had happened at Cayo Levantado at all? Bowden seemed convinced of all that, but why? None of the research Mattera had gathered made mention of the island, only that the pirate ship had sunk in Samaná Bay. In all the time they'd been searching, they'd never questioned Bowden's assertion that the wreck was at the island—or any of his other information, for that matter. Chatterton took out his cell phone and called Bowden, and two days later he and Mattera were on a plane to Miami to talk to Bowden about what he really knew.

The three men met for breakfast at a Denny's in South Miami. Chatterton and Mattera got straight to the point. They needed to know why Bowden believed the *Golden Fleece* lay in twenty-four feet of water. And they needed to know why he thought it had sunk at Cayo Levantado.

"How much do you know about the real story of the *Concepción*?" Bowden asked.

The *Concepción* was one of the three fabled treasure galleons on which Bowden had built his reputation. He was famous for the years of painstaking and beautifully detailed salvage work he did on her remains, an effort *National Geographic* had chronicled in a lengthy article penned by Bowden himself.

"We know the basic story," Mattera said. "But what does that have to do with the *Golden Fleece*? The *Concepción* sank fifty years before Bannister's time."

That much was true, Bowden explained. But for decades after

her sinking, no one could find the *Concepción* or the staggering treasure she carried. That changed in 1686, when a barely educated boat captain and former shepherd from Maine, William Phips, struck an unlikely deal with the king of England, and was granted permission to look for the wreck. During his journey, Phips put in at Samaná Bay, where he hoped to trade with the natives. There, his crew came upon the wreck of the *Golden Fleece*.

"They saw it?" Chatterton asked.

"Not only did they see it," Bowden said. "They saw it up close."

He reached into the oversized pocket of his Bimini Bay shirt, pulled out a folded sheet of paper and his eyeglasses, and began reading from the log of the *Henry*, one of Phips's ships.

> At three in the afternoon Capt. Phips sent his long boat and pinnace well manned and armed to cruise along shore and see if they could find any conveniency of careening. About two miles from the ship they found a wreck in four fathom water and burnt down to her gundeck, judging her to be a ship about four hundred tons, likewise found two or three iron shot which had ye broad arrow upon them, and several firelocks. . . . By all circumstances the wreck is judged to be Bannister the pirate who was careening her and surprised by some of our English frigates.

Chatterton and Mattera were impressed by the amount of information in this simple log entry. Here was an eyewitness sighting of the wreck of the *Golden Fleece*, made just a few months after her sinking, and in detail. A fathom equaled six feet, so the wreck would indeed be lying at a depth of twenty-four feet. There would be cannonballs aboard, some marked by an arrow, a symbol used by the Royal Navy. The ship would show evidence of having burned, and might still contain muskets used by the pirates to fire on the English force.

Every one of these details fascinated the men. Still, not one of them told where the wreck might be found. To that end, they asked Bowden perhaps the most important question of all: Why did he seem so convinced that the *Golden Fleece* had sunk at Cayo Levantado?

Bowden had an answer for that, too. Salvors had been looking there for decades, probably centuries; in the treasure business, that kind of generational constancy often was an excellent indicator. Also, the island's name, which meant levitate, suggested the place had long been used to careen ships. And then there was Miss Universe.

In the 1980s, a film crew had come to the Dominican Republic to shoot an episode of a television documentary series called *Oceanquest*. The host, twenty-five-year-old Shawn Weatherly, had recently been crowned Miss Universe, and would go on to appear on *Baywatch* and other television programs. For now, however, her job was to pull on scuba gear (and a tight-fitting suit) and "confront her deepest fears" by exploring some of the world's most dangerous underwater environments. It was Bowden's job, during the shoot, to help show her around.

He took Weatherly to Cayo Levantado. There, while exploring the western end of the island, she discovered a large ceramic jar on the ocean bottom, buried in mud but intact. Bowden had seen similar examples in books and auction catalogs. To his eye, the jar was European and dated to the late seventeenth century, just the kind of piece the *Golden Fleece* might have carried. He had searched the area many times since then, but had never recovered another artifact like it.

Mattera scribbled notes on the back of a placemat. *People*

looking at Levantado for centuries. "Levantado" means "levitate." Miss Universe. Chatterton didn't write down a word.

"Are you going to remember this?" Bowden asked Chatterton.

"Don't need to. I don't think your evidence cuts it."

Just because people had always believed something, Chatterton said, didn't make it so. In his experience, it was almost always by looking where others hadn't considered that the things most worth finding turned up. As for the island and its name, the place might have been used for careening, but not by a pirate of Bannister's caliber. Finally, while he remembered Shawn Weatherly—in glorious detail—the jar she found could have been dropped from any number of passing ships of the era.

Bowden shook his head. He told the men he had a strong feeling about Levantado. But to Chatterton that didn't matter; he didn't operate on feelings. He respected all that Bowden had accomplished in his career, but he respected evidence even more. And the evidence he and Mattera had put together over five months said the *Golden Fleece* wasn't at the island.

French chart of Samana Bay, circa 1802.
Cayo Levantado is called "Cayo Banistre."

Bowden sipped at his coffee. He put the cap back on his pen. Then, he pulled another paper from his shirt pocket, this one a photocopy of an old chart of Samaná Bay. It had been drawn during the French rule of Hispaniola, likely around 1802, and its labels were in French. But as he pushed it across the table, neither Chatterton nor Mattera needed help translating the name the French had given to Cayo Levantado. Clear as day, in big letters, it read "Cayo Banistre"—Bannister Island.

The men could only stare at the paper. This chart was more than a feeling or a best guess. This chart was real evidence, drawn by people from long ago who knew.

"I don't know what to say, Tracy," Chatterton said.

Bowden smiled.

"Maybe you guys missed something. We all do in this business."

Flying back to the Dominican Republic, neither Chatterton nor Mattera could remember feeling so lost. They had found every fence and fish trap within two miles of Cayo Levantado, yet couldn't locate a one-hundred-foot pirate ship with iron muskets, cannonballs, and maybe even cannons. During the six-hour drive back to Samaná, they tried to brainstorm other areas to search near the island, but all that remained were places that didn't have beaches in Bannister's day. They geared up and went to those places anyway, spending weeks mowing the lawn around rocky cliffs and jagged reefs and every other place the *Golden Fleece* never would have gone.

That left a single option: Redo the surveys they'd already done, as they believed Bowden implied that they should. None of them had the stomach for that. They knew they weren't perfect at mowing the lawn, but they also knew there was no way they'd missed a giant sunken sailing ship in an area as small as Cayo Levantado. But no one knew what to do next. It came as a welcome break to everyone when Chatterton flew back to the States to honor a commitment he'd made to attend a dive show.

It was there that he met up with Richie Kohler, his partner in the U-boat discovery. At dinner one night, he told Kohler about his quest for the *Golden Fleece* and her great captain, that he was throwing every part of himself at the problem, that he was willing to risk anything and lose everything to make it happen. That's how he and Kohler had broken through on the U-boat. That's how he'd always gone where others couldn't go.

"You're fifty-seven now, John," Kohler said.

"Exactly," Chatterton replied. "So I can't give an inch."

"You have a Plan B?"

Chatterton shook his head.

"I don't do Plan Bs."

Chapter 7

JOHN CHATTERTON

Tomorrow Is Promised to No One

John Chatterton seemed born to a storybook life. His father was a handsome, Yale-educated aerospace engineer, his mother an international fashion model. His family lived in Garden City on Long Island, New York, a privileged community where professionals built lives of big potential, and children could follow their dreams. John was smart, funny, and good-looking. Yet, nearly from the day he was born in 1951, he seemed indifferent to much of the world.

Kids seemed like kids to him. He had no beloved books, no special television shows, no favorite teams. He played with other children but had no best friend. Even at age eight the ordinary bored him, and so much of what he saw in Garden City seemed ordinary to him.

But all of that changed when he met the ocean.

Nearly every summer day, John's mother drove him and his younger brother to a beach on Long Island's south shore. There, looking out over the horizon, he saw a world that stretched forever, a place that looked different and endless every day no matter where he happened to stand. When people asked why he liked the beach so much, he told them he went there to see things.

John began exploring the beach. He built labyrinths in sand, hunted flounder with spears he made from scratch, tried to walk so far he couldn't remember his way back. Kids in Garden City hardly knew what to make of his summertime stories. He stabbed fish? He looked out over the ocean? He tried to get lost?

When John was nine, his parents bought him a diving mask and snorkel. He spent the summer using it to explore the ocean. Wherever he turned he saw something unexpected, unknown. When school resumed in the fall, academics could not compete. The ocean was an alien world—his world—and now John knew how to get inside it.

It was around this time that his parents divorced. More than ever, his mother relied on her father as a role model for her sons. Rae Emmett Arison was a retired rear admiral who had been awarded the Navy Cross during World War II. When John asked his grandfather about being heroic, Arison told him he had not done anything special, just what he thought was right. When John asked if he could be brave someday, his grandfather assured him he could.

During middle school John began to hitchhike, sometimes for thirty or forty miles in a random direction, until he arrived at an old abandoned house or a shuttered factory, and he would explore inside, even when getting inside was dangerous, imagining the lives of the people who'd lived and worked there. To John, this was history—better than textbook stories of presidents and kings, because he could stand there; he could feel these places for himself. To John, the feeling of a place was the reason to go.

In 1965, John entered Garden City High School, and it was more of the same—memorizing, regurgitating, accepting the story. He cut classes and did just enough to get by. And while he never became a serious problem, teachers said his problem was the most serious of all—he had a good mind but didn't use it the right way.

John's father warned that this was no way to get into Yale, yet by junior year John wondered whether he should attend college at all. The biggest questions of the day were about Vietnam, but few who claimed to have answers had been there. He considered enlisting, but had little interest in fighting before he had judged the war for himself. As the grandson of a hero, he could have landed a navy desk job, but what could he see from there? Then he came up with a plan.

He could be a medic, the guy who helped wounded soldiers in the field. That way, no matter what he discovered, he could be helping people rather than killing them, all from a place front and center, a place where he could see. School counselors tried to talk him out of it; go to college, they told him, ride the war out. But the world was on fire and there were people and places to know— how was he to know them if he didn't jump off from somewhere? Vietnam was his somewhere, and he intended to go.

In early 1970, Chatterton reported to the 249th General Hospital in Asaka, Japan. It was more than two thousand miles from Vietnam, but he saw the faces of war every day. They arrived by the busload, young American soldiers missing the backs of their heads or with shattered spines or torn-away faces—men who'd once had lives. Sometimes, as Chatterton washed them, they asked him what kind of husband a cripple might make, or if their parents could stand to look at them now. Chatterton had joined the army to find answers, but all he could say was, "I'm so sorry, buddy. I just don't know."

But he had to know. After six months in the neurosurgical

ward, he requested a transfer to the front lines in Vietnam. The wounded at Asaka begged him to reconsider. "Don't fuck things up," they said. "You have a life." But with every arrival he believed he knew less about how human beings could do this to one another, not more. And one day, in June 1970, he wasn't there anymore. When patients asked about Private Chatterton, they were told he was on an airplane bound for Chu Lai in South Vietnam.

Chatterton was taken to a firebase near the Laotian border. Minutes later, he was told a medic had been killed. "Get your gear," an officer told him. "You're up." Chatterton had been part of the 4th Battalion 31st Infantry of the American Division for all of an hour, and already it was his turn to go.

None of the men in Chatterton's platoon seemed happy to see him. Not one of them shook his hand. They just told him, "Let's go," and started walking, never turning to see if he followed, never believing he'd put his ass on the line. The platoon's other medic wouldn't even grunt at him. "They don't know me," Chatterton thought, but his legs shook so badly he wondered if they knew something he didn't. For miles, across crocodile-infested rivers and bombed-out villages, he tried to remember if his grandfather had believed he could be brave.

Near a village, the platoon stopped walking. To Chatterton, these men looked more like Hells Angels than soldiers, all long hair and dirty beards and ripped pants. Suddenly, shots rang out and everyone fell to the dirt, returning fire from wherever they could. When the bullets stopped the men went back to walking, no change in their expressions at all. Chatterton could hardly breathe. As he ran to catch up, he worried that he could never go for a wounded man now that he knew how much he wanted to live.

The next morning, as the men crossed a rice paddy, sniper fire rang out from a hillside. Two rounds ripped through the hips of squad leader John Lacko, a twenty-eight-year-old paperhanger from New Jersey. Bleeding, Lacko lay in the grass to hide himself while the others took cover behind a dirt mound. Someone yelled for the medic.

"Fuck it, I'm not going out there," the other medic told Chatterton.

Lacko lay exposed in the open field. Anyone who helped him would be an easy target for the enemy. "By killing a medic they demoralize a platoon," a friend had told him, and now the Vietcong were waiting to do just that.

Chatterton's chest heaved. He could not swallow. His body went light.

And then he ran.

He ran with everything he had, into the open field and straight for Lacko. Bullets shredded dirt and grass all around him but Chatterton kept going, his legs burning and his aid pack thrashing while the platoon returned fire to cover him. He kept waiting to die—maybe he was dead already—but his legs kept moving and the world went silent except for his breathing, until he slid beside Lacko in the grass.

"Hang in there," Chatterton said.

He checked Lacko for a severed artery, then looked back over the field to the platoon.

"We gotta get back," he told Lacko. "We gotta go."

Chatterton was six foot two, but at 165 pounds he could not hope to carry the heavier man over his shoulders. Instead, he scooped his arms under Lacko's from behind and began to drag him into the open field. Shots rang out; mud and grass spit up. Chatterton knew he would die now but kept dragging, trying to cover fifty yards that stretched over all Vietnam. All the while, he kept waiting to fall but his legs kept pushing, and even when he could no longer feel his body he kept pulling and digging until he was back to the platoon and behind the dirt mound. Dehydrated and exhausted, he hardly heard the Cobra attack helicopters as they arrived and unloaded on the enemy. But he felt the men in the platoon rub his shoulder and move dirt from his eyes, and he heard them call him "Doc."

For the next two weeks, Chatterton made every patrol. The men warned him that this was a fast ticket to a body bag, but he didn't hear them. All he knew was that he was good at his job and that the work was important. He kept volunteering, not just to join the platoon but to walk point—to be first in line during patrols—unheard of for a medic. It exposed him to booby traps, land mines, and sniper fire, but it also put him out front, where a person could see. Time and again, he ran to pull his men out. The world came alive when a person got a chance to be good.

It took just a week or two for Chatterton to find the answers he'd come for: America didn't belong in Vietnam. The soldiers were heroes. Human beings were animals. Yet he still kept walking point, still kept looking to see how people lived and died, how they made decisions, and the accountings they gave of themselves when things mattered. Over the months, he compiled a short list of truths he saw reflected in the lives and the dying around him— his principles for living:

— If an undertaking was easy, someone else already
  would have done it.
— If you follow in another's footsteps, you miss the
  problems really worth solving.
— Excellence is born of preparation, dedication, focus,
  and tenacity; compromise on any of these and you
  become average.

— Every so often, life presents a great moment of decision, an intersection at which a man must decide to stop or go; a person lives with these decisions forever.

— Examine everything; not all is as it seems or as people tell you.

— It is easiest to live with a decision if it is based on an earnest sense of right and wrong.

— The guy who gets killed is often the guy who got nervous. The guy who doesn't care anymore, who has said, "I'm already dead—the fact that I live or die is irrelevant and the only thing that matters is the accounting I give of myself," is the most formidable force in the world.

— The worst possible decision is to give up.

After a year, mostly in the field, Chatterton went back to Garden City on leave to see what the army would do with him next.

He could hardly speak, and spent most of every day on the floor. Sometimes, he broke down sobbing. Then he would turn silent. He never made it back to Vietnam. Instead, he served out his obligation at Fort Hamilton in Brooklyn, telling shrinks what they wanted to hear, marrying and divorcing a woman he hardly knew, wondering what had become of a person who once had needed to know.

For five years, Chatterton moved between hourly jobs, never staying anywhere long, never really connecting. By 1978, it occurred to him that his life could slip away like this, bound up in anger and dark memories, and that it dishonored the men who hadn't come back from Vietnam to be pissing away life this way.

He took a job as a scallop fisherman in Cape May, on the southernmost tip of New Jersey. At sea, the fishermen combed through piles pulled up by dredges, keeping the scallops and kicking the garbage over the side. To Chatterton, it was the garbage that mattered. "Mind if I keep that?" he'd ask. Soon, his house was overflowing with cannonballs, muskets, broken china, and flintlock pistols.

Scallops were gold until 1981, when the market for the mollusks collapsed, but by that point Chatterton knew he wanted to earn his living from the water. He enrolled in a commercial diving school in Camden. When his girlfriend, Kathy, asked what the profession entailed, Chatterton confessed he had no idea.

To be good at commercial diving, the instructor said, a person had to do underwater construction, welding, and repairs. To be great, he had to improvise in hostile environments, find a way when things seemed impossible, solve problems that changed by the minute. "That's what I did in Vietnam," Chatterton thought. "That's where I'm at my best."

After graduating in 1982, he landed a job with a commercial diving company that was doing work in New York Harbor. There, he demolished concrete, welded support beams under South Street, and installed pile wrap beneath the Port Authority Heliport. Every hour demanded muscular expression and a nimble touch, often in caves or tunnels made black by swirling silt and sediment. Supervisors could see that Chatterton was different— not just because he slithered into difficult places or refused to quit even after his body went numb from the cold, but because of the way that he saw. During times of zero visibility, he used his body, helmet, and even his fins to decipher the contours of his work space, assembling the shapes he encountered into three-dimensional diagrams in his mind. By freeing himself from vision he came to see with his imagination, and that meant there was nowhere Chatterton couldn't go.

Even at home his mind was submerged. In the shower, he contemplated how objects fell through water; over breakfast he planned escape routes on blueprints he'd borrowed from work. By the time he splashed into the Hudson each morning, he seemed incapable of panic. It's not that he believed the worst wouldn't happen—he knew from Vietnam that it would. He just knew that when he became buried in sludge or could no longer breathe or got pinned to a wall, he would come out okay, because in his mind he'd already been there; in his mind he knew the way out.

The next few years passed happily for Chatterton. He married Kathy, and his career flourished. For the first time in his life, he was earning an excellent salary, had steady work, and enjoyed generous benefits, all at a job he loved.

Chatterton began showing up for recreational shipwreck charters run by local dive shops. Dive charters were populated by rugged men (and a few sturdy women) who carried sledgehammers and crowbars, and wore a knife on each leg. You didn't work with a buddy down deep—that was resort stuff for tourists—and you never touched another guy's shit. These divers studied deck plans of ships sunk by great violence; every weekend they swam among the bones of souls who had died at sea.

Soon, he was pressing deeper into the ocean, but charters to these places were rare, and there was a reason for that. At depths past 130 feet, people started to die—from the bends, nerve damage, deepwater blackout, hallucinations, panic, and fear. Sometimes the bodies were never found. Captains shunned greenhorns like Chatterton, wannabes who didn't understand how the deep could kill. Chatterton showed up anyway. But he was in small company. Of the ten million certified scuba divers in the United States, only a few hundred dove deeper than 130 feet—the true deep.

Chatterton loved the wrecks. Twisted and bent—some collapsed on their sides—they were snapshots of moments when men had lost hope, when plans and futures and families had changed. Each wreck was different, sometimes by the day, changing with the temper of the ocean. Many divers lived for the artifacts these wrecks surrendered—teacups, dishes, portholes, a bell—but to Chatterton the stuff hardly mattered. To him, shipwrecks were puzzles that rewarded a man in exactly the measure to which he challenged himself. The farther a person swam into a wreck, the more of its secrets she revealed. Before long, Chatterton was seeing things no one had seen before.

Much of what made him special happened before he arrived at the dock. He prepared relentlessly, studying deck plans, rehearsing scenarios, and imagining the shipwreck not as a structure but as a story—one with a beginning, a middle, and an end. By seeing the ship's final moments unfold in his mind, he could see how she broke, and that meant he could move into places that had ceased being places, he could reach areas accessible only to those who could see backward in time.

Soon, he felt ready to challenge the *Andrea Doria*, by many accounts the most dangerous shipwreck in American waters. Sunk in 1956 after colliding with the MS *Stockholm* off Nantucket Island, the massive Italian passenger liner lay on her starboard side in 250 feet of water. The ship's interior was deep, dark, and dangerous. Narcosis and the bends could result from the slightest mistake. Passageways and staircases were twisted and disorienting. Silt and particulate reduced visibility, sometimes to mere inches. The *Doria* had a reputation for giving divers whatever room they needed to kill themselves inside.

Before long, Chatterton was venturing into areas on the *Andrea Doria*, and other great wrecks, no other diver had dared. To him, the risk was the point: If he went somewhere easy, he knew what he'd find there, and how could a person look forward to that? By 1991, some were calling Chatterton the greatest wreck diver they'd ever seen. Charter captain Bill Nagle paid him the ultimate compliment: "When you die, no one will ever find your body."

In the summer of 1991, Nagle got a tip from a fisherman about a possible shipwreck located sixty miles off the New Jersey coast. He called Chatterton and they made a plan to check it out. The trip would cost several hundred dollars in fuel alone, and the odds of finding anything important were almost nil, but to Chatterton and Nagle, a man had to look. Who were you if you didn't go look?

They recruited a dozen other divers, each of whom paid one hundred dollars to help defray costs, and made their way to the site. Scuba tanks strapped to his back, Chatterton descended 230 feet to the bottom by himself, where he discovered a mostly intact World War II German U-boat. Chatterton knew his ocean and he knew his history; there was not supposed to be a U-boat within a 100-mile radius of this location. Wreck divers dreamed of finding a virgin U-boat. To discover one in American waters was the holy grail. All that remained was for the divers to identify the wreck, and they would make history.

When the team returned to the site, however, a diver died on the bottom, his body swept away by currents. Chatterton and the others risked their lives looking, but they couldn't find the man. The tragedy hung heavy over the group.

Nagle moved to replace the fallen diver with Richie Kohler, owner of a local glass business and a member of the Atlantic

Wreck Divers, a notorious gang of tough guys who wore match-ing skull-and-crossbones jackets, and raised hell on shipwrecks across the Eastern Seaboard. Kohler and his crew were accom-plished divers, but they were everything Chatterton despised. They seemed to care for nothing but artifacts, risking their lives to get a twentieth teacup when they'd already bagged nineteen. They mooned passing dinner cruises, used stuffed animals for skeet-shooting targets, leaped naked into the water. They returned to the same wrecks to do the same things over and over, and for that, Chatterton dismissed them out of hand.

If anything, Kohler detested Chatterton even more. "Who is this uptight asshole talking about excellence and art?" Kohler would ask. He knew Chatterton was an exceptional diver, but believed him to be missing the point. Shipwreck charters were supposed to be about fun, camaraderie, brotherhood. Without that, the sport became labor, and weekends weren't made for that. "Imagine the life this guy leads," Kohler told his buddies. "Fuck him and the boat he came in on."

Over Chatterton's protests, Nagle brought Kohler aboard the U-boat project. Working separately, Chatterton and Kohler pressed into the submarine, where they encountered hanging pipe and wire and conduit (any bit of which could have entangled and trapped them inside the wreck), dead ends and tangled passage-ways, and live explosives ready to detonate from a single wayward touch. Throughout the wreck, they found the remains of fifty-six German sailors, some of them still dressed, their shoes laid out on the floor, left right, left right. But no proof of the U-boat's identity.

The two men began working together, not just underwater but in government archives, at libraries, with historians and diplomats, and on the phone with old U-boat aces. Slowly, they began piecing together a history different from the official accounts. And they began to understand each other. As months turned into years, they did groundbreaking work, but came to realize that until they found conclusive proof inside the wreck itself, their theories about the submarine's identity were just a best guess, and neither of them had come this far, risked his life, to say "probably." For Chatterton and Kohler, it came down to this: A person could have theories about who he was; he could make predictions about what he might do in a given situation. But he'd never really know until he was tested. For Chatterton and Kohler, the U-boat was their test. The U-boat was their moment.

So they continued to return to the wreck, spending money they didn't have on fuel and expenses, taking time from their families. Two more divers, a father and son, died while diving the U-boat. Time and again, Chatterton and Kohler might have moved the bones of the fallen sailors or reached inside the dead men's clothes to search for a pocket watch or cigarette lighter engraved with the submarine's identity—those items sometimes survived for decades in a cold underwater environment. But neither diver was willing to do that. Swimming among the human remains, Chatterton and Kohler began to see these dead sailors not just as enemies but as someone's sons or brothers or fathers or husbands, young guys whose country was being destroyed by a madman and whose families never knew where they had died. Searching the bodies would have required disturbing the remains. So Chatterton and Kohler let the bodies rest. Their decision raised the risk that they, too, would die inside the wreck. But they were on the verge of doing something beautiful, and would have rather lost their lives than do it in an ugly way. They kept searching.

Soon, only Chatterton, Kohler, and a few others remained on the project. Chatterton began pressing into the most dangerous corners of the wreck—places so cramped and strewn with hanging debris it was hard for the eels who lived inside to find a way out. But with every dive he seemed only to drift further from an answer.

At home, marriages grew distant and strained. To save his family, Kohler quit the U-boat and hung up his dive gear. By 1995, Chatterton found himself at a crossroads unlike any he'd known. He had unleashed all of himself on the U-boat, all that he knew about diving and life. And he was failing.

In a fury of protest, he discovered and identified several new wrecks, enough to make any other diver's career, but he only sank further into despair. By 1996, his marriage to Kathy was over, he was nearly broke, and Nagle, whom he adored, had died a broken man. When people tried to console Chatterton, he told them, "I no longer know who I am."

But by 1997, Kohler had sorted out his family issues and returned to the project. Chatterton devised a final plan to identify the U-boat, one that incorporated all his principles for living—and that Kohler felt certain would be deadly. Slithering inside a room that looked impossible to exit, Chatterton freed a supply box that held a key piece of evidence, then found he'd run out of air. Holding his breath, he pushed the box through a narrow opening to Kohler, then removed his tank and made a desperate swim for his partner. A few moments later, the supply box gave up its secret and the U-boat had its name. The journey had cost six years, three lives, two marriages, and two life's savings. But Chatterton had his answer.

In the spring of 1998, a friend invited Chatterton to a party at a hotel in Manhattan, promising good food and the chance to meet a woman he knew. Chatterton hated formal wear and fix-ups, but he liked his friend and said he would go.

That Saturday night, he pulled up to the hotel on his burnt-orange Harley-Davidson Road King, and left his keys with the valet. Inside, he was introduced to Carla Madrigal, a forty-six-year-old operational systems manager for a major commercial airline based in Washington, D.C. She was pretty in the way Chatterton liked—naturally and without trying too hard—slender, with light freckles and high cheekbones, and wore a gold letter *C* that caught Chatterton's eye.

They talked for hours, hardly noticing the others. At the end of the evening, Chatterton asked to see Carla again. She asked why Chatterton kept looking at her necklace. He told her about a shipwreck he'd found at a time in his life when he'd felt lost. The wreck was the SS *Carolina*; he knew it by finding brass letters on the fantail that spelled out the ship's name, in a font he'd never seen before—the same font as the *C* on her necklace.

That summer, Chatterton agreed to join an elite team of American and British divers on an expedition to the HMHS *Britannic*, sister ship to the *Titanic*. Sunk off the Greek island of Kea, the wreck lay on her starboard side in four hundred feet of water, a depth at the very edge of what was possible for world-class divers. Even before it launched, the expedition was being hailed as one of the most ambitious in diving history. For his part, Chatterton would attempt to become the first diver ever to use a rebreather on *Britannic*.

Using solenoids, sensors, and a chemical absorbent to manage exhaled gas, rebreathers allowed divers to go deeper and work more efficiently than ever before. The technology was cutting-edge but still hadn't been perfected; several divers had died using the new apparatus. In experimenting with a rebreather during training for

Britannic, Chatterton nearly lost his life more than a dozen times. On the wreck, he'd need it to function flawlessly.

To many, his plan seemed suicidal. He intended to go to the boiler rooms to search for evidence as to why the ship sank so fast. If there was a scarier destination on the wreck, no one knew about it. According to deck plans, a diver would have to wriggle through a narrow fireman's tunnel, a passage so tight a person could not turn around. In deepwater-wreck diving, the inability to turn around was often the last experience a person ever had.

Chatterton wasted little time when he got to the wreck. Dropping down into a fracture in the *Britannic*'s bow, he found the fireman's tunnel and corkscrewed inside. It was even more narrow and tight than he'd imagined, just inches of room to either side. He checked his depth gauge: 375 feet. Crazy deep.

He moved slowly, past jagged pipe, tangled wires, fallen railing, and razor-sharp coral—the worst place he'd ever been on a wreck. A single misstep, one brush against an invisible obstacle or a slip into a hanging tangle, and he would be trapped. And it would be hours before they came looking for him, if anyone knew where to come looking at all.

For several minutes, he finger-crawled forward, covering more than a hundred feet before he arrived at the boiler room. Chatterton checked the rebreather's handset.

The screen was blank.

The computer controlling the rebreather had died. Now he had no idea what oxygen concentration he was breathing, what he needed to survive, or how to keep from dying. And he didn't have a bailout tank—the tunnel was so narrow he'd left it at the anchor line. He began to say good-bye to himself.

But was he supposed to just give up and scratch out a note to loved ones as he waited to drown? He'd seen others do that. He was not going to die that way. So he started adding oxygen manually. If he added too much, he could become toxic, convulse, lose his mouthpiece, and drown. If he added too little, he could pass out and drown. It would have to be a guess. He adjusted the mix, and waited to see if he'd live.

He stayed conscious.

Now he had to get out. Unable to turn around, be began to slither backward, inching out of the tunnel in the same painstaking way he'd come in. Every instinct demanded he rush, but he knew suddenness would tangle him in the hanging web of wreckage.

He emerged several minutes later, wondering if each breath would be his last. He swam to the anchor line, grabbed his open circuit bailout tank, and began his three-hour decompression ascent to the surface.

That night, Chatterton took a taxi to a small hardware store, where he purchased hacksaw blades and a soldering gun, and went to work repairing the rebreather back in his hotel room. Smoke billowed from under his door before Chatterton put out the small fire he'd started, but in a few hours he'd Frankensteined the rebreather back into operating form.

He was back on the boat and into the wreck the next day. Chatterton made a total of six dives that trip. The rebreather failed on three of them. He never did figure out why *Britannic* sank so fast, but he'd gone places on the wreck thought to be impossible to reach. And though magazines published pictures from the expedition, no photographer could capture a feeling like that.

In November 2000, PBS aired a two-hour special episode of its documentary series *Nova* devoted to the mystery U-boat. Chatterton and Kohler were its stars, and it became one of the highest-rated episodes in series history. One morning, not long after it aired, Chatterton felt an egg-sized lump on his neck while shaving. A surgeon did a needle biopsy, then called later that day and asked him to come back to the office. "I'm kinda busy, can we make it tomorrow?" Chatterton asked. He knew it was trouble when the doctor said no.

At the office, the surgeon told Chatterton he had a squamous cell carcinoma—cancer. He explained the pathology and recommended immediate surgery.

"You didn't say if it was benign or malignant."

"Malignant. You're going to need chemotherapy and radiation. You have a fifty-fifty chance of survival."

Chatterton went numb. He was just forty-nine years old. But as he got his coat to leave he thought, "I can live with fifty-fifty. I can come out on the right side of that."

He started chemo shortly after the surgery, riding his Harley in the snow to the treatments, then going to his underwater construction job the same day despite being too weak to swim. Carla joined him at chemo. She teased him about the attention the gay pharmacist lavished on him. "I don't think anyone else shows up here in black leather," she joked, but inside she was trembling.

After chemo, Chatterton began radiation, five times a week for two months. By the end he could not lift his diving helmet. But doctors were cautiously optimistic. Fingers crossed, Chatterton would make it.

A few weeks later, he was supervising a big job in Battery Park City in downtown Manhattan. This work site was different from the usual water locations. It was underneath the World Financial Center, across West Street from the World Trade Center.

Chatterton was in his company's trailer on September 11, 2001, when he heard a roar and then an explosion. He opened the door and looked up, where he saw an orange-and-black fireball shooting out of the side of the North Tower of the World Trade Center. He ran back into the trailer as debris began raining down on the corrugated tin roof. When those sounds finally stopped, he went back outside and into a world of mayhem and screams. He helped four Japanese tourists who were covered in blood. Dead bodies were everywhere.

Chatterton ran fifty yards to the communications shack and got on the radio—he had ten divers in the water and needed to get them out. He ordered the men to drop everything and return to the dive station. Then he ran back outside.

After all his divers got out of the water, one of them pointed to the South Tower.

"Here comes another one!"

Chatterton saw the second plane hit, and human shapes falling from the tower. By now, the fire department had taken over Chatterton's trailer and made it their command post. A short time later, the South Tower fell onto the trailer, killing five of New York City's top firefighters inside. Nearby, a man flailed in the river. Chatterton and his divers ran and pulled the man out.

For the next several hours, Chatterton helped people onto the ferryboats until there were no more boats coming in. He boarded the last one to leave that day, and looked back over a broken New York. In New Jersey, he found a ride to his condo and called Carla, who was in Argentina on business. She started crying and told him she had watched it all on television. She had feared the worst but never got the sense that he'd died, only that he'd been helping people. And she told him she loved him.

Chatterton returned to work a few weeks later, but his heart wasn't in it. The commute was bad, the memories bitter, and he was spending more time in management than in the water. He married Carla in January 2002. Then he hatched a plan.

He would become a history professor. He'd taken a few college courses after Vietnam, and had come to love the subject after diving so many historic shipwrecks. He enrolled at Kean University in New Jersey and quit his job as a commercial diver. It had been a twenty-year run, but for Chatterton the challenge was gone.

He got straight As his first semester, and was ready to start a second, when he received a call from cable television's History Channel. They were developing a show about shipwrecks and were looking for hosts. Days later, he and Kohler—once the archest of enemies—found themselves auditioning as a team.

Producers liked them and ordered eight episodes. The show would be called *Deep Sea Detectives*, and the premise was simple: Each week, the two divers would investigate a shipwreck-related mystery, doing research on land and diving the wreck underwater. Chatterton's powerful baritone would be perfect for the narration.

The show began airing in 2003 and was a hit from the start. Chatterton filmed between classes, but the schedule was tough on Kohler's family and business, so Kohler quit after eight episodes. He was replaced by thirty-five-year-old Michael Norwood, a handsome and accomplished British diver who had on-screen chemistry with Chatterton.

Chatterton and Norwood became fast friends. In December 2003, the show went to Palau, an island nation in the west Pacific, to investigate the USS *Perry*, a World War II warship sunk in 270 feet of water. The hosts would be joined by cameraman Danny Crowell, an experienced diver and a veteran of the U-boat adventure.

At the wreck site, Crowell moved down the anchor line,

followed by Norwood and Chatterton. Near the bottom, Norwood motioned with his hand across his throat—the out-of-air signal—which seemed strange to Chatterton; they'd been in the water for just a few minutes.

A moment later, Norwood's regulator fell out of his mouth. Chatterton immediately replaced it with his own backup regulator. Norwood started breathing the gas, but he was lethargic and his eyes were confused. Chatterton began trying to help Norwood up the line. He signaled and waved and pulled on him, but nothing he did got through.

Chatterton and Crowell struggled to get Norwood back to the surface. They began dragging him up the line, but Norwood's left hand was clenched so tight on the rope it was difficult to move him. They pried his fingers loose, muscling Norwood up a few feet at a time. A minute later, he stopped breathing, and this time his eyes stayed open, no fear or panic in them, just staring straight into forever. A moment later Norwood began sinking, his lungs filling with water.

Norwood's life now depended on reaching the surface. Rushing him up would likely inflict a lethal case of the bends, but he was drowning, so Chatterton inflated his friend's buoyancy compensator and sent him streaking up toward the boat. He and Crowell dropped back down to allow nitrogen to dissipate from their bodies, an agonizing but necessary wait. Chatterton prayed that when he surfaced he would find Norwood drinking a beer and telling a joke, the guy could really tell a joke, but he'd seen Norwood's eyes, and men didn't wake up from that.

When Chatterton finally reached the boat, Norwood was lying on deck, still in his gear, but dead. A rescue swimmer had tried to administer CPR but could do nothing to help him. Norwood was thirty-six years old and fit, a nonsmoker, vibrant.

Chatterton stared across the water, replaying events in his mind, searching for an explanation or justification or someone to blame, but there was no blame. Norwood had done everything right. This was the ninth diving fatality Chatterton had witnessed, nine human beings who had plans and people who loved them, and he began asking himself questions, right there on the boat. *Do I want to do this anymore? Have I grown too hardened to these fatalities to see what's really going on? Is diving worth dying for?* But by now, he knew how he'd answer once the shock lifted. *No one lives forever. A person has to be who he is. I'm a diver.*

The authorities in Palau attributed the death to a heart attack, but that was just a guess. When Chatterton returned to the States, he and Carla agreed that they should move to Maine to keep an eye on Norwood's widow, Diana.

Christmas felt different that year. In less than three years, Chatterton had battled cancer, watched the World Trade Center towers collapse around him, and lost a close friend in his arms. As revelers rang in 2004, he made an addendum to his principles for living:

— Do it now. Tomorrow is promised to no one.

To Chatterton, Norwood's passing meant the end of *Deep Sea Detectives,* but the History Channel renewed the series, eventually bringing Kohler back as co-host. In the summer of 2004, *Shadow Divers* (my book about Chatterton and Kohler's efforts to identify the U-boat) became a bestseller and was published in several languages. *Deep Sea Detectives* continued to earn excellent ratings, and the *Nova* episode ran often on PBS. In less than two years,

Chatterton and Kohler had gone from working-class unknowns to world famous scuba divers.

The television series continued into late 2005, when the History Channel decided not to renew. The show had run for five seasons and fifty-seven episodes, but its end left Chatterton, for the first time in more than twenty years, with no job. Friends and colleagues urged him to relax, catch his breath, and get out of the dive game. He was fifty-four now, still just four years removed from cancer and the World Trade Center, and too old in any case to keep making the life-risking dives he had trademarked.

Instead, he devised a plan with Kohler to go to *Titanic*. Work on that project wrapped up in 2006. Again, friends urged him to cash in his chips and stop risking. Use your money to purchase a future, they told him. Buy a Laundromat or an apartment building, something you'll just have to watch.

He looked into these ideas and others. All of them made sense. None of them made him feel like John Chatterton. But what was left for a diver who had identified a mystery U-boat, done groundbreaking work on *Titanic*, explored the *Lusitania* and *Britannic*, mastered the *Andrea Doria*? Was he to dive those wrecks again? He was fifty-five now. If his body held up he might have one more great adventure inside him.

So, he researched other shipwrecks and called divers from around the world, and over the months assembled a list of potential dive projects, each of which would have been challenging and interesting, not one of which would have been great. He passed his days lifting weights, eating salads, and running long distances at sunrise, doing all he could to be ready when his moment came. He tried to be polite when his financial adviser suggested buying a Dunkin' Donuts franchise.

Months passed that way, until he met Mattera in the

Dominican Republic and heard stories about the great Spanish galleons—treasure ships of unimaginable value and rarity and beauty, ships no one had been able to find. To search for one, he would be required to pledge every dollar he'd saved, join forces with a virtual stranger, work in a third-world country, embark on a mission that had crushed centuries of men. But as he reached over the breakfast table to shake hands with Mattera, he had only one idea in his mind: Do it now. Tomorrow is promised to no one.

Chapter 8

A PLACE EQUAL TO THE MAN

Driving over the speed limit and stopping at roadside gas stations for fill-ups and heat-lamp cheeseburgers, Carla Chatterton made it from Maine to New York in time to join her husband for the last day of the dive show he was attending. Carla was always a magnet at these events, calling to passersby to introduce them to John, manning the booths of friends (and sometimes strangers) to help pitch their products. Carla had just hours with John at the dive show, and she would do all she could to enjoy the time they had together. The months apart hadn't been easy for her.

Carla and John squeezed in an hour for dinner at the hotel; his flight back to the Dominican Republic left in just a few hours. In the seven months since the search for the *Golden Fleece* had begun, the couple had seen each other only a few times. Even *Titanic* had taken him away from home for just a month.

Near the end of the meal, a young boy and his father walked up to Chatterton's table. They were fans and wanted to know what Chatterton was working on.

"Can you keep a secret?" Chatterton asked.

When the kid nodded, Chatterton said he was looking for a pirate ship that belonged to one of the great swashbucklers of all time. When he signed an autograph for the boy, he inscribed it, "Stay inspired."

Chatterton landed in Santo Domingo early the next morning, then set out for Samaná. The road, like so much else in the

Dominican Republic, was beautiful and treacherous all at once, an obstacle course of mud slides, stray dogs, and, occasionally, a body lying beside an overturned motorbike (scooter and motorcycle accidents were common here). By the time Chatterton pulled up to Tony's to meet his friends for lunch, all he wanted was a cold beer. But the cooler at Tony's had fried during a blackout, and as Chatterton sat down at the table, Mattera delivered sour news to go with the place's warm ale.

The lower end of one of the *Deep Explorer*'s engines had been damaged while Chatterton was away, a five-thousand-dollar repair. It would take a week or more to get a replacement part. And there was more. The magnetometer cable had shredded again. A new one had been ordered for just under four thousand dollars.

Chatterton stared at his menu. To Mattera and the others, it was clear that these expenses, and these frustrations, were becoming too much for Chatterton, and they wondered whether this latest financial blow might push him out of the project.

"I've been doing a lot of thinking about our operation," Chatterton said. "I've gotta be honest with myself. And I've gotta be honest with you guys."

Hearts sank around the table. At least Chatterton had been man enough to come back and quit in person.

"We've been looking in the wrong place," Chatterton said. "We've been thinking about this all wrong."

The wreck of the *Golden Fleece*, he insisted, would never be found near Cayo Levantado, the island where they'd been searching for months. It didn't matter if history said she'd sunk there. It didn't matter if Bowden believed she'd sunk there. History and Bowden were wrong.

"Everyone's been looking for a pirate ship," Chatterton said. "But this isn't about finding a ship. It's about finding a man."

Chatterton asked the others to think hard about Joseph Bannister. In just a few years, the captain had stolen his own ship, outmaneuvered two governors of Jamaica, evaded an international manhunt, and then, despite being outmanned and outgunned, defeated the Royal Navy in battle. To do any one of those things, a man had to plan meticulously, prepare relentlessly, and demand the highest level of excellence of those around him. To do them all, he had to be great.

"So we need to look for a place that's worthy of this guy," Chatterton said.

And that wasn't Cayo Levantado. Which is why Chatterton knew no one would ever find the *Golden Fleece* there. To him, Bannister had been on the mission of a lifetime. His life was at stake. He would not have chosen to put himself or his men anywhere less than perfect.

"So our job is to find that perfect place."

"What about the chart Tracy showed you, where Levantado is called Bannister Island?" Kretschmer asked.

"Forget it," Chatterton said. "Wreck's not there."

"What about the Miss Universe jar?" Ehrenberg asked.

"Forget it. Wreck's not there."

"So where is it?" Kretschmer asked.

The pirate ship, Chatterton explained, was in Samaná Bay, that much was certain from the treasure hunter Phips, whose crew had spotted the *Golden Fleece* there just months after her sinking. But if Chatterton was right in his thinking, it would be somewhere far from Levantado. Somewhere almost impossible to see.

But the bay was about twenty-five miles wide. There could be a hundred good places for a pirate ship to careen in an area that large. To survey all of them could take years. But that didn't worry Chatterton. The team wouldn't need to search every viable location—only the great ones, those that were nearly invisible.

"Great," Ehrenberg said. "Now we're looking for places we can't see."

"Bannister got there," Mattera said. "Anyone here saying we can't?"

No one wanted to say that.

But that still left the matter of how to handle Bowden, who seemed convinced that the *Golden Fleece* had sunk at Levantado, and didn't appear eager to entertain suggestions to the contrary. And Bowden was boss—his lease, his water, his pirate ship.

"This is bigger than Tracy," Mattera said. "If we keep doing things his way we'll still be scratching our asses at Levantado when we're all in Depends. Chatterton's right. We have to change our thinking. This is on us now."

So the men made a plan. Chatterton and Mattera would scout for new locations away from Cayo Levantado, but still inside Samaná Bay. Ehrenberg and Kretschmer would work on repairing the *Deep Explorer*. And none of them would stop until they found a place that reflected Bannister's genius, a place equal to the man.

At the end of lunch, as everyone walked to their cars, Mattera called out to Chatterton.

"John," he said, "I'm glad you're back."

The next morning, Chatterton and Mattera walked down to the small, stony beach area beneath the villa and pushed their inflatable Zodiac boat into the bay. The twelve-foot rubber craft, with its hard fiberglass bottom, was much like the ones used by U.S. Navy SEALs, and was capable of maneuvering in depths of less than one foot. It was the perfect quick-hit vessel with which to zip around Samaná Bay, and a fine substitute while the *Deep Explorer* was in repair.

The partners' job now was to look beyond the practical and toward the beautiful. For months, they'd limited their searches to well-hidden areas near Cayo Levantado that had good beaches for careening, excellent places for cannon defenses, and waters roughly twenty-four feet deep. This time, they dispensed with criteria. Instead, they would go strictly by feel.

They explored inlets and bays and tiny islands on the first day, each place more scenic and unspoiled than the last. Not one of them measured up. Near sundown one day, they could see Garcia-Alecont standing in the sand and waving to them in the distance. When they reached him, he delivered some news.

A government contact had warned him that at least one group of treasure hunters was gearing up to search Samaná Bay for the *Golden Fleece*. Details were sketchy, but the source said he believed these rivals to be heavy hitters who had deep pockets and government contacts of their own.

"Where in Samaná Bay?" Mattera asked.

"Cayo Levantado. Someone watched you working out there. They think you left too early."

"You've gotta be shitting me."

"No. And that's not all. They think the *Golden Fleece* could be one of the greatest shipwrecks ever found."

"They're not going to find shit at Levantado," Chatterton said. "But I still don't want anyone in our area."

"Not on our watch," Mattera said.

Garcia-Alecont asked how the men intended to stop it.

"I don't know yet, Victor," Chatterton replied. "I can put up with a lot, but I can't put up with thieves. No one is going to steal the *Golden Fleece* from Tracy. And no one is going to steal her from us."

That evening, Garcia-Alecont threw a party at the villa for family and friends, as he often did on the weekends. Guests partied past midnight. The next morning, Chatterton announced that he, Ehrenberg, and Kretschmer were moving out. He gave little explanation other than to say they'd already overstayed their welcome and did not wish to take advantage of Garcia-Alecont's kindness. They would be moving into a small apartment in downtown Samaná, four thousand pesos (about one hundred dollars) a month, no hot water. When Mattera pressed for a better explanation, Chatterton told him the all-night parties at the villa were distracting and not good for their business, which was to find the *Golden Fleece*.

They were soon back on the Zodiac and into the bay. This time, they steered toward the outer edge of their search area, several miles west of Cayo Levantado along the northern coast. Still they could find no perfect place for Bannister to careen, and that is how it went for the next few weeks: moving their boat into places that looked to be great, but never finding anything better than good.

One afternoon, Chatterton cut the Zodiac's engine and let the boat drift on the waves. Neither he nor Mattera was the type to feel sorry for himself. But each now wished for just a little of the luck that William Phips had when he parked in Samaná Bay and stumbled onto Bannister's ship.

And that got the men to thinking.

Phips had gone to Samaná Bay to trade with locals on his way to search for the lost galleon *Concepción*. That meant there had to be hundreds of natives living in the area at the time, and it was near certain that some—or even most—of them had witnessed the battle between Bannister's pirates and the Royal Navy. Since Hispaniola belonged to the Spanish at the time, reports of the battle might have been filed with authorities back in Spain.

"I know where to get those reports," Mattera told Chatterton. "Buy me dinner at Fabio's and I'll tell you."

A few hours later, Mattera laid out his plan. A few days after that, he was on a plane headed for Madrid.

Mattera enjoyed few luxuries more than Europe's high-speed trains, and he spent most of the two-and-a-half-hour ride from Madrid to Seville gazing out the window, watching olive plantations and rust-colored soil fly past him at nearly two hundred miles per hour. In the deliberate rhythms of a speeding train, he did his best thinking, and his thoughts now were that he'd done the right thing to come looking for his English pirate in Spain.

In Seville, Mattera caught a taxi to the General Archive of the Indies. Standing at the entrance to the grand building, which dated to 1584, he imagined couriers arriving on horseback, delivering documents written by explorers, conquistadors, and shipwreck survivors. He'd been here before, researching treasure ships and dreaming of gold.

He was lost within moments of walking in the door. The grand building contained hundreds of thousands of documents comprising more than eighty million pages of original papers, each of which seemed as likely a starting place as any other. He drifted like a boat cut from its line until an attractive woman in her thirties tapped him on the shoulder. She introduced herself as an archivist, and asked, in good English, if she could help.

"Yes, I'm looking for—"

Mattera's voice boomed off the cavernous interior. He toned down to a whisper.

"I'm looking for any reports from Samaná Bay, on the northern coast of Hispaniola, from June 1686 to around June 1688. It can be from merchants."

Mattera figured that any account of the battle would have reached Spain before a year had passed. He added an extra year to make sure he didn't miss anything.

"Are you a treasure hunter?" she asked.

No one had ever asked Mattera that question.

"I guess I am," he replied.

The archivist smiled, then led Mattera through the building, taking him past floor-to-ceiling shelves of documents and papers. Only a small part of the collection, she said, had been cataloged on computer or copied to microfiche; the rest was available only by hand, as it had been for hundreds of years. The secrets to the galleons were here, yet Mattera saw little security, and he always noticed security—it had been his life's work until now.

The woman helped Mattera comb through old books and folders. She parked him at a table that looked as long as a football field and left him alone with the documents, some of which hadn't been handled in centuries.

For hours, Mattera worked at that table, searching for mention of Bannister or pirates or a battle involving navy ships. The archivist checked on him often, translating strange and curlicued words written in old Spanish, bringing him more binders. She read passages aloud to him: an account of a passenger making a confession to a clergyman as a hurricane pummeled her ship; a navigator's doubts about his captain's decision; a crewman's fear that nearby lands were inhabited by cannibals. All dramatic and fascinating, but not what Mattera was looking for.

The next morning, Mattera was first in the door, but his friend hadn't yet arrived, so he made a journey—and it was a journey in this place—to a section he'd visited the last time he was here, when he was researching lost galleons that he and Chatterton might pursue. That was in the early days of their partnership, when they dreamed in the hundreds of millions of dollars, and sunken Spanish treasure ships called to them from across oceans. Retracing his previous steps, he found his way to a binder that contained information on his favorite of all the lost Spanish galleons, the *San Miguel*.

She'd sunk in a storm in 1551, one of the earliest of Spain's great treasure ships to go down, and was carrying mostly gold, not silver. That, alone, had been enough to capture Mattera's attention. But it was the contraband that gripped him. According to Mattera's earlier research, it was likely that the *San Miguel* also hauled priceless Inca and Aztec treasures, to be sold on the lucrative European black market by the conquistadors who'd stolen them. That didn't surprise Mattera; he'd grown up among thieves and smugglers, some of them legendary. He knew what it meant to have a license to steal.

By his estimate, the *San Miguel*'s cargo was worth at least five hundred million dollars. Given the ship's history, he thought it might eclipse even the famous *Atocha* discovered by Mel Fisher off Key West in 1985. Most intriguing of all, he believed the ship sank near Samaná Bay, in waters leased by Bowden. As far as he knew, Bowden had never searched in earnest for her.

Thumbing through the file on the *San Miguel* brought back memories for Mattera. The last time he'd been here, he'd believed nothing could pull him away from his dream of finding a lost galleon. Now, he put the papers back in order and replaced them on the shelf. There were still answers in this file on the *San Miguel*, he could feel it, but his archivist friend had arrived, and he had a great pirate to go find.

Mattera pored over more binders and folders. By afternoon, it had become clear to him that he was not going to find any Spanish mention of Bannister's ship. Still, he read through every document, looking for any timely reference to pirate ships. He found a few, but none that could be linked to the *Golden Fleece*. By day's end, he was exhausted, and he still had a train to catch for Madrid that evening.

On his way out, he stopped by the archivist's desk, where he reached into his bag and gave her a small tissue-wrapped gift. It was a ceramic tile, about ten inches square, painted with Salvador Dalí's *Figure at a Window*. It showed a young woman gazing out over the bay of a Spanish seaside town. Mattera had always loved the painting because the girl seemed hopeful, like she knew something beautiful was coming, even if she couldn't see what it was at the moment. Mattera felt that way inside libraries and archives. He'd always been able to depend on these places, to find stories that moved him, to rescue him from a dangerous life. Waving good-bye to his friend, he worried for himself. Before Bannister, he'd believed there was nothing he couldn't see if only he found the right window. Now it seemed he was running out of light.

Chapter 9

JOHN MATTERA

Waiting for Jacques Cousteau

Everyone kissed in John Mattera's family. His father kissed his three sons when they visited him in his butcher shop. His mother, Ann, kissed the kids when they came home on the bus from Holy Rosary Catholic Grammar School. John's two younger brothers kissed him when he lent them his baseball glove. Once, after an insurance man made a cold call at the house, John kissed him good-bye.

That was the way in the South Beach neighborhood on the east shore of Staten Island, a community of Italian and Irish families, and in the late 1960s, one of the safest places in New York. Ladies could walk home at midnight by themselves. Home owners left their front doors unlocked. The South Beach area was home to some of the highest-ranking figures in the Gambino crime family, the most powerful mafia family in the country. Gambino boss Paul Castellano lived two miles from John; underboss Aniello Dellacroce's house was just down the street.

These men, and their world, seemed as natural a part of the landscape to John as the cement ball field at the American Legion post or the sand flats on Mills Avenue. In line at the supermarket, he heard ladies talk about loyalty; riding the school bus, he heard kids discussing respect. Men with nice haircuts and new cars met for breakfast at local diners, even in the late afternoon.

John's father, John Sr., worked more than seventy hours a week at Matty's Quality Meats, the butcher shop he owned on Hylan Boulevard, but he would still play catch every day with John and his brothers in the backyard. John loved the stories of his father's childhood, especially those about fighting his way through the Prospect Park section of Brooklyn. As the only Italian in the neighborhood, he'd learned to use his fists and wits to survive. "Me and you together back then?" John's dad would say to him. "No one could have beat us."

After grade school one day, John and some friends threw a smoke bomb into a local coffee shop. Cutting through the neighborhood, John was on the verge of a perfect getaway when a dark blue Lincoln Continental cut him off. Glaring at him from the driver's seat was Tommy Bilotti, a captain in the Gambino family with a reputation for being the toughest guy in a very tough neighborhood.

"Come here!" Bilotti ordered.

John walked up to the window, panting.

"Did you do that at the restaurant?"

"Yeah."

"Why did you do that?"

"I don't know."

Bilotti glared at John. Even at age eight, John had heard stories about what Bilotti did to people who did bad things.

"You Matty's son?"

"Yeah."

"Then get the fuck outta here. Go."

John ran, faster than he could ever remember moving, but even as the wind blew in his face and his feet flew above the ground, he understood that the bad guys who lived nearby had power and could do things the police or even his father couldn't, and that they cared about respect; he knew that for sure because he wouldn't still be running if Tommy Bilotti didn't respect his dad.

John's parents paid good money for him to attend Catholic school, but by second grade it was clear John wasn't making the most of his opportunity. Yet, on many days after school when his friends went to shoot baskets or trade baseball cards, John rode his green Schwinn Pea Picker to the two-room South Beach branch of the New York Public Library, where he immersed himself in history books, especially those on the Revolutionary War. He loved the idea of the underdog rising up against the king—what guts that took!—and even though kids teased him for spending time that way, he forgave them because they didn't know the stories hiding inside that tiny building.

One night, John's father sat him down in front of the television, poured a bowl of Wise potato chips, and showed him a new program. It featured mini-submarines, scuba divers, exotic fish, a giant boat, seaplanes, foreign accents, underwater dirigibles, faraway lands, helicopters, dashing music, and a great white shark—and that was all in the first two minutes. This was *The Undersea World of Jacques Cousteau*. From that day forward, John never missed an episode, planning not just his days but his months around the new ones. Cousteau's world, and his journey around the globe on the ship *Calypso*, were a leap into history, danger, daring, mystery, and new worlds all at once.

Most kids who loved Cousteau wished they could be on an adventure like that. What John wished for, more than anything, was to be on an adventure like that with his father. But even at age eight, he worried about whether his dad would ever get that kind of chance. John Sr. worked six and a half days a week, twelve or thirteen hours a day. It gave John and his brothers a good life, but what kind of life did it give his dad?

In fourth grade, John's class took a trip to Fort Wadsworth, a former military installation in the shadow of the Verrazano-Narrows Bridge. According to the tour guide, the place had figured in the Revolutionary War, which was all John needed to hear. Wherever he looked, he saw the ghosts of patriot soldiers, cleaning their muskets and pushing tobacco into their pipes, poised to defy the king. John hung on the guide's every word, but what he really wanted to know was how such a place could be here, just six blocks from his house.

After school, John and his friends rode their bikes back to Fort Wadsworth, where they climbed and explored, and imagined firing at enemies until the night had turned black and America had prevailed. And this is how John's life went for the next four or five years—enduring school, hitting the library or Fort Wadsworth, waiting for Jacques Cousteau.

At thirteen, John took a job at a local florist's shop to supplement the money he made from working at the butcher shop his dad owned. Kids teased him about the flowers. He wondered why it wasn't in him to use his fists to silence bullies, like his father had.

In the playground one day, several seventh graders, including Albert, the biggest kid in the school, started taunting John about carnations. He wanted to tell them that working at a florist's shop showed good character. Instead, he said, "I'm going to fight every one you. After altar boy practice Saturday morning. At the top of the hill." His legs shook so badly he could hardly walk home.

Saturday morning, John's father drove him to the fight. At the bottom of the hill, he put a hand on his son's shoulder.

"You don't have to go."

John got out of the car and walked up the hill.

Albert was waiting, along with several henchmen.

"You ready?" John asked.

"Yeah."

And John swung, with fists that reached back to his father's childhood in Prospect Park, with arms that had lifted legs of veal since grade school, with the spirit of the soldiers at Fort Wadsworth and the determination of the crew of the *Calypso*, and he hit Albert square in the jaw, knocking him down. Then he walked back down the hill and got into his father's car. Tears streamed down his cheeks.

"I won," he told his dad.

Ann Mattera had grown up poor, and eating away from home had been a luxury for her as a girl, so it was with pleasure that she took her sons to Skippy's hot dog truck whenever it parked nearby. It was there that John spotted a sign on a shop advertising scuba diving lessons.

"Go in and see what they say," Ann said.

John wolfed down the hot dog, wiped ketchup-onion sauce from his mouth, and ran to the shop. Inside, he smelled the neoprene of new wet suits and saw framed photos of divers. A man of about thirty looked up from the counter.

"What's up, Big-time?" he asked.

"I want to learn how to do scuba diving."

The man looked John up and down, especially his Catholic school uniform.

"How old are you?"

"Fourteen."

He handed John an application, then provided the lowdown. His name was Floyd Van Name, and he owned the place, Diver's Cove. Scuba lessons cost forty dollars, no refunds. They lasted sixteen weeks. Scuba was not for the timid, at least not the way Diver's Cove did it, no refunds. He'd need a physical. His parents would have to sign the forms—don't even think about signing yourself. "I don't care if you do wear a suit and tie, I'll know."

John nodded, started walking toward the door, then turned back.

"You like Jacques Cousteau?" he asked Van Name.

"What do you think?"

After a summer of scuba lessons, arranging flowers, and boning out legs of veal, John began classes at St. Peter's Boys High School on Staten Island. His teachers were sharp and the resources excellent, but John's thinking was mostly underwater. At every chance, he took the bus to Diver's Cove, asking questions of veteran divers and handling equipment he'd have to work double shifts to afford. His checkout dive came on an old wooden shipwreck in Spring Lake, New Jersey. Down deep, he pried loose a glass bottle that looked to be more than one hundred years old.

"What wreck is this?" he asked Van Name after surfacing.

"It's called the Spring Lake wreck."

"How did they know it was going to wreck in Spring Lake?"

"No, that's just what we call it. It's been here forever. No one knows its real name."

At school, teachers continued to pile on homework, but John was at work on a bigger problem. Using microfiche, periodical guides, and finally an old *Collier's* magazine, he pieced together a solution, which he wrote on an index card and took to the dive shop.

"You know that wreck in Spring Lake?" he asked Van Name.

"What about it?"

"It was an old merchant ship. Sunk in 1853. Her name is the *Western World*."

Sophomore year began with fists flying. Seniors on the baseball and wrestling teams had heard about John's reputation for toughness and decided to relieve him of it. John pounded each of them. By Christmas, he had been suspended three times for fighting.

One person who noticed was a freshman named John Bilotti. He and John had always liked each other, but this was the first time they'd attended the same school. It was John Bilotti's father, Tommy, who had cut off John's escape route after he'd thrown a smoke bomb in the coffee shop. Tommy Bilotti had enjoyed a big rise in the ranks of the Gambinos since then, and was now one of the most feared gangsters in all of New York.

One day, John and John Bilotti got to talking. There were kids at school who needed money—for cars, girls, concert tickets. Each of the boys had saved cash from working; there was no reason they couldn't lend it to classmates. They could charge the going rate in South Beach: four points a week, with the principal due after twenty-six weeks.

They started by lending a few bucks—fifty here, one hundred there—and that went well so they branched out. If their old men found out there would be trouble—neither father wanted his son earning money that way. But by now, customers were coming to them.

After a few months, John was earning hundreds a week. By the end of sophomore year, John and his friend were collecting on tens of thousands of dollars in loans, and it was a sweet business.

They didn't have to break legs or make threats. People just paid them back.

But the business really took off after John got his driver's license. Able to reach more clients, he and John Bilotti began to lend out tens of thousands of dollars. They didn't believe they were hurting anyone. And they were good at it.

Brimming with confidence, the two friends began investing in legitimate businesses, and even purchased an after-hours club they were too young by law to enter themselves. By seventeen, John was making more money than the principal of his school. Still, he never missed a shift at his dad's butcher shop.

John used some of that money to sign up for weekend dive charters to dangerous shipwrecks in New York and New Jersey waters. Though he could drive himself, he always asked his father to take him. It was fun to share the adventure—to be on the way to important places together. Driving home from the docks, John's father pressed him for details. He wanted to know everything that had happened underwater; often, John Sr. knew more about the history of the wreck or the details of her sinking than anyone on the charter. John loved that about his father, but it made him ache for his dad, too. "Take diving lessons and go with me to the wrecks," he'd say, and his dad would always answer, "Oh, man, I'd love to, pal. When I get the time, I will." But John knew better—his father had a family to support, and Matty's Quality Meats couldn't run without Matty, so the best John could do was to keep telling his father the stories, and to leave in all the details.

While John was putting money on the streets, his classmates were choosing colleges. He'd thought about it, too, but was disappointed by his transcript: all average, except for history, for which he'd received As. But John knew that people didn't go to college on history alone.

After graduation, he bought a white 1971 Ford Mustang Boss 351, his dream car. One morning, he used it to take his father to breakfast at their favorite luncheonette, Jean and Tony's. After the meal the Mustang wouldn't start. John asked his dad to give the car a push so he could start it with the clutch. When John got rolling, he looked in the rearview mirror to see his dad bent over, huffing and puffing.

Ann took her husband to doctors and they arrived at a diagnosis: lung cancer. John was floored by the news. Though he smoked three packs a day, John's dad was only forty-six and had always been strong and fit. John had no doubt his father would beat it.

They went back to the butcher shop, the two of them, every day. For a few months, his dad seemed fine, and that made sense to John, he'd seen cancer up close, in chucks of beef that looked normal until you opened them up and saw huge yellow sacs inside, and in those cases you just wrapped the meat back up, called the guy who delivered it, and sent it back.

But then his father started losing weight. He died early in 1981, at age forty-seven. John was eighteen. He didn't cry at the funeral. He just looked out at the world, knowing it was finally too late for his father to have an adventure, and nothing seemed in color anymore.

John Mattera took over his father's butcher shop, but he no longer cut meat with precision. For years, people had known him for his perpetual smile; now, he mostly stared at the ground. Four months later, his mother sold the shop. People began to steer clear of Mattera. One who did not was Tommy Bilotti, the father of his friend. Whenever Mattera stopped by the house, Tommy would put his arm around him, inquire after his mother, ask if there was anything he could do for the family. Sometimes, he'd put a few hundred dollars in Mattera's pocket, but when Mattera tried to pay him back, he'd only say, "Get outta here before I hit you." By now, Tommy lived in a twelve-thousand-square-foot waterfront mansion.

Mattera and John Bilotti grew closer, becoming best friends. Their money-lending business grew. If anyone accused them of stealing customers, they issued this response: *I don't give a fuck for you.* If anyone pressed harder, Mattera would say, "Do something about it." Almost no one did.

One exception came when Mattera was twenty, after he got into a beef with a twenty-six-year-old Gambino associate, the nephew of a made guy from another of the New York crime families. A few days later, Mattera found his apartment broken into and his guns, all legally owned, stolen. He countered by breaking into the apartment of the man he'd argued with. There, he found every one of his guns, along with forty thousand dollars in cash. He took it all.

Not long after, the man and two of his partners grabbed Mattera at gunpoint and took him to a closed-down Fine Fare Supermarket. Pushing him into a meat locker, they tied him to a chair and put a gun to his head.

"Where is the money?"

"What money?"

The men began punching and kicking Mattera.

"Where is the fucking money?

They knocked Mattera over in his chair and began stomping his head, throwing him into walls, and kneeing his face until Mattera was sure they would kill him.

"Where is our goddamn money?"

"Go fuck yourselves."

One of the men pulled out a nine-millimeter Smith & Wesson Model 59. "I'm dead," Mattera thought. But instead of pulling the trigger the man raised the gun in the air, then brought it down behind Mattera's ear. Blood oozed onto the meat locker floor.

Another man pulled out a stun gun and shocked Mattera. Then he called to his friends, "Get the bat."

The men left the room. Lying in a pool of his own blood, Mattera thought, "If they were going to kill me I'd be dead already. So when I get out of here they're finished."

The men didn't return. A nearby store owner came in with a bag of ice, put Mattera in a taxi, and sent the driver to the hospital. In the emergency room, doctors stitched up Mattera and told him he was lucky to be alive.

John Bilotti picked him up a few hours later.

"My father wants to see you," he said.

By now, Tommy Bilotti was acting underboss of the Gambino family, the second highest position in the organization, and running much of Staten Island, parts of Brooklyn and Manhattan, and the docks. At his front door, he stared at the turban of bandages on Mattera's head and asked his wife to excuse them.

"Tell me what happened and don't fucking lie to me. Were you dealing drugs?"

"I swear, Tommy, never."

"Don't fucking lie to me."

"Tommy, I swear, no drugs. He broke into my house. I broke into his house."

"And you took one hundred fifty grand from him."

"No. I got forty thousand."

"What else did you get?"

"My guns."

"You found your guns in there?"

"Yeah."

"Okay. I'll take care of it."

Mattera knew this was supposed to be the end of the conversation. But he couldn't leave it there.

"Tommy, with all due respect, this is something I need to take care of myself."

Bilotti thought it over.

"Okay," he said. "But I'm going to tell you two things. First, I want you to make a measured response—don't go crazy, don't kill anyone, don't fuck up your life. Second, when you're better, I'm going to kick the shit out of you. Because that's what your father would do."

Mattera's father, in fact, never would have hit him, but it touched Mattera that Tommy was trying to help in a fatherly way.

Mattera got up to leave. Tommy called after him.

"Measured response."

On the Fourth of July, Mattera found out that the man who'd stolen his guns and beat him was going to be watching fireworks with his fiancée near the beach. In late afternoon, Mattera got into John Bilotti's Cadillac and the two men drove to the site. By the time they arrived it was dusk. No one said a word as Mattera moved through the crowd carrying a baseball bat. He found the guy drinking Sambuca with friends.

"What the—" the man said at the sight of Mattera, but before he could finish Mattera hit him in the mouth with the bat, knocking out all of his teeth, and breaking his jaw and cheekbone. Mattera reached back to hit him again but feared he'd already exceeded a measured response. He dropped the bat and walked back to the car. Police arrived a few minutes later. Though it had happened in front of hundreds of people, no one had seen a thing.

Two weeks later, the man's uncle contacted Tommy Bilotti and arranged for a sit-down. The meeting was set for a Staten Island pizzeria owned by the man Mattera had pummeled. That man would be represented by his uncle. Mattera would be represented by Tommy.

The sit-down occurred a few weeks later. Mattera, John, and Tommy were led to the back of the pizzeria, which was decorated in glass and mirrors, the furniture in salmon leather.

"Disgusting," Tommy said. "This is Staten Island, not the inside of I Dream of Jeannie's bottle."

The injured man spoke first, counting off Mattera's offenses. Mattera did the same. Then, the made guys spoke.

"Tommy, I think a certain amount of restitution has to be made here," the uncle said. "This kid stole a lot of money and did a lot of damage. He needs a big-time beating. What's right is right."

Bilotti thought it over.

"I'll tell you what's going to happen," he said. "This pizzeria your nephew owns? It's closed now. That arcade he owns? I own that now. This is your relative? You like him? You take him. He goes back to New York with you. This day is the last day he's on Staten Island. If I see him here again you can come after me because I'm going to kill him. And anything the Mattera kid took is his."

The uncle seethed but knew Tommy was within his rights according to the unwritten and ancient laws of organized crime. Mattera could hardly believe it. He was at the center of a quintessential mob sit-down like he'd seen in the movies. And he'd won.

A few months later, Mattera dropped by the Bilotti house. Tommy, as always, asked him in for breakfast. In the kitchen, Tommy fried an omelet, put bread in the toaster, and then, swinging from the ground up, hit Mattera across the face with an open hand, leaving him sprawling and dazed on the floor.

"That's the beating I owed you," Tommy said. "Your dad didn't want you in trouble. Now pick yourself up and eat eggs."

Mattera's business expanded rapidly after that, and though he was young, single, and flush with cash, the darkness of his father's passing still hung over him. At night, he wrote letters to Lloyd's of London requesting copies of registries for missing ships they'd insured. His happiest days were when packages arrived, post-marked in colorful stamps from England, stuffed with pages of clues as to where some of these ships might be found.

Not long after Mattera turned twenty-two, he roughed up a tough guy who'd stolen money from him. Word on the street was that the guy had a gun and was looking for him, so Mattera made sure he had a gun, too. They found each other on McClean Avenue. From a distance of ten yards, the man drew his weapon and started firing at Mattera, and Mattera responded in kind. Each man emptied his gun, somehow missing the other. Then they began punching, and even as he landed blows, Mattera thought, "What am I doing here? Where am I going to end up in this life?"

But whenever he made a move to get out—by opening an auto towing company or his own butcher shop—he drifted back to his lending business. It was then that Tommy Bilotti was promoted again, from acting to full underboss, just under the big boss, Paul Castellano. If ever there was opportunity to make big money, that time was now.

Still, neither John Mattera nor John Bilotti made a move to expand. Mattera continued to run the new butcher shop he'd opened, and it was there, in mid-December 1985, that a friend rushed in and told him that Tommy Bilotti had been killed in midtown Manhattan, shot in cold blood outside Sparks Steak House, along with Paul Castellano. It was an audacious assassi-nation in front of New Yorkers doing their Christmas shopping. Newscasters were calling it the biggest mob hit since the 1929 St. Valentine's Day Massacre.

Mattera took off his apron, grabbed a Browning Hi Power

nine-millimeter pistol from the meat locker, and closed shop. He drove to Tommy's house, found John inside, and put his arm around him. For the next eight hours, he stood by the door with his weapon and waited, ready to protect his friend in case anyone had ideas about hurting another Bilotti.

Shortly after the murders, John Bilotti was called in for a sit-down with Sammy "The Bull" Gravano, the new underboss of the Gambino family. War was breaking out and word had it that John Gotti, who had ordered the killings of Castellano and Bilotti, and was the new boss, wanted to make peace with those who might have a grudge against him. Many viewed John Bilotti as a fine mind and loyal son who was not likely to allow his father's murder to go unavenged. The way Mattera and Bilotti saw it, there were only two potential outcomes from a sit-down with Gravano: Bilotti would be killed, or he would become a made member of the family. Bilotti could not decide which of the two he preferred least.

So he decided not to show.

The decision would displease Gotti, so Mattera and Bilotti went on the lam. For months, they moved between rural Pennsylvania, upstate New York, and Staten Island, never staying in one place for more than a day, never going anywhere without weapons. On the road, they discussed baseball and cars, dated girls, and drew up plans for new businesses.

Again, Gravano urged Bilotti to come in for a sit-down. That's when Mattera and Bilotti had a serious talk.

A life in organized crime, or even on its fringes, rarely ended well. One after another, neighborhood guys went to jail or wound up buried in the sand flats or lived in constant fear. So, yes, if Bilotti sat down with Gravano, there was a chance he would be killed. But there was also a chance the Gambinos would listen when he said that he and Mattera wanted nothing to do with the life.

A sit-down was scheduled. Bilotti would not swear allegiance to Gotti nor would he ask to be made. He would simply deliver his message: He wanted out.

On the night of the meeting, Mattera and another friend armed themselves heavily in case the worst happened. They would follow Bilotti to the sit-down and wait outside. If Bilotti came out at the end of the meeting, they would all go for pizza. If he did not, Mattera and his friend would go in with guns blazing.

A tan Cadillac picked up Bilotti and set out toward Brooklyn. Mattera and his friend followed in the distance. They lost the Caddy going over the Verrazano-Narrows Bridge, but picked it up again at the Ninety-Second Street exit, then followed to a small bar in Brooklyn called the 19th Hole. Bilotti and three men walked into the bar.

A half hour passed.

Then an hour.

Mattera's friend wanted to go in shooting, but Mattera held him back—maybe the men were still talking. Finally, four figures emerged and got into the tan Cadillac, but in the dark Mattera couldn't tell whether one of them was Bilotti. So Mattera and his friend followed the car. Near Eighty-Sixth Street, the Cadillac pulled over.

Mattera's heart pounded. All he wanted now was to see his friend's face, but no one was moving in that car.

Then, he heard a click.

Slowly, a door on the Caddy swung open and a man got out. He began walking, quickly, toward Mattera.

Mattera reached for his gun, but he recognized the man's gait. It was Bilotti.

"You almost got them to shoot you," Bilotti said. "But I love you."

"You okay?"

"Yeah. Let's get pizza."

Crammed around a tiny table at Spumoni Gardens in Brooklyn, Bilotti told his friends what happened. He and Gravano had talked for more than an hour. Gravano told him the family couldn't function at war with itself—guys were getting killed and he wanted to make sure Bilotti wasn't involved. Bilotti looked into the eyes of one of the most feared killers in organized crime and said, "I don't want any part of this business. My father didn't want me in this business. You leave my friends and my family out of it, and we have no intention of getting involved." Gravano looked him up and down and said, "Well, then, it's done between us."

A few months later, Mattera walked into Magnum Sports on Staten Island, the largest indoor shooting range in New York. He struck up a friendship with Pat Rogers, a forty-year-old detective sergeant in the New York City Police Department, and the best shooter Mattera had seen. Rogers rarely missed—two rounds center mass almost every time—and he was smart and interesting, someone Mattera could talk to.

Rogers began mentoring Mattera at the range, five sharp every morning, the two of them cranking off hundreds of rounds until each was standing in brass. It wasn't long before the owner of Magnum offered Mattera a job—for less in a month than he used to make in a day—and Mattera took it.

At the range one day, Mattera helped a customer with a broken mainspring on his .45 automatic, no charge, happy to do it. The customer asked if Mattera might be looking to become a police officer, a reasonable question given the venue. Mattera was intrigued by the idea. Of course, he presumed he'd never qualify given the life he'd led. But then he got to thinking. Despite all his capers, he'd never come under police scrutiny for anything more than a traffic violation.

He showed up the next day at the Westhampton Beach police station on Long Island. The customer with the broken .45 turned out to be the town's chief of police. The man took Mattera's photo and had him sign papers, then took him across the street to a courthouse, where a judge told Mattera to raise his right hand and swear to uphold the laws of the state of New York.

"No one back on Staten Island is going to believe this," he thought. "Even I don't believe this."

He made the pledge. They handed him a badge and a police ID card, and told him to report to the police academy in a month.

Mattera was a natural in the classroom. By graduation, he carried a ninety-nine average and was named valedictorian. Westhampton Beach hired him on provisional status. There was a hiring freeze on full-time employees, but that wouldn't affect his hours or pay, and he took the job. Soon, he was out on the streets working a beat.

Other cops didn't see what Mattera did. If there were bad guys packing guns, Mattera knew. If college kids were selling drugs, he knew. If a senior citizen out for a stroll was really casing a home in order to rob it, he knew.

No one on Staten Island could believe he'd become a cop. Made members of the Gambino family threw friendly punches into his arm and said, "What did we do wrong with you?" The one person who seemed most happy for him was John Bilotti. "It doesn't surprise me," he told Mattera, who picked him up one day and took him for pastries in his police car. "You always could do whatever you wanted."

Mattera loved being a cop—making pinches others missed, thinking like a bad guy in order to do good—and he did it for two years until it became clear that, due to the hiring freeze, he would always be provisional. By this time, however, he was thinking bigger about law enforcement.

He went to live in Missouri and Arizona in order to learn from Jeff Cooper and Ray Chapman, the fathers of modern combat shooting. This was the Ivy League of gunfighting, and Mattera took to it right away. And he made friends at the school. One of them, through contacts at government agencies, arranged for Mattera to do covert work overseas, the kind that required a man who wouldn't flinch.

Working as a contractor for the U.S. government, Mattera traveled to Nicaragua, Turkey, Montenegro, and a dozen other high-risk countries, distributing propaganda, protecting shipments, and training security details. He worked mostly in war zones, always in the shadows.

In his early thirties, he flew to a third-world country hostile to the United States to conduct covert surveillance. A contact he trusted there betrayed him, leaving him pinned in a burned-out building and surrounded by armed insurgents eager to collect the rich bounties paid for the heads of Americans.

His only hope for survival was to make it back on foot to the American Embassy, more than a mile away. But he didn't dare try it in daylight, so he passed the hours running through New York Mets lineups he'd memorized as a kid, and counting off the things he'd meant to do in life but hadn't yet made time for. When he needed to calm himself for his nighttime run—one he likely wouldn't survive—he thought about shipwrecks, and of how beautiful it would be to find one that no one knew was there.

After dark, Mattera walked, slowly and purposefully, to the embassy. He waited for shots to ring out but the road remained silent. Six hours later, he was on a flight back to the States. On the government airplane, he kept his hand on his gun and promised himself that no matter what, he wouldn't put off until tomorrow what his heart told him to go for today.

After Mattera returned home, his uncle died of lung cancer, just as Mattera's father had a decade earlier. People at the funeral tried to console him, but no matter what anyone did, Mattera could not stop crying. It was the first time he'd cried since before his father died.

By 1992, Mattera had attended dozens of law enforcement–related specialty schools, covering everything from the operation of submachine guns to explosive room breaching to the latest in hostage negotiation. That year, he took a job with a security company in Virginia.

He provided executive protection for CEOs, celebrities, and dignitaries, and he flourished. Soon, he was earning at the top of the pay grade, all for doing what came naturally. He did this work for years, building a reputation and protecting the kinds of people who appeared on the cover of *Time* magazine.

In 1998, Mattera married Denise, a woman from Staten Island who had a five-year-old daughter, Danielle. On his farm in Virginia, he would unroll a "treasure map" (really, a plan of his property), put Danielle on his tractor, and set out looking for gold. Time and again, they found foreign coins Mattera had buried in advance, which thrilled the little girl. Once, after inspecting the date on a piece of treasure, she asked Mattera why the coin was only three years old. "I don't know," he responded. "Treasure is a mysterious thing."

By 2000, Mattera had a baby daughter, Dana. Sensing that he could build something special for his family, he and a partner bought the security company outright. They had more work than they could handle, and soon, Mattera was taking home more than a million dollars a year. If a celebrity or CEO needed protection, Mattera himself was available at rates that made him among the highest paid bodyguards in America.

Now he could see the mountain. If he and his partner continued to push, there was no limit to where they could go. Giants in the industry put out feelers to see if Mattera and his partner would sell, but Mattera had long since made up his mind. Building this company was his chance to do something historic.

There were costs, however, to doing it. He often worked twenty-hour days. High-risk projects—his company's sweet spot—ate away at his stomach, making him dependent on a milk shake of Mylanta, Excedrin, and Advil. Tensions were building with Denise.

When a buyout offer from a global security giant arrived in 2002, Mattera and his partner listened. By putting his name to the contract, he would walk away with three million dollars in cash, and the buyer would pay him a consulting salary. At age forty, he could live on the interest from his savings alone.

The offer was generous, but the chance to build his business into something world-class was too rare for Mattera to give up. His partner, however, wanted him to sell, and he wasn't the only one. Some of Mattera's friends and family also urged him to get out, reminding him of people they knew who regretted not taking the sure thing. The buyer needed an answer.

In a law firm conference room in Manhattan, Mattera signed his name to a pile of papers, and in a moment his company was gone. Walking the streets outside, not headed in any particular direction, he couldn't shake the sense that, after a lifetime of challenging big worlds, he'd gone and sold himself short.

His marriage, already strained, began breaking, and he and Denise separated. Even Mattera's guns let him down; he took them to the range but could never muster the will to unpack them. He waited for these feelings to pass, reminded himself of his good fortune. Yet, when it came time to drive his $125,000 Mercedes, he couldn't think of anywhere to go but Jean and Tony's, where he ordered the same bacon and egg on a roll he and his father had loved to eat there on Saturday mornings when John was a boy.

As the months passed, it occurred to Mattera that he might be chasing the wrong things in life. Money was great and success important, but at bottom, he loved history. It was the one thing that spoke to him, and yet he'd never set out after it himself. He'd come close through the years—by diving unexplored shipwrecks and solving small mysteries in great archives—but even then he was still one step removed, an observer looking back through the distance. What he really wanted, and had since grade school, was to do something historic himself, to add an enduring story of his own.

He might have done that by rising to the top in organized crime, but he hadn't wanted to live a life of violence. He might have done it by taking his security company global, but what kid would want to read about that in a hundred years?

That's when he moved to the Dominican Republic. Diving the waters around Santo Domingo, he began to feel like himself again. He started Pirate's Cove, an exclusive resort for scuba divers. And he began dating Carolina Garcia. She loved history as much as Mattera did. Soon, Mattera came to love Carolina.

And then he came up with a plan.

He would set out in search of a galleon, a treasure ship loaded with gold and silver that had sailed between the New World and Spain in the sixteenth and seventeenth centuries. He bought a boat and equipment and did a thousand hours of research. In 2006, he joined forces with Chatterton, the most driven and relentless person he'd ever met. Together, they pledged their savings to the project, which would make them rich and the toasts of the diving world.

And then, on the eve of the search, he'd thrown it all over to look for a pirate ship.

The sudden change of plans risked his treasure dreams and his savings—political winds were blowing hard against salvors, and every week spent searching the seas cost thousands. But Mattera had no choice. Finding a Golden Age pirate ship was rarer than stepping on the moon. Only one had ever been discovered and positively identified. But it was the pirate, even more than the ship, that took hold of him. To Mattera, Joseph Bannister couldn't have become the most wanted man in the Caribbean and defeated the Royal Navy in battle without meaning to do something historic himself. And for that, Mattera was willing to risk whatever it took to go find him.

All that remained was to tell Carolina his plan. Over dinner at a seaside restaurant, he told her all he knew about Bannister and the *Golden Fleece*. And he told her what the search could cost him.

Carolina took his hand.

"I'm with you," she said. "I think you've been searching for this pirate for a very long time."

Chapter 10

THE ORACLES

Mattera flew back to Santo Domingo after his journey to the archive in Seville, but he didn't go on to Samaná to rejoin his team. Instead, he made phone calls to old men in America, living legends of treasure hunting who knew things a person couldn't learn from books. He doubted that any of them had chased a pirate before—these men lived for silver and gold— but he believed in wisdom and experience, and in that way, they were oracles to him. Soon, he had appointments to see the best of them.

He flew to Florida and checked into a hotel in Key Largo. At a lobby kiosk, he saw a brochure for the Pirate Soul Museum in Key West. "See real pirate treasures from the Golden Age!" "No quarter given!" Mattera stuffed the flyer into his pocket. Key West was one hundred miles to the south. He had people to see the next day. But pirates were calling, so he started driving.

Standing in line outside the museum, he took in the passing parade of bohemians, artists, and tourists. To him, Key West was laid-back and glorious, a place he could live for up to a week before going crazy and needing something to do.

He paid the $13.95 entry fee and walked back in time. In the first few rooms, he saw authentic pirate swords, pistols, treasure, cannons, rum bottles, and tools, including a gruesome amputation kit. The museum even had a globule of quicksilver—mercury— captured from pirates and entombed in a small jar of water. All of it dated to the Golden Age of Piracy, between 1650 and 1720. But the rarest items were still to come.

Hanging on one wall, ominously lit, was an original Jolly Roger, the infamous skull-and-crossbones flag flown by pirates, and one of only two known surviving examples in the world. Near it lay the only pirate treasure chest in America, complete with hidden compartments and belonging to captain Thomas Tew, number three on *Forbes* magazine's list of the Twenty Highest-Earning Pirates (estimated career earnings $103 million), who was said to have been disemboweled and killed by a cannon shot during battle. On another wall, Mattera saw an authentic English proclamation from 1696, offering five hundred pounds for the head of pirate Henry Avery; the piece was likely the oldest wanted poster in existence.

The museum had been put together by Pat Croce, the former owner of the Philadelphia 76ers, from his personal collection. "This guy might love basketball," Mattera thought as he stood before a 1684 first-edition copy of Exquemelin's *The Buccaneers of America*. "But he loves pirates more."

Mattera didn't leave until he'd read about the great pirates, and they all lived here: Morgan, Blackbeard, Kidd, Anne Bonny, "Black Sam" Bellamy, "Calico" Jack Rackham. Each one's career seemed more thrilling than the last. Yet, walking out the door into the blinding Key West sun, Mattera couldn't help but smile, because he knew a pirate captain who could top them all.

The next day, Mattera walked into Manny and Isa's restaurant in Islamorada, about twenty-five miles south of Key Largo, and shook hands with a quiet, slightly built eighty-year-old man named Jack Haskins. Few names were better known in the treasure business, yet Haskins had never been the classic treasure hunter.

A researcher first, he had done work that had led to the discovery of some of the greatest Spanish galleons ever found. In talking to others about treasure, Mattera always heard the same things about Haskins: first, that he knew more about finding old shipwrecks than anyone in the world; second, that he was a decent and honest man, a rarity in the business; and third, that he'd been taken advantage of throughout his career.

Haskins recommended the conch chowder, and the two men got to talking. In treasure, he said, information was paramount. A person could own the latest technology, operate the finest boat, and have the deepest pockets, but little of that mattered without knowing where to look. And that always came down to research.

Haskins's own research had begun in Seville, at the General Archive of the Indies, the place from which Mattera had just returned. As a young man, he'd made a pilgrimage there, armed only with an English-Spanish dictionary and a hunger to find a galleon, and over the next few years made himself fluent in the archaic language and script that told the story of the great Spanish treasure fleets.

Soon, treasure hunters began paying Haskins to do research in Seville. He stayed for weeks at a time, completing assignments, then copying thousands of other documents, some of them seemingly at random, until he'd built an archive of his own—one that filled even the bathrooms and reached to the ceilings of his small Florida home. He used some of that research to find shipwrecks himself; by many accounts, he was as fine a treasure hunter in the water as he was in the stacks in Seville. But perhaps Haskins's greatest contributions came from the groundbreaking research he did that helped lead to the discovery of the galleons *Atocha*, *Concepción*, *Tolosa*, *Guadalupe*, *San José*, and *Maravilla*.

Many thought Haskins had never received the credit, or treasure, he deserved. At times, his finances had run so low he'd been forced to sell his scuba gear. Supporters urged him to fight for his rights, sue, throw a punch, anything; attorneys offered to take his cases for free. But he'd seen enough combat on PT boats in World War II, and he was a gentle soul. Instead of fighting, he returned to the archives, finding things no one else could find, diving his own wrecks, selling enough antique coins to survive. Now almost eighty, he was renowned in the world of treasure—not just for his ability to find valuable shipwrecks, but for his instinct to forgive those who'd wronged him.

Mattera ordered a piece of key lime pie and sat back and listened to Haskins talk treasure. Modern gold and silver, Haskins said, could not compare in beauty or presence to the old gold and silver found on galleons, which had been mined using mercury, a dangerous process no longer permitted but which produced a remarkable purity. The imperfection of handmade early Spanish coins, or "cobs"—no two were exactly alike—made discovery endlessly interesting. The amounts of contraband carried by some treasure ships still staggered Haskins's imagination.

"But I know you want to talk about pirates," Haskins said. "Why don't you follow me home and we'll do that. I want to show you a few things."

Mattera pulled into the driveway of a modest house built on stilts, a must in the flood-prone area. A narrow set of stairs led to the front door, which Haskins climbed carefully—there was no railing, so he held the side of the house for support. Inside, copies of centuries-old Spanish documents towered high in every room— hundreds of thousands of pages written in a near-indecipherable hand. There was little else in the place, not even a television.

"I married once, briefly. Never had any kids," Haskins said. "Mostly, it's been just me, my cats, and my research."

Every few minutes, Haskins picked a random page from a

random box and read aloud to Mattera—about cargo lost from a doomed galleon, the worries of a captain on the eve of his journey back to Spain, the accounts of survivors who had seen their loved ones vanish during storms. All of them came from the logs of treasure ships, many still out there waiting to be found.

In the kitchen, Haskins poured Mattera a cup of coffee.

"You're working in Samaná and looking for a pirate," Haskins said. "Which means you must be looking for our friend Mr. Bannister."

Mattera smiled.

"You know about Bannister?"

Haskins did. He'd come across mention of the pirate and his ship, the *Golden Fleece*, while researching the *Concepción*. He'd even done research in Seville on the wreck, just as Mattera had the previous week. That alone made Mattera feel like he was playing in the big leagues. But it worried him, too. If a historian like Haskins couldn't track down Bannister's ship, what chance did he have on his own?

"What can I do, Jack?" Mattera asked. "I'm running out of ideas."

Haskins sipped from his coffee and thought it over. Shipwreck research, he said, wasn't just about looking through books and records. In the case of Spanish galleons, it was about understanding the nature of the target, the treasure ship—why she sailed when she did, what she feared, the shortcuts she used, the chances she took. In the case of the *Golden Fleece*, perhaps it meant understanding the same things about a pirate ship.

Haskins showed Mattera more documents and maps he'd acquired over a lifetime of research, then walked Mattera back to his car. Standing in the driveway, the men shook hands. Mattera needed to leave—he could see Haskins was tired—but he couldn't go without asking one last question.

"Do you feel like you got ripped off all these years, Jack?"

For a moment, Haskins didn't reply. Then he smiled.

"I just loved the wrecks."

Mattera's next appointment, the following morning, was a three-hour drive north of Key Largo, but he was eager to make it. Seventy-five-year-old Bob Marx was one of the most successful treasure hunters ever. A former marine, underwater archaeologist, and the author of dozens of books on treasure and shipwrecks, he listed nearly one hundred major discoveries on his curriculum vitae, and that was just the short version of the document. By turns bombastic, brilliant, and profane, he'd discovered, among other things, the sunken city of Port Royal, Jamaica; the Spanish galleon *Nuestra Señora de las Maravillas*; lost Mayan temples in the jungles of Central America; and ancient Phoenician ports and wrecks in Lebanon.

Few men knew more about shipwreck hunting, or had seen more of the business, than Marx. He'd recovered millions of dollars in treasure, lectured in more than forty countries, and been knighted by the Spanish government for sailing in a replica of Columbus's ship the *Niña* from Spain to San Salvador, a journey that had risked his life. When customers purchased his treasure, they received a certificate of authenticity signed "Sir Robert Marx."

In recent months, Mattera had become friendly with Marx, but it hadn't always been that way. In 1998, Marx had insulted Mattera, whom he did not know, at a book signing. Years later, when Marx showed up at a dive conference Mattera was sponsoring in the Dominican Republic, Mattera told him, "You're too old for me to punch you in the face, Bob, but I can still yell at you," and gave him an uncensored piece of his mind. To Mattera's surprise, Marx apologized for the long-ago incident. That meant a lot to Mattera, given that he owned twenty-eight of Marx's books and considered him a pioneer—and that Marx clearly didn't remember the event.

But that was a long time ago. Now Marx was waiting for him in the driveway and waving him in.

"Are you packing?" Marx asked. He wanted to know if Mattera had brought a gun.

"Yeah, it's in the glove compartment."

"Good. We might need it. There's some crazy bastard after me, don't ask why. Just bring the piece."

Marx was a hero to Mattera, so he did as he was asked.

The men walked up a pathway lined with shards of ancient pottery, the detritus of countless Marx scores.

"In the old days, everyone in the treasure business lived within about two or three miles of right here," Marx said. "I don't care if you worked in the Bahamas, Florida, Cuba, you were based here. All the astronauts were involved, 'Hot Lips' Houlihan from *M*A*S*H*—you name it. This was the place to be."

Inside the house, Marx introduced his wife and co-author, Jenifer. Mattera had read her work and spoken to her on the phone; if anything, she was even more impressive than her husband. The couple wanted to show Mattera around the house, but he stood frozen in the dining room. He stared at a bronze disk about the size of a grapefruit resting on a high shelf.

"There it is," Mattera said.

The mariner's astrolabe predated the sextant and had been used as early as the late 1300s to determine latitude at sea. Coveted by treasure hunters, archaeologists, collectors, and museums, a single example could fetch as much as half a million dollars at auction. Marx had a dozen of them lined up beside the one Mattera was beholding.

And that was just the start of the treasures Mattera observed on his way to the kitchen: a piece of pre-Ming dynasty china (circa 1200) with delicate dancing dolphins; pristine olive jars taken from sunken galleons; a jade burial suit that dated, by Mattera's estimation, to around 200 B.C., used to bury royal members of China's Han dynasty. Mattera couldn't begin to calculate the value of that piece, if a value could be placed on it at all.

The men walked outside and crossed a small path to Marx's office, which had once been the slave quarters on an old sugar plantation. Here, Mattera saw an even better kind of treasure—tens of thousands of books on double-deep shelves that seemed to stretch forever.

"Don't touch those horses!" Marx called out when Mattera moved past sculptures recovered from a centuries-old Portuguese ship. "They're a hundred grand apiece, don't fucking break them!"

On a bench near Marx's desk, Mattera saw a copy of a coffee-table book about Marx's discovery of ancient Phoenician artifacts; on a nearby table, he saw hundreds of those very artifacts, and others millennia old, laid out on display.

"I'll sell you whatever you want," Marx said. "Friends and family price. I'll throw in a certificate of authenticity, too. There's an X-rated section in the back. The ancients loved that shit."

For the next several hours, Marx told stories about treasure hunters, past and present. Each was laced with adventure and close calls, but most of them underlined what Marx had said decades earlier—"Treasure is trouble"—a line that had become gospel in the business. Outsiders took the saying to mean that treasure hunters usually ended up broke, which was true, but not what Marx meant. The trouble he was referring to resided in the hearts of the unlucky few who found treasure—to the weight that gold and silver placed on the soul. Time and again through history, treasure turned honorable men greedy and brought out the worst in the well-intentioned. Just the sight of it caused reasonable people to sever marriages, friendships, and partnerships; to cheat investors; to fight for more than their fair share. In this way, gold and silver performed alchemies of their own. By mixing with human instinct, they could turn even the pious base.

Mattera could have listened to Marx's stories all day, but he'd come to talk about pirates, and he pressed Marx on the subject. Marx, in fact, had mentioned Bannister and the *Golden Fleece* briefly in one of his books, and now Mattera wanted to know more.

"There's no map or secret instructions for finding the *Golden Fleece*," Marx said. "If you're going to get her, you've gotta understand what these guys were doing. You gotta know the pirates."

Marx himself had come to learn a lot about piracy when, in 1964, he fulfilled a childhood dream by salvaging the sunken city of Port Royal, Jamaica, the fabled pirate haven lost in an earthquake in 1692. It was in Port Royal that Bannister had stolen his own ship and turned pirate. It was from Port Royal that the manhunt for him had been directed.

"Pirates from all over the world went to Port Royal," Marx said. "Big things were happening there. Your guy was part of all that. He was there in its heyday. That's gotta tell you something."

Mattera spent the rest of the afternoon talking to Marx, absorbing his stories. In late afternoon, the men went to another of Marx's offices in town, where the old treasure hunter showed photographs from his career. By the time they left, it was near dark, but Marx was still going strong as ever, limping from gout as they made their way to the car, still firing off profanity-pocked stories of treasure derring-do. It was clear to Mattera that the man would never retire—that treasure was not something Marx did but rather something he was. Like William Phips in the late 1600s,

Marx seemed to exist on confidence—on an inborn instinct to take rather than ask from the sea. Retire? And do what, take a Perillo bus tour of Europe? Get an early-bird price on a meal? In the end, Mattera thought, it didn't matter if guys like Marx got too old to actually find the stuff; they weren't really in it for the treasure. In the end, they seemed in it to set sail, to search for things others didn't dare look for, to be "Sir Robert" instead of Bob.

Mattera had one more appointment to keep. In ways, he looked forward to this one most of all.

Carl Fismer had a reputation for being a maestro in a business full of great storytellers. He was also known for his honesty and integrity; as with Haskins, his close friend, it had probably cost him several fortunes. He'd worked on some important wrecks, including *Concepción*. And he'd worked in Samaná Bay. Many said that "Fizz" knew even more about human nature than about treasure.

Generations of salvors knew Fizz's story. He'd worked for General Motors in Cincinnati but despised it; every day seemed the same to him there. He moved to Florida in 1968, after his wife, who'd been his high school sweetheart, was killed in an automobile accident. She was just twenty-six. Punching the clock didn't feel right to Fizz after that. He gathered his two young children, packed his car, and drove south.

In Sarasota, he joined the fire department, the closest thing he could find to a paying adventure. Practicing body recovery on a fireboat, he came across a shipwreck, a small freighter busted open and showing its copper pipes. Fizz and the other firemen salvaged what they could. In the end, the haul netted the men a total of $6.40, but the idea that he could take money from water inspired Fizz, and from that day he was hooked.

For months, he visited every library and bookstore within a day's drive of Sarasota, reading everything he could on Spanish galleons and sunken treasure. He built his own magnetometer, a hodgepodge of transistors and wires that turned out to be better at picking up local radio stations than metal, but it just made him hungrier still. For six years, he searched the waters near Sarasota but found almost nothing. Only then, at age thirty-six, did he drive to the Keys, not to go looking for treasure, but to find the man who had practically invented the hunt.

Art McKee was considered the grandfather of American treasure hunting. He'd found several Spanish galleons in Florida waters in the 1940s, part of the fabled 1733 Fleet, and had been featured in *Life* magazine, on *The Dave Garroway Show*, and in newspapers, magazines, and newsreels. Before McKee, few in America knew that real-life treasure hunters existed. McKee had built a treasure museum next to his house in Islamorada, and that's where Fizz found him, riding on a lawn mower. By now, McKee was in his sixties.

"I want to be a treasure hunter," Fizz told him, "and I'm willing to work for free to learn the business."

"I bet you're a diver," McKee said.

"Yes, sir."

"What else can you do? Are you a boat captain? A mechanic? Have medical training? Can you cook?"

"No, none of that."

"Everyone's a diver. Got too many of those."

Fizz got into his car and drove back to Sarasota, where he enrolled in an emergency medical technician course, earned his boat captain's license, learned to work on small engines, and volunteered to cook for fifteen firemen a day at the firehouse. Two years later, he drove back to Islamorada, where he found McKee, again, on the lawn mower.

"I'm Carl Fismer. I want to be a treasure hunter and I'm willing to work for free to learn the business."

"I bet you're a diver."

"Yes, sir."

"What else can you do?"

"I'm a boat captain, I fix small engines, I'm a state-certified paramedic, and I cook. Meatloaf is my specialty."

"Good. You're on my next trip."

And with that, Fizz began to learn from the master. It was the start of a career that would take him on adventures across the world.

Mattera found Fizz's address in Tavernier, a small town about seven miles south of Key Largo, and knocked at the door of a small house beside a winding canal. A stocky, tanned, and handsome sixty-eight-year-old man answered the door. He sported a neatly trimmed gray beard, Hawaiian shirt, khaki shorts and deck shoes, and a heavy silver coin around his neck.

"Come on in and let's talk shipwrecks."

Mattera looked around. On every shelf, atop the television, behind the coffeemaker, he saw shipwreck artifacts. On the TV stand, he spotted a silver coin, its date clearly marked—1639.

"That's the second-best coin I ever found," said Fizz.

"I'm guessing the best one is around your neck."

"You guess good."

Fizz knew Mattera wanted to discuss pirates, so they sat at the kitchen table, where Fizz said the best stories got told.

"Let me hear what you got," Fizz said.

And Mattera told him the story—about Bannister and the *Golden Fleece*, about searching Samaná Bay with Chatterton, about doing exhaustive research in libraries, archives, antiquarian bookstores, and rare-map dealers.

"I'm lost, Fizz. I don't know what to do next."

Fizz got Mattera a beer.

"What are you best at, John?"

"What do you mean?"

"What do you love doing when you're looking for a wreck? Is it the survey work? Diving? Digging? What gets you?"

"It's the history. The research."

"Then you need to keep doing that."

But Mattera had already done months of research and read everything he could find, and he told Fizz so. That's when Fizz told him a story about Jack Haskins.

Like many treasure hunters in the late 1960s, Haskins had been working to find the *Atocha,* a Spanish galleon sunk off the Florida Keys in 1622. For centuries, salvors believed the ship to be lost off the village of Islamorada, in the central Florida Keys, but no one could find a trace of her there. So Haskins, a historian in his heart, went to Seville.

He threw himself into the stacks there, unearthing thousands of pages of documents, many of which hadn't been handled since the seventeenth century. He spent years going through the papers but never found anything that helped further the search.

"That's when most guys would have given up," said Fizz. "But not Jack."

Haskins kept reading, even the most obscure papers—ones that didn't even seem worth the price of a photocopy in Seville. One day, he ran across a single sentence buried in one of those thousands of papers. It mentioned a place called Marquesas Keys, off Key West, about eighty miles from where most treasure hunters in search of the *Atocha* were working at the time. Haskins shared that information—it was his nature to share—and it helped lead treasure hunter (and former chicken rancher) Mel Fisher to the wreck. Soon, the *Atocha* became the most famous treasure ship of all time.

"She's been worth half a billion so far," Fizz said. "Jack got almost nothing, but that's another story. One of the richest treasure wrecks ever was found because he never gave up on those papers."

The first fishing boats began returning to dock, so the men went out on Fizz's screened porch to watch them come in. They talked for hours, Fizz telling stories from a lifetime in the business, and in the cracks and unspoken spaces Mattera heard subtext, and this is what he took Fizz to be saying:

Treasure shows who you really are. It strips away every façade you've constructed, every story you believe about yourself, and reveals the real you. If you are a miserable, lying, greedy, worthless fuck, treasure will tell you that. If you are a good and decent person, treasure will tell you that, too. And you needn't find a single coin to know. It's enough to get close to treasure, to believe it within reach, and you'll have your answer, but once it happens it can't be lied about and it can't be bullshitted away. For that reason, treasure is crisis, because what you get in the end is yourself.

When the men finally got up to say good-bye, Mattera asked about the coin on Fizz's necklace. Fizz pulled it from his shirt. It was an eight escudo from *Concepción*, a wreck he loved because it had been lost twice to history but never abandoned.

Driving over long bridges back to his hotel, Mattera watched the Keys disappear behind him, local joints such as Craig's Restaurant and Doc's Diner giving way to Starbucks and Denny's. His time with the oracles had come to an end, and though none of the men could show him to Bannister's wreck, each had pointed him in the same direction, to history, and they told him not to let go.

Chapter 11

THE GOLDEN AGE

A weathered ship sails through the Caribbean in the late seventeenth century, chicken coops and empty barrels cluttered about her decks, a handful of rough-hewn crewmen scrubbing, painting, and unwinding rolls of line. Aloft in the masts, a lone sailor scans the seas, looking for others.

Late in the day, the lookout spots the white sails of a smaller vessel in the distance, and soon, he can make out her flag—English. He calls for his captain, who trains his looking glass. He can see that she carries six cannons, typical of a merchant vessel, but he is even more interested in whether she rides high or low on the water. This one rides very low, meaning she is full of cargo, and to this captain, that is what matters.

The captain issues orders and his crew snaps into action. Two of the men open a chest containing a collection of flags from around the world, fish out the English Red Ensign, and hoist it to the top of their mast. Three others dress in women's clothing and begin sauntering around the bow. Below decks, 130 men arm themselves with weapons and explosives. At the helm, the captain orders his ship to set course, slowly, for the merchant ship in the distance.

By now, the merchant ship captain is looking back through his own telescope. He is excited to see the red English flag in the distance. This is his forty-man crew's chance to trade supplies, exchange stories, and share drinks with fellow countrymen. But he is wary, too. He is carrying a valuable cargo of silver, sugar, and indigo, and knows that pirates hunt in these shipping lanes.

So the merchant captain keeps watching the English vessel. When the two ships close to within five hundred yards, the women on board the larger vessel throw off their clothes and start running, only they are not running like women, and in a moment they muscle a wood-colored tarp off the sides of their ship, revealing an additional twenty-four cannons. Dozens of men rush up from the decks of the larger ship, some to guard posts, others to masts, still others to the stern, and in a sudden and screaming ballet they trim sails so that the large ship now knifes through the sea, making white foam as she hurtles toward the smaller merchant ship.

The merchant captain yells for his crew. And then he sees what he has spent his career dreading: the onrushing ship lowers its English flag and hoists a new one, blood-red and emblazoned with an hourglass. This is a pirate flag. The hourglass makes a warning—*if you resist, your remaining time on earth will be short. And bloody.*

The merchant captain orders his men to their guns. Before they can act, the pirates fire a cannon. The seas explode, a thunder so loud it seems to collapse the skies, and out of a billowing cloud of gray smoke a six-pound black iron ball screams over the bow of the merchant ship, a preview of what is to come if they fail to surrender. The smell of burning sulfur fills the air.

It takes minutes for the smoke to clear, but when it does the pirate ship is just three hundred yards away and closing fast. Now the merchant captain can see pirates streaking up from the holds, twenty at a time, until more than a hundred line the decks, screaming and waving swords and firing muskets into the sky.

The merchant captain's instinct is to flee, but he is heavy with cargo and slow. Still, if he could run for just a few hours he might slip away under cover of night; there was always hope in the night.

He orders his crew to speed away, to get the ship moving for all she's worth, but no matter how fast she sails the pirate ship stays with her, gaining with every maneuver. Now just two hundred yards away, the pirate captain finally shows himself, stepping onto his bow dressed in gray breeches and a tan waistcoat, a heavy gold chain around his neck. Calling into a speaking tube, he demands that the merchant captain surrender or face the fires of hell.

The merchant captain now must decide whether to fight. A single well-placed shot from one of his cannons could stop the pirates. Two might destroy them. But if he fails, he knows how the rest would unfold; he has heard accounts of pirate attacks since boyhood.

The pirates would fire their cannons at his masts in order to disable, but not ruin, his ship and her cargo. They would strafe his decks with musket fire, looking to kill and maim as many crew as possible. As they drew closer, they would hurl shrapnel-filled cast-iron hand grenades, fire-starting bombs, and flaming stink-pots (a rancid concoction of rotting animal flesh, tar and pitch, and other putrid ingredients). Some of these fireworks would kill or disable his crew; others would blanket his ship in smoke.

When the pirates got just a few yards away, they would use grappling hooks, swords, axes, pikes, and pistols to fight off defenders and pull the ships close. Swarming onto the merchant ship, they would hack and shoot, slash and bite anyone who resisted them. Even if the merchant captain and his crew fought well, it usually ended badly for captains who chose to fight pirates.

And that was if the captain was lucky enough to die in the fight.

If he survived, the pirates might boil him alive, cut out and eat his still-beating heart, pull out his tongue, crush his skull until his eyeballs disgorged, hang him by his genitalia, throw dice for the privilege of chopping off his head. If a merchant captain surrendered peacefully, however, the pirates might set him and his crew free, invite them to join their crew, even return the ship. Nothing, however, was guaranteed, which was the pirates' most terrifying quality of all.

"Answer, dogs!" the pirate captain orders, his men training their cannons and muskets on the merchant ship.

The merchant captain has no more time for thought. By surrendering, he places his own life, and the lives of his crew, in the hands of madmen. But he also can count. The pirates outnumber him three to one. They have thirty cannons; he has six. He remembers the stories he heard growing up. So, as do most merchant captains in his position, he puts down his guns and surrenders.

The pirates board, and the merchant captain and his crew are made prisoner, chained together on the deck. None is surprised when the pirates relieve them of their clothing and valuables, then plunder the ship of its cargo. But the crew is startled to hear the pirate captain address them directly.

"Speak up plain, lads. What treatment from your captain have ye?"

For a time, the merchant crew stays silent. Then, one by one, they begin to tell the pirates about their captain. When they finish, the pirate captain walks up to his counterpart.

"And so, sir," he says, "the same shall happen to you. . . ."

"John?"

Mattera's heart pounded at the sound of his name. Ready to meet his own fate, he looked up to face the pirate captain. Instead, he saw Carolina, bleary-eyed and in her negligee.

"It's two in the morning," she said.

"I'm researching. Is it really that late?"

"Yes, really. Can you make room for me?"

Sitting cross-legged on the dining room floor of his Santo Domingo apartment, Mattera was surrounded on all sides by piles of books and papers on pirates. It had been a week since his trip to see the oracles in Florida, and he'd done little but study pirate history since then.

"Come here, my pirate princess," he said.

He pushed aside a pile of books and pulled Carolina into his circle. He described the pirate attack he'd just envisioned, pieced together from these resources. He'd known tough guys in his life, some of them legends, but few came close to these men.

Even pirates, Carolina said, needed sleep, so she insisted that Mattera hang it up for the night. Since he'd begun this phase of his research, he'd spent every evening working past midnight.

Mattera took a quick shower, brushed his teeth, and put on his boxer shorts and T-shirt. In bed, he kissed Carolina good night and waited for sleep.

And waited.

He turned onto his side and adjusted his pillow. He flipped onto his other side and pushed down a sheet. Maybe he needed a drink of water—

"John?" Carolina said, "I was wondering . . . if you're not too tired to talk . . . what's so interesting about these pirates?"

Mattera smiled and sat up in the bed.

"You really want to know?"

"Mmm-hmm."

"Then listen to this."

Pirates were born in ancient times, on the day men first loaded cargo onto ships—or maybe the day before. They came from Greece and Rome, China and North Africa, and almost every other country on the map—bandits of a thousand eras who sailed with a single purpose: to steal everything they could from ships too lightly defended, or too terrified, to fight.

The pirates Mattera cared about came from a special time and place. They hunted prey on the Caribbean and the Atlantic from the mid-seventeenth century to the early eighteenth century, the Golden Age of Piracy. It was these men who swashbuckled and plundered in the books and movies of generations, and who haunted and thrilled the dreams of youngsters. It was these men whom Bannister commanded.

They flourished for much of the seventeenth century, taking prizes and striking terror into the hearts of merchant seamen, especially the Spanish, who controlled much of the trade and shipping in the Caribbean and Atlantic. Many countries considered the pirates to be the "scourge of mankind." England loved them. By harassing Spanish ships, pirates made room for English trade and expansion. In the bargain, pirate ships took hard and violent men off the streets and put them to work, then brought back stolen goods to English markets and sold them on the cheap. Pirates spent handsomely to outfit their ships, and paid generous bribes to English officials. They drained their purses in port like men just days away from the gallows, which many of them were. If England shook her fist at these rogues, she did so with fingers crossed, bulging coffers, and an eye toward expanding her empire.

Many of the pirates got rich. If Spanish seamen happened to be terrorized or killed in the bargain, few in England seemed heartbroken about that.

And the pirates could bring the terror. In a letter to the secretary of state, one English witness wrote: "It is a common thing among the privateers . . . to cut a man in pieces, first some flesh, then a hand, an arm, a leg, sometimes tying a cord about his head, and with a stick twisting it until the eyes shoot out, which is called woolding."

Another described the methods of a notorious French pirate: "L'Ollonais grew outrageously passionate; insomuch that he drew his cutlass, and with it cut open the breast of one of those poor Spanish, and pulling out his heart with his sacrilegious hands, began to bite and gnaw it with his teeth, like a ravenous wolf, saying to the rest: I will serve you all alike, if you show me not another way."

The years following the English conquest of Jamaica were glorious for pirates and privateers, who preyed almost at will on Spanish shipping. Even Spanish towns weren't safe from these marauders, who were capable of assembling forces of a thousand or more and invading places thought to be impregnable. Often, the Spanish could do little but surrender and pray for mercy. In Port Royal, gold and silver spilled out of the taverns and brothels onto the streets. The Golden Age of Piracy had dawned.

And with it came great captains, men of charisma and vision who schemed on the grandest scales. None dreamed bigger, or led more men, than Welshman Henry Morgan, who launched a series of great invasions against the Spanish. In just four years, he led rough and wild crews, sometimes by the thousands, on raids against Porto Bello, Maracaibo, and, in one of the great military triumphs of the age, Panama. For this, he became exceedingly wealthy, and a hero in both Port Royal and England.

Stories of Morgan's ruthlessness were legion. One witness reported that, when a prisoner refused to cooperate, Morgan's men:

strappado'd him until both his arms were entirely dislocated, then knotted a cord so tight round the forehead that his eyes bulged out, big as eggs. Since he still would not admit where the coffer was, they hung him up by his male parts, while one struck him, another sliced off his nose, yet another an ear, and another scorched him with fire—tortures as barbarous as man can devise. At last, when the wretch could no longer speak and they could think of no new torments, they let a Negro stab him to death with a lance.

When another man refused to talk, "they tied long cords to his thumbs and his big toes and spreadeagled him to four stakes. Then, four of them came and beat on the cords with their sticks, making his body jerk and shudder and stretching his sinews. Still not satisfied, they put a stone weighing at least two hundredweight on his loins and lit a fire of palm leaves under him, burning his face and setting his hair alight."

For every person who witnessed such horrors, a thousand more heard about them. Reputation became the pirate's sharpest sword.

For a time, it seemed as if the glory years for pirates might last forever. By 1670, however, new economic winds were blowing in the Caribbean and Atlantic. Legitimate trade had become increasingly profitable to the merchant and ruling classes. Uncertainty on the high seas and in the shipping lanes was bad for business, and was putting the fortunes of powerful merchants, and even England herself, at risk. And there were no greater purveyors of uncertainty at sea than the pirates and privateers.

In 1670, England and Spain signed the Treaty of Madrid. Among other things, it called for England to condemn piracy—no more privateer licenses, no more safe havens, no more markets for stolen Spanish goods. In return, Spain made concessions to English trade and shipping.

The treaty provided England with new commercial opportunities, some big enough to grow an empire. But they required peaceful and predictable seas. English officials shook fists and swore vows to eradicate the pirates, but through the 1670s, little meaningful action was taken. Pirates still had deep roots in the Caribbean, and continued to supply locals with cheap goods, contraband, and a steady flow of income. To great swaths of the population, especially the commoners, the pirates remained the good guys.

And they were getting better at their craft. By 1680, pirates were causing great disruption to the legitimate trade moving into and out of Jamaica. The governor called for Royal Navy warships. By 1683, they had arrived, four in all, including the *Ruby*, a 125-foot giant killer that could carry forty-eight cannons and a crew of 150. She anchored at Port Royal and would be directed by Governor Thomas Lynch, who had been charged with destroying the pirate scourge.

But it would take more than just the hoisting of sails for these warships to take on this enemy. More than twelve hundred pirates were thought to be operating out of Port Royal alone. They had faster ships, could slip into shallower waters, knew the waterways and inlets and escape routes better, and had more experienced captains. And the pirates knew they would hang if they were caught.

Still, the sheer power of the navy frigates was enough to scare many pirates away. To those who remained, the rows of cannons aboard the navy ships anchored in sight of Port Royal spoke a simple truth: *We are the hunters now. You are the prey. It is just a matter of time before we catch you. And when we do, you will die.*

Governor Lynch sent the warships into heavy patrol, not just around Jamaica but to Hispaniola, Cuba, and other pirate strongholds. Often, the frigates returned empty-handed, but with every cruise they gained experience and savvy. Soon, they were catching pirates, most of whom chose to surrender rather than risk annihilation in battle. Pirates continued to flee from Port Royal and other safe havens; for those who remained, the prospect of the gallows loomed larger than ever. Every month, it seemed, England got better at exterminating these rogues of the sea.

Nevertheless, if a man were willing to go up against the Royal Navy, defy the will of a nation, spit in the face of wealthy merchants and plantation owners, give the middle finger to a governor, and sail in a world increasingly hostile to his kind, he might still make a fortune as a Caribbean pirate. To do it in 1684, however, he would need to be better than good, and brave in exceptional measure.

"And that was when Bannister made his move," Mattera said. "He had everything, Carolina—respect, admiration, money, a future. He risked it all to turn pirate. Why would he do that?"

His fiancée didn't answer.

"Carolina?"

Mattera could tell by her breathing she'd fallen asleep. Reaching over, he pulled up her covers and kissed her cheek.

"There was something calling to Bannister," he said, rolling over and putting his head on his pillow. "It was more than money or power. There was something else going on with this guy."

The more Mattera learned about pirates, the more interesting he found their portrayal in Hollywood films and popular culture. Some things the movies depicted were true, others were fantasy, and still others were rarely shown.

Pirates, for example, were not known to make prisoners walk the plank. They found it easier to kill a man by hacking him with a sword or shooting him—and then throwing him overboard, no theatrics required. And they never buried treasure or made maps leading to it; they spent their money, often as fast as they could steal it.

But they did love parrots and taught them to talk, and kept them as pets during voyages. And they went into battle carrying as many weapons as possible—not to look cool but because guns of the day often misfired and took time to reload.

Mattera loved the language of the pirates, and even found a book dedicated to the subject. Pirates never said "Arrgh" or "Shiver my timbers" (which almost certainly originated, like so much supposed pirate language, in Hollywood movies from the 1950s). They did use terms and phrases such as "Ahoy," "A merry life and a short one," and several curses, oaths, threats, and greetings, each of which Mattera enjoyed. He scribbled down these favorites to yell at Chatterton when next he saw him:

— Eat what falls from my tail!
— Damn your blood!
— I'll cleave your skull asunder!
— I'll cut you in pound pieces!
— I come from hell and I'll carry you there presently!

Some other things Mattera had learned from the movies turned out to be true as well. Pirates employed hooks and wooden legs as prosthetics, and patches to cover eye sockets, often for injuries suffered in battle. They wore a range of outfits, from the drab and practical to the most fanciful flourishes of gold, crimsons, blues, and reds, including feathers, gold chains, silk shirts, and velvet trousers. (Often, their getups depended less on sartorial instinct than what they'd recently stolen.) And they swore, drank, gambled, and womanized as if any night might be their last. "Whenever they have got hold of something, they don't keep it for long," wrote one contemporary observer. "They are busy dicing, whoring and drinking so long as they have anything to spend. Some of them will get through a good two or three thousand pieces of eight in a day—and next day not have a shirt to their back." Mattera had known guys like that growing up.

Pirate views on race and gender fascinated Mattera. Black people sailed often on pirate ships during the Golden Age. In fact, black sailors often composed a large minority of men on board. Their status, however, depended on the time. Early in the Golden Age, black men aboard pirate ships were more likely to be slaves—either working as such, or as prisoners captured from ships and to be traded at market. Later in the era, however, many black men aboard pirate ships—perhaps even most of them—were full-fledged pirates, with all the rights and privileges of their white counterparts. They led charges into combat, earned equal pay, stood side by side with Blackbeard himself during battle—all 150 years before slaves became free in the United States.

But for all the racial equality, pirates almost never sailed with women. Just four or five are known to have worked as pirates during the Golden Age. Two of them—Mary Read and Anne Bonny—became famous, dressing as men and fighting alongside one of the most celebrated of all pirate captains, "Calico" Jack Rackham. Almost without exception, pirates viewed the presence of women aboard their ships as a distraction and a potential source of conflict and jealousy. On some pirate ships, the penalty for secreting a woman aboard was death.

Mattera could not get enough of these men. He absorbed pirate customs, cataloged their weapons, diagrammed their ships. All the while, he marveled at their criminal instincts. Wherever he looked he saw Gambino in them.

Like the gangsters Mattera had known growing up, the pirates worked to avoid violence and fighting. It wasn't because they were frightened (they weren't) or believed they couldn't win (they almost always had bigger crews, stronger fighters, and better weapons than their prey). It was because bloodshed was bad for business. A battle at sea could result in casualties, ruin plunder, even cost the pirates their own ship. It also attracted the attention of the law. To steal quietly always paid best.

Most pirate victims understood whom they were dealing with and gave up on the spot. For their cooperation, they often were treated fairly, even generously. But there were also those who, for money or principle or pride, tried to flee or put up a fight. That's when the pirates rained down their particular brand of terror, one designed to echo across oceans.

By squeezing a man's eyes from their sockets, roasting him on a baking stone, or extracting and eating his still-beating heart, pirates did more than punish resistors or force them to turn over hidden booty. They also sent a message to the rest of the world: *Do not struggle against us. We are crazy. It always ends better if you just go along.* To guarantee they were heard, they often spared a lucky few, sending them home to spread the terrible word.

Not every pirate captain tortured or punished resistors so cruelly. But enough of them did it enough of the time that by the seventeenth century, the only weapon a pirate often needed was the design sewn into his flag. Unmistakable even at great distances, it announced not a fait accompli, but that a choice was at hand.

Mattera lost himself in these stories. Still, he was looking for something even deeper about pirates—for an insight into their lives. So he began asking a different kind of question, one he'd posed to every interesting person he'd met since he was a boy: How did you get here? The voices that began sounding from inside his books began to tell a singular story.

A young Englishman of the late seventeenth century might expect to earn his living as a farmer or carpenter or baker. If he were good with his hands he might become a tailor or a smith. But if he had a strong constitution and an appetite for adventure, he could step off the end of his country and find work on one of the many merchant ships that carried cargo and passengers to a world that was expanding by the day. A merchant seaman visited strange lands, stared down nature, saw places and creatures his peers could scarcely imagine. In the process, he learned to become a first-rate mariner, able to navigate treacherous waters and find his way by the stars.

It could be the hardest of lives. Often, the work was backbreaking, the conditions miserable, and the pay barely enough to survive. Perhaps worst of all, merchant captains exercised absolute authority over their crews, often treating them brutally and holding back what little salary they earned. If anyone objected—and even when they did not—the captain might whip, torture, imprison, or starve them. Much of this treatment was protected by admiralty law, which granted a captain near autocratic power over his crew. Such laws were deemed necessary to maintain order (and profitability) aboard the ships, but such unchecked authority opened doors to abuse and created a legion of predators at the helm.

Aggrieved seamen might leave the trade, but those who desired to stay at sea had few options. One was to join the navy, where provisions and pay were a bit better, and the workloads more humane. Discipline, however, might be even more severe aboard a navy ship. And there was always the chance a sailor might die in battle for a cause he might not agree with, or even understand.

The other option lay in the shadows. It called to the daring and it promised a far different life. To find it, a merchant sailor need only step to the other side of the harbor, to the other side of the world, to where the pirates lived, to the place where a common man could turn king.

Many pirates became wealthy, earning hundreds or even thousands of times more than a merchant seaman, sometimes overnight. They formed large crews, often exceeding one hundred, making for easier workloads and more carefree environments. They chased adventure, became comrades, lived life on their terms. Cruelty by pirate captains was almost unknown.

Of course, there were dangers to turning pirate, especially in the late seventeenth century. They risked life and limb on every voyage, and often hanged for their crimes. Still, if a man possessed a certain boldness, if he dreamed for himself glorious things, chancing the gallows made sense. By Bannister's time, nearly three-quarters of all pirates came from the ranks of the merchant seamen, strong young men adept at sea, tired of bad treatment, and with little to lose. That made them a formidable force before they ever left port, a gang of the angry who, on the right day and with the right leader, might even take on the Royal Navy.

Of all Mattera's pirate books, the one he loved most was the oldest and tiniest, *The Buccaneers of America*, written by onetime pirate

Alexandre Exquemelin, and first published in 1678. It was skinny enough to pocket, so he took it on a trip to the grocery store one morning with Carolina. Flipping through pages while Carolina inspected the produce, he found this sentence: "When a ship has been captured, the men decide whether the captain should keep it or not."

"Carolina!" he called.

"*Siento*—sorry," he said to startled customers, then made his way past the bananas and papayas until he could whisper in Carolina's ear.

"I think I've got it. I think I found what I've been looking for."

At his apartment, he tore through Exquemelin and other books. He'd been through many of these volumes before, but always for the swashbuckling stuff. This time, he turned to the chapters on pirate organization and politics. He'd always presumed them to be the dreariest sections. From the moment he began reading, they opened his eyes.

Before every voyage, pirates gathered together to commit an unthinkable act: They made every crewman an equal. From the greenest of lookouts to the captain himself, no one would own rights over any other or possess privileges unavailable to all. The men would eat the same meals, earn similar wages, share the same quarters. The captain would exercise absolute authority only in battle; at other times, he would guide the ship according to the pleasure of the crew.

And that was just the start of the madness.

Having made everyone equal, the pirates now put almost everything to a vote. To choose where to stalk prey, they voted. To decide whether to attack a target, they voted. To determine the rules of the ship, the punishment for wrongdoers, division of booty, to maroon or shoot traitors, they voted. And every man's vote counted the same.

One might have expected these men, who lived lawless lives in the shadow of gallows, to cast their ballots in unpredictable ways. Yet, time and again through the decades that spanned their Golden Age, the pirates seemed to vote exactly alike. Mattera could see the patterns right away. Using his orange highlighter, he began underlining rules that seemed to govern every pirate ship that sailed in the era:

— Captains were to earn no more than two or three
  times that of the lowliest deckhand.
— Every man was to have an equal share of food, liquor,
  and other provisions.
— Battle injuries would be compensated according to
  body part. On one pirate ship, damages were paid as
  follows:

Lost right arm	600 pieces of silver or six slaves
Lost left arm	500 pieces of silver or five slaves
Lost right leg	500 pieces of silver or five slaves
Lost left leg	400 pieces of silver or four slaves
Lost eye (either one)	100 pieces of silver or one slave
Lost finger	100 pieces of silver or one slave
Internal injury	up to 500 pieces of silver or five slaves
Lost hook or peg leg	Same as if original limb was lost

— Anyone caught stealing from the ship's plunder
  would be punished, including by being marooned on
  an uninhabited island.

— Anyone caught cheating another crewman would have his ears and nose slashed by the aggrieved party, then turned out at the next port.
— No women were allowed on board. Anyone sneaking a woman onto the ship would be killed.
— Disputes between crewmen would be settled onshore by duel.
— Bonuses would be awarded for courage in combat, the sighting of prey, boarding a target ship first, and other heroics.
— Punishments would be inflicted for cowardice, drunkenness, insolence, disobedience, rape, and any other action that undermined the ship's primary purpose — to steal.
— Any unsettled issues would be put to a vote.
— Every man's vote carried equal weight.

One after another, these ideas seemed incredible to Mattera. He tried to imagine Paul Castellano accepting just two times the salary of the lowest Gambino foot soldier, or John Gotti taking the votes of street corner bookies. The criminal bosses Mattera had known killed men who aspired to be their equal. Now, he was reading about pirate captains who wouldn't take an extra pig's foot for dinner, and didn't get a cabin to themselves.

Mattera couldn't get enough of these captains. Each needed to be fearless in vision and unflinchingly brave, and willing to visit terror on targets that resisted attack. Yet, the captain served at the pleasure of his crew. He was elected by popular vote and could be deposed by the same. If he were too lenient or too cruel, too aggressive or too passive, if he refused to be guided by the will of the ship, he was out and might be punished, even marooned, for his failures. And this was true even if, like Bannister, he owned the ship.

All of this had a thrilling ring to Mattera. The votes, the equality, the absence of kings — this was democracy, a century before the concept took hold in America.

To Mattera, it made sense for a regular guy to turn pirate. But what of Bannister? He already had money, power, and autonomy. His future was made. By turning pirate, he risked all of that. And he risked his life. Before, Mattera couldn't figure why a made guy would make such a leap. But he understood it now. There was freedom aboard these pirate ships, one hundred or more men inflamed with the idea that anything was possible for anyone. Bannister might have been a gentleman, and he might have had his future ahead of him. But he'd likely never gotten inside a feeling like that.

Mattera could have kept reading forever, but he believed he had his answer. By week's end, he would rejoin Chatterton for their search for the *Golden Fleece*. But this time things would be different. This time, they were going to look somewhere entirely new.

Chapter 12

THE SUGAR WRECK

"Gentlemen, we have direction."

Presiding over a strategy breakfast he'd called at Tony's, Mattera asked his teammates to imagine themselves back in the Golden Age, when the greatest and most daring pirates had made their names.

"We need to think like them," he said. "If we can think like pirates, we can find them."

That's when he started to talk about democracy.

The pirates had sailed in the seventeenth century, but they were men ahead of their time, professional lawbreakers who made inviolable laws for themselves. Mattera read to the men from pirate constitutions, described their voting rights, and underlined their foundational idea—that any man might become rich if he dared, but that no man should ever become king.

His companions listened rapt throughout. Then they asked him: How does this help us find the *Golden Fleece?*

Mattera's answer was simple: It all came down to Bannister and his motivations.

Bannister was more than a great pirate—to Mattera, he was a man enthralled by democracy. No other motive so elegantly explained why a gentleman captain, likely in his thirties or forties and with a future secured, would risk everything to go plunder on the high seas. Maybe he loved money. Maybe he loved adventure. But he must have known one thing for sure: Men came alive when they were made equal. A hundred of them together could take on the world.

Yet, in the 1680s, as empires joined forces to drive pirates to the bottom of the sea, a man like Bannister couldn't be certain that democracy would survive, or even that future generations would know such an audacious idea had taken hold. To make people remember, he would need to do something epic—something history couldn't ignore. Pillaging more ships wouldn't cut it. Stockpiling treasure would leave no mark at all. But fighting the Royal Navy would have impact. Defeating them in battle would make equality echo through time.

And that, Mattera said, changed everything about how the team might search for the *Golden Fleece*. For nine months, they'd been looking for the perfect place for a pirate ship to careen. Now they would look for the perfect place for a pirate ship to *fight*, an area of land where Bannister had placed cannoneers and musketeers and waged a battle for the ages.

Chatterton agreed.

"Bannister believed," Chatterton said. "He wasn't running from the navy; he was waiting for them. If we find Bannister's battlefield, we find his ship nearby."

The four men laid out a map of Samaná Bay on the table, but none could immediately point to an area they hadn't already searched. But that was just on paper. Armed with new insight, they would return to their boats and start looking back toward the shores.

Leaving the restaurant, Heiko Kretschmer pulled Mattera aside and told him how moved he was by the pirates' story. At age eighteen, he'd risked his life fleeing East Germany, first by hopping a train to Czechoslovakia, then stowing away aboard another train bound for West Germany, likely never again to see his family, all for a taste of freedom and a chance to see the world.

"In those days," Kretschmer said, "I dreamed about democracy."

Chatterton and Mattera combed the banks of Samaná Bay for the next week. They found several potential battlefields, but none good enough for inspired pirates to make history in a stand against two Royal Navy warships.

That weekend, Garcia-Alecont threw a party at the villa. Chatterton was among the first to show up, a bottle of wine in each hand. He didn't intend to stay—he and Mattera were scheduled to search the bay at five-thirty the next morning—but didn't argue when Garcia-Alecont's wife pulled him inside and introduced him to guests. For the next several hours he talked diving, recounting his adventures. Even as he laughed and described key moments, it all seemed like a lifetime ago to him now.

When the party finally wound down, Chatterton grabbed a last glass of wine and stepped onto the veranda, where he stood, under a bright moon, looking out over the channel. Mattera joined him.

"What are we missing?" Chatterton asked.

Mattera couldn't answer. He couldn't do anything but look out over the water. Then he put down his wineglass.

"Get in the boat," he said. "Get Victor."

"It's two in the morning. . . ." Chatterton said.

"We need to go. Now."

Twenty minutes later, the three men were in the Zodiac and heading across the channel to Cayo Vigia, a small island just six hundred yards from the villa. Mattera cut the engine and let the boat settle onto a sandbar by the island's northern hump.

Cayo Vigia, as seen from the villa where Chatterton, Mattera, and crew stayed during much of their hunt for the *Golden Fleece*.

"Holy shit," Chatterton said.

The men stood up in the boat and looked around. From every direction, the Zodiac remained hidden to the world.

"If I'm a pirate looking to careen, this is my place," Garcia-Alecont said.

"And if I'm going to have a fight for the ages, I fight from right here," said Chatterton.

The three men took stock of the island. At most, it stretched five hundred yards east to west, one hundred yards north to south. Yet, the water was deep, about twenty-five feet, almost up to its beach. Its eastern end rose high above the water, where cannon batteries could be camouflaged in dense overgrowth and fired, unseen, at enemies. And it was less than a half mile to the mainland, where freshwater could be found.

Mattera could only chuckle. He and Chatterton had been looking at this island from the villa every day for the past nine months. But it had never crossed their minds that a big sailing ship like the *Golden Fleece* might be capable of maneuvering in here. Yet, when one stood on the spot, it was clear that a large vessel could do that—if she were helmed by a man of daring and nerve. Even the smallest mistake or sudden current could force a big sailing ship to run aground.

Mattera began scribbling notes in his small leather notebook, but Chatterton held up his hand.

"Start the engine. We need to move," Chatterton said.

He pulled the cord and took the tiller, guiding the Zodiac from the island to a point about 125 yards off its northeastern tip.

"Guys," Chatterton announced, "we are now over the so-called sugar wreck."

The sugar wreck was a debris field worked for a few days by Carl Fismer in the mid-1980s. He'd learned of it from a Dominican treasure hunter whose family had owned land in Samaná for centuries. When Fizz dove the site, he found a sugar urn, delicate and intact, that looked to have come from the late 1600s—hence, the nickname "sugar wreck." To him, it appeared that the urn, and the scattered debris that spread for a hundred yards around it, might have come from a merchant ship, and since he was looking for treasure galleons at the time, he put the wreck on hold. Fizz didn't get back to the site before his lease in the area ended, but Bowden had done his own work there, recovering Delftware pottery, a pistol, cannonballs, medicine bottles, axes, and several handblown onion-shaped wine bottles. Chatterton and Mattera had seen these artifacts at the lab, pushed off into a corner, stepsisters to Bowden's more glorious finds. Still, they remembered them. Every piece dated to the late seventeenth century. Not one was a day newer than 1686, the year Bannister did battle with the Royal Navy.

"Guys," Chatterton said. "Why can't the sugar wreck be the *Golden Fleece?*"

The men could see it all in front of them now. Bannister had careened at the island, the most perfect and invisible place in Samaná Bay. The Royal Navy tracked him there, but the island's elevation, tight quarters, and dense overgrowth gave the pirates an advantage in battle, and they'd leveraged every bit of it to hold off the navy warships. Sometime during the fight, or perhaps just after it, the *Golden Fleece* moved off the island before sinking at this very spot. Perhaps Bannister had tried to get away in her, or maybe she'd burned her lines and drifted before going under.

The three men looked at one another. There was every chance the *Golden Fleece* was directly under them now.

Mattera reached for the bottle of beer he'd brought along. He opened it and splashed some over the side.

"This is for the dead guys below," he said.

Garcia-Alecont started the engine and steered back toward shore. On the beach, Chatterton and Mattera stood in the surf, happier than either could remember being in a very long time, looking out over their future, looking back at an island that had been there all along.

If the world still used telegrams, Chatterton and Mattera would have sent one to Bowden asking the critical question: Why can't the sugar wreck be the *Golden Fleece?* They certainly weren't going to do it by phone or email. Only a trip to Santo Domingo to ask Bowden in person could do justice to a question like that.

So they drove the wild and bumpy roads back to the

Dominican capital city, marveling throughout at Bannister's ingenuity in choosing Cayo Vigia, imagining the sinking hearts on the Royal Navy ships as they took cannon fire from invisible guns mounted high on the unlikeliest island.

And what an island it was! By now, Chatterton and Mattera had studied it on charts and satellite photos. At its narrowest, it stretched just thirty-eight yards north to south, but it was long and lean, nearly a quarter mile east to west. From the air, Vigia looked like a whale, its muscular front end swooping down into a lean and elegant body, then widening again at the tail, swimming toward the open Atlantic, an island in motion even as it stayed perfectly still.

It even had a footbridge.

Constructed in the 1960s, the half-mile-long concrete and steel structure connected Cayo Vigia to a resort at the mainland, but few used it. The island had little beach to speak of and was mostly grown over with trees. Occasionally, tourists ventured over, and sometimes amorous couples made an adventure of it. But mostly, it was just a dead end. For that reason, the people of Samaná called it the "Bridge to Nowhere." For Chatterton and Mattera, Nowhere was the only place that mattered.

Every mile they drove, the men grew more eager to see the look on Bowden's face when they told him he already had the *Golden Fleece*. They didn't doubt he'd ask questions, but they'd prepared answers, fact upon fact that would be hard to argue with, even by someone stuck in his own way.

They sat down with Bowden at Adrian Tropical, an upscale café in downtown Santo Domingo. Chatterton didn't waste time.

"Tracy, let me ask you a question," he said. "Why can't the sugar wreck be the *Golden Fleece*?"

Bowden raised an eyebrow.

"Cayo Vigia is the perfect place to careen a vessel, install shore batteries, and fight the Royal Navy," Chatterton said. "And every artifact you brought up from the sugar wreck is period to Bannister's time."

Bowden smiled. Taking a small notebook and a pencil from his shirt pocket, he motioned for the details. The men said they saw it like this: Bannister had careened his ship on a swooning dip on the northern side of Vigia. Tucked into this place, the *Golden Fleece* became invisible, not just to passing ships, but to the world. The pirates had access to freshwater from a nearby stream. In the channel's calm waters, crewmen hunted turtles and scrubbed their ship's hull without struggle.

But Bannister hadn't relaxed. He put two cannon batteries—and probably most of his pirates—into the wooded hills on the island's eastern point. One hundred feet above water, these men scanned the horizon with telescopes and sharp eyes, looking for enemies, knowing they could spot trouble hours before trouble found them. After a time, they spied two Royal Navy frigates approaching in the distance. Against one, they stood a slight chance. Against both, they would need a miracle.

Even then, there was still time to go peacefully. By surrendering now, Bannister could place his fate, and that of his men, in the hands of a Port Royal jury. But Bannister hadn't come to surrender. Instead, he ordered the pirates to their battle stations. Then he sounded the trumpet and told his men to open fire.

Cannonballs and musket shot rained down from the island; to the men on the navy ships, it must have seemed they'd been attacked by the forest itself. Returning fire, the frigates tacked into the channel near the site of the villa and dropped their anchors, positioning themselves to destroy the *Golden Fleece*. For two days, the battle raged, the pirates leveraging every bit of the island's advantage, the navy pounding back, until the frigates ran out of powder and shot and, already suffering twenty-three dead and wounded, turned back for Jamaica. At some point, the *Golden Fleece* came off the island and, badly damaged, sank less than two hundred yards away—right at the site of the sugar wreck.

Now Bowden looked thrilled. He scribbled notes.

"So, what do you think, Tracy?" Mattera asked. "Looks like you've had your pirate ship all along. The sugar wreck is really the *Golden Fleece*."

Bowden buttered his toast.

"Bannister really was a hell of a captain," he said. "But you know what? I want to talk about you guys."

And he told Chatterton and Mattera they'd done a hell of a job, that they'd showed dedication, creative thinking, and courage, that not many men would have stayed with such a difficult search.

And then he told them they were wrong.

The sugar wreck, he said, could not be the *Golden Fleece*, and he began to count off his reasons:

— Cayo Vigia is not included in histories that mention the *Golden Fleece*.
— Shipwreck hunters have always looked for Bannister's wreck at Cayo Levantado.
— Many artifacts salvaged from the sugar wreck were intact, unlikely on a ship destroyed in battle.
— Miss Universe found a period English jar at Cayo Levantado.
— The sugar wreck site is away from the island, not in a careening place.
— The French chart refers to Cayo Levantado as Cayo Banistre.

And, most important of all:

— The sugar wreck is too deep.

"Excellent points, Tracy," Chatterton said. Then, he spoke to each of Bowden's objections, short and direct:

— It's true that Cayo Vigia is not included in histories that mention the *Golden Fleece*, but neither is Cayo Levantado or any other specific location.
— The crowd is usually wrong.
— No one knows how much damage the *Golden Fleece* took—all that's known is that she burned and sank.
— The Miss Universe jar could have fallen overboard from a passing ship of the era.
— The *Golden Fleece* could have come off the careen to fight the navy or attempt an escape.
— The French chart was drawn up in the early nineteenth century, more than one hundred years after the battle, by people who weren't present for the fight.
— The sugar wreck is of the same period and culture as that of the *Golden Fleece*; to believe it unrelated to the battle would be, at best, relying on coincidence.

Bowden made notes on these points, nodding and saying "Oh, I see," or "I hadn't thought about that." Then he pressed the men on the issue of the sugar wreck's depth. Men working for treasure hunter William Phips, he reminded them, had seen the *Golden Fleece* sunk in twenty-four feet of water just months after the battle. By contrast, the sugar wreck lay in forty-four feet.

"That's true," Chatterton said. But he noted that Phips's men never said whether it was twenty-four feet to the top or the bottom of the wreck. If he meant the top, one would expect the *Golden Fleece*, broken down by nature over more than three hundred years, to be in forty-four feet of water, exactly where the sugar wreck was.

Bowden put down his pencil and told the men they'd done inspired work. And, again, he told them they were wrong. The sugar wreck was not the *Golden Fleece*. It would be a good idea to go back to Cayo Levantado and keep searching for her there.

Chatterton looked ready to leap across the table and strangle Bowden, so Mattera leaned forward and spoke in a measured way, telling Bowden that, with all due respect, there was no way the *Golden Fleece* was at Cayo Levantado. But before Bowden could answer, Chatterton jumped in.

"All you want to do is look where everyone's looked before, Tracy, where everyone's already been. With that kind of thinking, you're never going to find this wreck. You're never going to find anything."

Bowden's face reddened. He looked disturbed by Chatterton's tone, but calmly explained that little about the sugar wreck felt right—the depth, the location, the history.

"This is not about feelings!" Chatterton said. "It's about evidence, hard work, and research."

"That's your opinion," Bowden replied.

"No. It's about evidence, hard work, and research. All of the pieces have to fit. I've found more than a wreck or two myself, Tracy, important ones. Not once did I do it by feelings or intuition or any other voodoo bullshit."

Both Chatterton and Bowden looked ready to get up and leave—not just the table but the project. Before that could happen, Mattera told Bowden he wanted to discuss another issue, and was going to take his chances and speak frankly.

"We've got it on good information that other crews might be coming to Levantado to search for the *Golden Fleece*. As you know, we don't think the wreck's at that island. But sometimes all it takes is a bullshit story."

Bowden nodded—he'd heard people tell those kinds of stories before. But Mattera wasn't finished. He also said he'd heard that Cultura was looking to trim down every treasure lease in the country, including Bowden's, and that the agency wanted to bring in new blood—young guns who could help cover the vast areas that, for years, had been underworked. Mattera judged by Bowden's eyes that he'd heard the same. And feared it.

"So what do you suggest I do?" Bowden asked.

"Accept that the pirate ship ain't at Levantado," Chatterton said. "It's at Cayo Vigía."

"Work the sugar wreck," Mattera said. "Pull up more artifacts. Prove it's the *Golden Fleece*."

But Bowden didn't look eager to do any of that. If he blew time working at Cayo Vigía, and someone else found the *Golden Fleece* at Cayo Levantado, everything he'd worked for over a lifetime might be tainted: his reputation, his legacy, his honor. And he didn't seem willing to go out like that—not on a mistake, not on anything less than sure. Instead, he thought Chatterton and Mattera should return to Cayo Levantado and prove conclusively that the *Golden Fleece* was not there before he committed to another theory.

Chatterton jumped up from his seat.

"You're asking us to prove a negative! How can we show you something that's not there?"

"Keep looking," said Bowden. "Maybe you missed something. Maybe the mag's not working right. . . ."

"What about the four hundred other things we found there?" Chatterton said. "Are you saying we found every goddamn fish trap and license plate around all of Levantado, but somehow missed a one-hundred-foot pirate ship?"

"We just need to be sure."

Chatterton, ready to explode, stormed off to the restroom.

"Your partner is a hothead," Bowden said. "I don't know if I can work with him anymore."

Mattera leaned forward.

"Listen, Tracy. I've got an idea. Why don't we mag the sugar wreck? Do some serious salvage on her. Come up with proof. It wouldn't take long."

But Bowden didn't seem convinced. If claim jumpers were coming, if Cultura was taking back leases, this was not the time to abandon Cayo Levantado, where everyone else would claim the pirate ship sank, and he told Mattera that as he paid the check and left for home. When Chatterton returned from the restroom, he didn't even ask where Bowden had gone.

Chapter 13

I Hope We Can Stay Friends

Chatterton and Mattera spent the rest of the day buying supplies in Santo Domingo. Neither spoke of the lunch with Bowden, but each knew what the other was thinking—that this arrangement with the old treasure hunter could not continue.

Carolina cooked dinner for them at her apartment. The men steered the conversation away from business, but when she asked how things had gone that afternoon, Chatterton couldn't stay quiet. Bowden, he said, was never going to give up his belief that the *Golden Fleece* was at Levantado.

"The wreck's not there and I'm not wrong," Chatterton said. "I'm done with this guy."

Mattera could hardly believe what he was hearing. Chatterton was a lot of things, but he was not a quitter. After dinner, Mattera pulled Chatterton into the study, where he urged his partner to be patient. "Tracy is a stubborn old man," he said, "but he's not dumb. You've gotta let him come to the sugar wreck himself. You've gotta let it be his idea, too."

That only frustrated Chatterton more, and he let it be known at high volumes. Mattera didn't always put up with his partner's yelling, but he knew Chatterton was really yelling at Bowden. And that his partner was right.

"Hang in there with me, John," Mattera said. "This is not about Tracy."

But Chatterton wasn't buying it. To him, Bowden could have

been standing inside the Lost City of Atlantis, and he wouldn't have believed it if he'd already made up his mind he was somewhere else.

After brushing his teeth that night, Mattera poured a handful of Advil into his mouth, then washed it down with Mylanta, the same kind of concoction he'd used to endure the twenty-hour days at his security company, when a single misstep could have cost him his future.

He awoke the next morning to a voicemail message from Bowden, who wanted to talk. Without Chatterton.

"That's it," Mattera told Carolina. "Tracy's quitting. He's done with us. The whole thing is falling apart."

The two men met for coffee an hour later. But Bowden didn't talk business. Instead, he told Mattera about his life.

The scuba diving craze hit America in the 1950s, and Bowden found it fast. After graduating from Abington High School near Philadelphia in 1957, he bought his first piece of gear—a wet suit with a wide yellow stripe that had to be glued on by hand—and headed to the creeks and quarries in the Pocono Mountains. There was little in the way of scuba instruction then; a person tried to teach himself enough to survive, then went underwater to see if it worked out.

To make a living, Bowden worked as an apprentice electrician, earning a good salary and with excellent prospects for the future. His mind, however, was on diving, not diodes. When someone told him there were hundreds of shipwrecks off the New Jersey coast, he loaded his car full of gear and didn't stop driving until he got to the ocean. There, he pushed his way into fallen ships; some of them hadn't been seen since the day they'd gone down. Each year, he added more wrecks to his résumé. But he distanced himself from other divers. To him, they were secretive, petty, and cliquey: the same complaints Chatterton would have about the same kinds of people nearly two decades later.

So Bowden went it mostly alone. He dreamed of finding something old—not World War old, but epochs old, from the days that shaped civilizations. But how to do it? There were no classes or instruction manuals for finding those kinds of ships in those days, no mentors looking for protégés. Bowden had to figure things out for himself, and that wouldn't be easy while carrying a full-time job. By now, he'd become a master electrician, but more than ever, his heart wasn't in it. Even the blueprints he carried to electrical jobs looked like nautical charts to him.

In 1969, when Bowden was thirty, he told his boss he was taking a two-week vacation to go look for the HMS *De Braak*, an eighteenth-century shipwreck thought to have sunk at the mouth of the Delaware River, and with possible treasure onboard. His boss tried to talk him out of it, but Bowden was already out the door.

He didn't find treasure. He didn't even find the wreck. But the rush of having looked stayed with him. In 1976, he set out for the Dominican Republic, where great galleons lay, and was granted exclusive rights to search for ships in a wide-ranging area, the first such arrangement ever made by the country. But officials said they'd be watching him. Any missteps and he was finished. Any breaches of trust and he would be gone.

In less than two years, Bowden located and identified the wrecks of two Spanish galleons in Samaná Bay, the *Nuestra Señora de Guadalupe* and, just eight miles away, the *Conde de Tolosa*. The ships carried more than twelve hundred passengers and crew between them, many of whom had planned to make lives abroad. Most had converted their worldly possessions into gold, jewelry, and coins, which traveled easily along with their dreams. After Bowden found the wrecks, much of their treasure became his.

In 1979, *National Geographic* ran a twenty-six-page feature, "Graveyard of the Quicksilver Galleons," about his work. Penned by famed marine historian Mendel Peterson, the piece took readers underwater with Bowden and showed, in glorious color, what a man could find if only he threw over his life to go look. It included a gold medallion bearing the cross of the Order of Santiago, framed by twenty-four diamonds, which Peterson later called the greatest artifact ever pulled from the sea. Mattera had read the *National Geographic* story as a teenager, imagining himself as Bowden.

Many presumed Bowden to be in it for the money, but he seldom sold what he found. He told people he was chasing a feeling—the moment when, after years of struggle, and after a thousand people say you're crazy, you see something sparkle in the water and grab on to it. Treasure. A person is never the same after that.

Bowden worked his lease area for the next several years, doing groundbreaking work on the eighteenth-century French warship *Scipion* and other important wrecks, but often finding nothing at all. That didn't stop others from envying his life—one in which they imagined him cruising the Caribbean, wind in hair and cognac in hand, in search of the next lost treasure. Few thought about the life he lived every day.

He was away from home almost all the time, which made a normal existence impossible and his marriage a challenge. It was hard for him to have a meaningful conversation about his job—almost no one in the world did what he did, or could even imagine it. Even the treasure itself had a tragic patina: Much of it came from wrecks in which people had died violently at sea.

Still, he could not dream of doing anything else. So he kept working, and in the late 1980s, he struck again, this time on *Concepción*, one of the greatest treasure wrecks of them all.

William Phips had arrived there first, in 1687, and cleaned out as much of the ship's silver as seventeenth-century technology allowed. Soon, the wreck became lost to the ages, and it stayed lost for almost three hundred years, until Jack Haskins's research helped lead treasure hunter Burt Webber to the wreck in 1978, in an area about eighty miles offshore dubbed the Silver Bank. Webber salvaged what he could, after which the government awarded the rights, briefly, to Carl Fismer, and then to Bowden. Although he hadn't found the wreck, Bowden's touch on it made all the difference. Soon, *Concepción* was showing more of her silver: thousands of coins worth millions of dollars that no one had seen since 1641.

But it came at a lonely price. Radios and television didn't work in the Silver Bank. There were no movies or videos aboard Bowden's salvage vessel, just old newspapers. No one could get away for a jog or even a smoke by themselves. During these two-week trips, over and over again for years, it was just eight or nine men together on a sixty-five-foot boat, alone and crowded, inescapably, all at once.

And that was just during the day. At night, it became difficult for Bowden to push away the idea that he was anchored over a mass grave site. More than three hundred people had perished aboard *Concepción*, along with countless others who had died nearby in ships broken by the Silver Bank through the ages. Sometimes, he would awaken at two or three in the morning to go out and check his boat's lines, not because he believed they hadn't been tied well, but because he knew anything could happen out there, especially on moonless nights.

On one trip, an elderly investor who'd come along shook Bowden awake in the middle of the night. "Tracy," he said. "I was standing on the back deck. I heard voices. I heard so many voices." Bowden told him to keep away from the railings but didn't argue with the man. "Most of these ships wrecked in hurricanes," Bowden told him. "I can't imagine what those people went through."

For years, Bowden kept working the *Concepción*, bringing up silver and selling little of it, fighting off hurricanes and solitude. Filmmakers put him in documentaries. His artifacts went into museums. In 1996, *National Geographic* ran another feature, this one written by Bowden himself, about his experiences on the *Concepción*. And he kept working the galleon, taking treasure and artifacts others never could reach. He thought a lot about Phips during those long stretches out on the Silver Bank, about what it meant for an ordinary guy to go after something great.

Bowden could have told these stories to Mattera for hours, but he stopped himself.

"I've taken too much of your time already, John," he said. "What I really wanted to say is that I hope we can all stay friends."

Chatterton spent the next several days reading books about the conquistadors, especially Francisco Pizarro, who showed up in Peru with fewer than two hundred men and vanquished thousands of the enemy—an empire seized in moments.

At the same time, Mattera typed up ads to place in scuba diving magazines on behalf of Pirate's Cove, his once-thriving dive charter business. It was time, he told Carolina, to face reality. The *Golden Fleece* likely would never be found, not because it wasn't there, but because his partners couldn't come together. Chatterton seemed to have lost patience—with Bowden, the search for the pirate ship, and the Dominican Republic. Bowden also appeared to have lost patience—with Chatterton, with him, with their crazy ideas.

So, Mattera had come to his senses. By reviving Pirate's Cove, he could do what he'd originally intended: support himself in a Caribbean paradise by taking high-end clients to storied and beautiful shipwrecks.

He awoke three hours later than usual the next morning. He didn't shave or brush his teeth; he just sat at the kitchen table, reading about the New York Mets on his laptop and eating his bowl of cold cereal.

Finally, he drove back to Samaná, where he was to meet Chatterton for dinner. But what kind of dinner would it be? Without crew, notebooks, or place mat diagrams, all that was left was the pizza at Fabio's, and a person didn't drive to the tip of nowhere for that.

Still, he went. A few hours later, when he reached cell phone coverage, he received a voice mail from Bowden, who said he'd thought things over and wanted to further salvage the sugar wreck. They would work for two weeks, the typical salvor's cycle, and discover what they could. To Mattera, it seemed like a miracle. This was what he and Chatterton wanted most of all.

He dialed his partner as fast as he could.

The two men made a plan on the phone. They would do a detailed side-scan sonar and magnetometer survey of the sugar wreck, then salvage as many artifacts from the debris field as possible, looking for anything that would confirm the ship's identity as the *Golden Fleece*. If they found so much as a coin or pottery shard or anything newer than 1686—the year of the pirate ship's sinking—they would rule out the sugar wreck as Bannister's ship. But neither expected that.

Work began in earnest on the sugar wreck site several days later. Chatterton and Mattera scanned and magged the area, making detailed maps Bowden could use to pinpoint the search. Salvage began shortly thereafter. Bowden joined the men for the work.

From the start, the mood was collegial, especially between Chatterton and Bowden. Over the next week, crews pulled up hundreds of artifacts from under the muddy bottom, many of them pristine: muskets, knives, a broadsword with bone handle, jugs, Delftware china, Madeira wine bottles, and cannonballs. Each piece seemed more impressive than the last, not just for its delicate beauty, but for its age. Not one dated later than 1686.

At night, the two partners relaxed at the villa, looking out over the work site. In the distance, a great sailing ship appeared, her white sails stretching into the sky. The men watched her draw closer, until she'd entered the mouth of the channel. She was perhaps one hundred feet long, about the size of the *Golden Fleece*, and she maneuvered beautifully in this tight space. She anchored just past the island and parallel to the bridge, likely to resupply and take on freshwater, just as ships had for centuries here. To Chatterton and Mattera, the ship seemed a gift, a demonstration of all they'd believed. A ship of her size could come here after all, if only her captain had vision.

The two-week salvage operation on the sugar wreck concluded a few days later. While crews pulled gear from the water, Chatterton and Mattera asked Bowden for his opinion: Was the sugar wreck the *Golden Fleece*?

Bowden told them that while all the artifacts were period to the *Golden Fleece*, the fact that the wreck was off the island and not in a careening place, and especially that the wreck was too deep, continued to trouble him. For those reasons, he still needed to be certain the pirate ship wasn't at Cayo Levantado before doing more work on the sugar wreck.

Chatterton walked away. Mattera looked straight into Bowden's eyes.

"Tracy, you know that people are looking to steal this wreck from you. And you know the government wants to cut down everyone's leases. You can really help yourself by notifying Cultura you found the pirate ship. The wreck's not at Levantado. It's right here."

But Bowden held firm.

A few days later, Chatterton was back in Maine, making arrangements to dive real shipwrecks, getting to be John Chatterton again. Mattera flew back to the States, too, showing up at a gun range in Pennsylvania, shooting at targets long after they'd shredded and stopped being targets anymore.

A month passed that way. Then, in early December 2008, Mattera received a phone call from Bowden reporting news from Cultura: An archaeologist had found the *Golden Fleece*.

At Cayo Levantado.

Chapter 14

DRIFTING AWAY

B owden sounded shaken on the phone, but this was his information: A report had been filed at the lab in Santo Domingo
by a Dominican-based archaeologist who had long researched
shipwrecks, and even hunted treasure, in the country. Not only
had he found the *Golden Fleece* at Cayo Levantado, he'd supplied
the precise location.

Mattera went nauseous. He swore to Bowden that the discovery was impossible—that he and Chatterton had gone over every
square foot around Cayo Levantado—but mostly his mind was
swimming, searching the area all over again, dragging the magnetometer across Levantado and all that was fair in the world,
telling himself it was inconceivable that he and Chatterton had
found everything at the island but the one thing that mattered.

Mattera asked if he could get the location the archaeologist
had supplied. In a barely audible voice, Bowden said he would try.

Mattera's next call was to Chatterton. He laid out the facts as
he knew them. Chatterton asked how fast Mattera could get to
Miami International Airport.

"Why?" Mattera said.

"So we can go back and prove this is bullshit."

On the airplane, Chatterton and Mattera analyzed the devel-
opment. Neither had expected an archaeologist to take a shot at
the *Golden Fleece*, and yet it made sense. By making this discovery, the man could make a case, in the name of academia, for the

Dominican government to grant him salvage rights over Bowden. He had a fine reputation. No doubt he would contribute artifacts to a museum or a university to justify his claim jump.

The rest of the flight was spent trying to figure out where on the island the archaeologist had made his discovery, trying to imagine a spot they had missed. Every few minutes, one of the men would ask, "Did this sonofabitch really find it?" and the other would answer, "No way."

They sat down with Bowden later that day in Santo Domingo. He looked worn, but he came with important information: the place where the archaeologist had reportedly found the *Golden Fleece*. The man hadn't supplied any GPS coordinates, just a photograph and a description of an area at Cayo Levantado near the western beach. But that was enough for Chatterton and Mattera. They recognized the location. There was nothing there.

"Give us a few days," Mattera said. "We'll prove it."

Before Bowden could object, Chatterton and Mattera were out the door and on their way to Samaná, ready to shoot down the archaeologist's claim.

On the road to Samaná, Chatterton and Mattera received a call from Garcia-Alecont, who had spoken to a government contact. The new claim was putting pressure on Cultura to seize the *Golden Fleece* from Bowden and declare it an archaeological site—wherever she happened to lie. Officials now understood the rarity and significance of Bannister's ship, and believed the wreck might be better curated by an academic than by treasure hunters. Chatterton and Mattera had feared these days were coming, when politicians and armchair wannabes elbowed in and stole treasure from real guys who worked the waters every day.

And there was more bad news.

As Garcia-Alecont understood it, the push was intensifying

now at Cultura to cut down the size of Bowden's lease area. Indeed, the agency had taken similar action recently against another leaseholder, and appeared ready to do it to every treasure hunter working in country. By putting more salvors to work over smaller areas, Cultura could expect better production, along with increased lease payments. There was no telling which areas they would seize first.

"So what do we do?" Mattera asked.

Garcia-Alecont had no answer, just an opinion: Get to Cayo Levantado and deliver the strongest possible proof that the pirate ship was not where the archaeologist claimed it to be. The longer the lab believed it was there, the more likely they were to take it from Bowden. And then none of the rest would matter.

"We're on the road, Victor," Mattera said. "We're already going as fast as we can."

The next morning, Chatterton, Mattera, Kretschmer, and Ehrenberg took the *Deep Explorer* to Cayo Levantado, wondering how they would live with themselves if someone else had found a pirate ship in a place they'd sworn it could never be.

Chatterton slowed the engine as the boat settled near the westerly end of the island. He navigated the rest of the way by using the photograph Bowden had supplied, trying to match the image to the island, calling out directions to Kretschmer at the wheel. They finally reached the spot, a place a couple hundred yards offshore, and dropped anchor. Ehrenberg reviewed the team's data files on his laptop. Months earlier, they'd surveyed the entire area and found no targets, and therefore, no shipwreck.

Still, they pulled on their dive gear to make sure.

They set up a grid and searched the bottom—visually and with metal detectors.

Methodically.

And again.

They found ceramic bricks and pieces of wood, all of which came from a shipwreck that was centuries old. But no one worried about that. They'd discovered these remnants months ago, during one of their surveys of the island. By shape and dimensions, the pieces couldn't have belonged to a ship larger than one-third of the *Golden Fleece*. This was the wreck of a sixteenth- or seventeenth-century island-hopper, not a great sailing vessel built to cross oceans and carry a hundred pirates.

Back on the boat, the team made a plan. They would send a report to the lab, including photographs, bathymetric surveys, magnetometer histories, and multicolored sonar images, an account so thorough it would rule out the site for good.

Heading back to the villa, the men got to thinking. There was no guarantee that Cultura would accept their proof that the archaeologist was wrong. Even if it did, other salvors or academics or treasure hunters were likely to follow with their own claims to the *Golden Fleece*; to Chatterton and Mattera, it made sense for rivals to show up now, as word must have leaked that Bowden was hot on the pirate ship's trail. If enough rivals made similar claims, even if those claims were bullshit, Cultura could take the wreck from Bowden. The only defense was to find the *Golden Fleece*. And the best shot to do that was to convince Bowden to finish salvage at the sugar wreck site, and to do it now. If there was smoking gun evidence still under the mud, they would find it.

Mattera called Bowden, assuring him that the archaeologist's report could not be correct, and imploring him to further salvage the sugar wreck site. Bowden seemed buoyed, but still concerned that others might descend on Cayo Levantado looking to claim the *Golden Fleece*.

"Exactly," Mattera said. "Which is why you have to act now."

Bowden agreed that action had to be taken. But he wanted Chatterton and Mattera back at Cayo Levantado. Mattera's neck tightened so quickly his vision blurred.

"This is really bad, Tracy. There's no way Chatterton is going back to that island."

"He's a hothead—"

"I'm not going to listen to that anymore," Mattera said. "Chatterton is my partner. You need to forget Levantado."

But Bowden didn't sound like he was going to forget the island. When they hung up, Mattera could only think, "He's lost confidence in us. He doesn't believe in us anymore."

That afternoon, at Fabio's, Mattera told Chatterton about the call. He expected his partner to explode or storm out or to call Bowden and scream or quit, but it was worse than that. Chatterton just sat there, eating his pizza, looking through Mattera and out onto the street. Minutes passed this way, each longer than the last, until a familiar sound came from the television in the corner of the restaurant. Only now did Chatterton glance up, to see himself, starring in an episode of *Deep Sea Detectives*, the History Channel television series about two divers who solve shipwreck mysteries around the world, and he watched it, not because he enjoyed seeing himself on the screen, but because every one of the shows he'd filmed had an ending that made sense.

Chatterton called Mattera's cell phone late that evening. He said he'd given up on Bowden, but could not put up with the idea of poachers stealing something they hadn't worked for—something they were incapable of finding themselves. And yet, that's likely what was coming now that word was out that Tracy Bowden was after the *Golden Fleece*.

One morning, after Ehrenberg lost data on the computer, Chatterton exploded, accusing his friend and roommate of slovenly work and an unfocused mind.

"Screw this guy. I'm going home. It's not worth it," Ehrenberg told Mattera. "I don't get paid. My payoff doesn't come until we find something. And we sure as hell aren't finding treasure now. I don't need this."

Before Chatterton could throw Ehrenberg over the villa's balcony, Mattera stepped between them, pulling the usually easygoing Ehrenberg aside and urging him to stay.

Ehrenberg went inside to cool off. Chatterton followed him a few minutes later, and the men shook hands.

But the peace was short-lived. That afternoon, Chatterton lit into Kretschmer for requesting time off to spend with family.

"Now?" Chatterton yelled. "Are you fucking kidding me, Heiko?"

"You know what, John?" Kretschmer said. "I'm done. I have a job waiting for me at the oil refinery. It's a steady job. It pays. I'm leaving."

Again, Mattera jumped in, asking Kretschmer to stay on. But Kretschmer shook his head. His nights were tortured by mosquitos; there was no Internet or hot water in his apartment. He missed his family, and he had an offer for a good job, no crazy bosses.

Mattera couldn't afford to lose Kretschmer any more than he could Ehrenberg; Kretschmer fixed everything, was the first to work in the morning and the last to leave at night, and was one of the nicest, easiest guys Mattera had known.

"You gotta take the good with the bad with Chatterton," Mattera said. "He and I have different styles. But he gets more out of people than anyone in the world. He gets things done."

"He's making me crazy," Kretschmer said.

"He's making me crazy, too," Mattera replied. "But we gotta remember that this sonofabitch is the one who's going to help us make history. He squeezes more out of a three-week operation than most guys could in a year. You have to agree with that, Heiko."

Kretschmer nodded.

"If you leave, we're done," Mattera said. "Worse than that: I lose a good friend, because I'll have to kill you. So stay."

Kretschmer took a breath and began to laugh.

"Okay," he said. "For you I stay."

Lying in bed that evening, sweating because the air conditioning had died, Mattera opened a book he'd read twice already: *Benedict Arnold's Navy*, about the American general's stand against a British fleet on Lake Champlain in 1776. He read into the night, worried for Arnold, a hero in America's greatest year, and the coming decision that would ruin the good life that Arnold had made.

It was now just a week before Christmas, and no one had to say it: They needed a break, from this place, from this search, from one another. So they decided to go home to spend time with families and do things that counted. No one believed other salvors would show up at Cayo Levantado during the holidays; that's not how the lazy worked.

It took more than twenty hours for Chatterton to travel from Samaná back to Maine. When he got home, he kissed his wife, fell onto his living room couch, and marveled at how every light and appliance and toilet just worked. He went scallop diving off the rocky coast behind his backyard, stacked wood for his fireplace, and selected the right bottle of wine. At night, he lay silent in bed, unplagued by mosquitos and sweat. He took long, hot showers in the mornings.

Only after Christmas, when Chatterton had been home for a week, did Carla ask, "So, where's our pirate?" Of course, she knew he hadn't found Bannister yet, and she didn't mind. He'd loved that about her since they met. She'd never complained about his work—the travel, the time away from home, the danger—never asked him to be who he wasn't. But now, he could see that his life was wearing on her. More than once during the search for the pirate ship, Carla had said, "You work all the time," and it was true, he was hardly home anymore, but any less effort and he'd lose the *Golden Fleece*. Every day, he wanted to tell Carla he didn't need this bullshit in the Dominican Republic anymore, that his decision to hunt pirates and treasure now seemed a mistake, that he couldn't believe the choices he'd made at a stage in his life when days, never mind years, couldn't be thrown away. But what good would whining do? Instead, he just told her that it's one thing to go up against the ocean—if the ocean beats you, okay. But to be held back by a stubborn old man? That's not how the world should work.

The crowd was lively for Chatterton's talk at a northeast dive shop, and he did not disappoint. Jumping into his story about finding the mystery U-boat, he gestured with his hands to describe his first moments inside the lost German sub and twisted his body to show how he'd slithered out with his life.

At the end, people lined up to have him sign books, DVD covers, and T-shirts. They asked his advice and told him he'd been an inspiration. Time went fast for Chatterton here.

At home, he received a phone call from Terry Kerby, the director at the Hawaii Undersea Research Laboratory. Kerby had an idea for a television documentary: an investigation into whether a two-man Japanese midget submarine had fired torpedoes at the battleship USS *Arizona* during the attack on Pearl Harbor. To Chatterton, the idea was a winner. It had everything he loved: history, mystery, and deep diving. And an ending. He thought it perfect for PBS and its documentary series *Nova*, which he'd been a part of before.

"Sounds like a great project, Terry. Let me get back to you."

On New Year's Eve, Carla made a dinner at home for their closest friends, including Diana Norwood, the widow of Chatterton's former co-host on *Deep Sea Detectives*. She served a Stilton cheese, a whole Arctic char, and homemade cheesecake with fresh Maine blueberry glaze. It was the kind of meal Chatterton dreamed about when he was in Samaná.

Not long afterward, Chatterton and Carla went to an event for an organization that introduced badly wounded and disabled veterans to scuba diving. The group would be exploring a shipwreck in the Caribbean. As a Vietnam combat veteran, Chatterton felt honored to contribute.

On the dive boat, he geared up with the other veterans. He worried about how he might help them underwater and rehearsed rescue scenarios in his head. The group was led into the water by another dive instructor, Chatterton bringing up the rear. His attention soon turned to a young man, paralyzed below the waist, who strained with his arms to pull himself through the water. By the time he reached the wreck he was nearly exhausted. Chatterton signaled to ask if the diver wanted to return to the surface, but could see in the man's eyes he didn't want to give up, so Chatterton followed him inside the wreck.

Unable to kick, the man reached for a piece of railing and began pulling himself along, and when he ran out of railing he grabbed pipes or door frames, and in this way he began to streak through the ship, free and powerful and faster than even Chatterton could swim. By using the wreck to propel himself, the man now darted through passageways and corridors. When Chatterton finally caught up to him, he saw pride in the young guy's eyes, and he remembered what it felt like when a person found a way to do something that looked impossible to do.

In Santo Domingo, Mattera booked new reservations for his dive center. Each transaction was pleasant—just a phone call, a date on the calendar, and a thanks. He took beach walks in the mornings, smoked Cohiba cigars in the afternoon, ate dinner with Carolina by candlelight. Not once did his fiancée lose her temper or curse Tracy Bowden or wish the entire country to be swallowed by the sea. Perhaps she didn't realize the spectacular extent to which he and Chatterton were failing.

Sometimes, Mattera's thoughts drifted back to the galleons, and he wondered if he might have found treasure by now if he and Chatterton hadn't detoured to go look for the pirate ship. One morning, he called Francisco, a dive instructor he knew, and invited him to the Santo Domingo harbor, just down the road from his apartment. For years, Mattera had heard stories about galleons that had sunk while tied up in the harbor. He'd even gone diving there once before. Now, on a whim, he went back to check the place out.

At the mouth of the Ozama River, the men pulled on their wet suits. Just a few yards away, cars and trucks flew past on the Paseo Presidente Billini, horns blaring and lights flashing as drivers hurried to everywhere. As the vehicles passed, Mattera wondered how many of them might imagine a four-hundred-year-old galleon sunk here, silent for centuries under this city of fast-moving lives.

Soon, he and Francisco had descended twenty feet to the bottom. Sand and particulate mushroomed up from the floor, making it impossible for either man to see more than a few yards in front of his mask. It took just a minute before they lost sight of each other.

Mattera began to sweep his metal detector over the bottom, listening for the sounds of treasure. What might it be like, he wondered, to find a gold coin down here? Would he be able to read the date? Would it shine—

Mattera stopped. Ahead, he could see the faint outline of a massive object, brownish and heavy, moving toward him, slowly but definitely, as if aimed. As the object drew closer it appeared to be an ancient wood timber of the kind he'd seen in his books about galleons. He swam toward the object and reached for it— here was his treasure—but when his hands arrived they took hold of a face, there was a face on this object and holes where there once had been eyes, and in a moment the thing crashed over Mattera, tearing the regulator from his mouth and sending him sprawling, and as he screamed into the water he could see that this wooden timber was really a horse, drowned and decomposing and floating out to the Caribbean Sea.

When Mattera surfaced, his first instinct was to call Chatterton, who loved this kind of story, but he stopped himself. He worried that it would sound like he was drifting away from their pirate project, and worse, he worried that it was true.

Chapter 15

DROWNING

When the men returned to Samaná in early January 2009, Chatterton learned that Mattera had booked more customers for the dive center. In a tone and volume Mattera didn't appreciate, Chatterton accused him of losing focus on the only thing that mattered, the pirate wreck. But when Mattera asked for a better idea about how to make use of their time, Chatterton couldn't answer.

That afternoon, Mattera received a phone call from Kretschmer. A salvage boat belonging to Burt Webber, one of treasure hunting's biggest names, was maneuvering off Cayo Levantado. It wasn't clear what the vessel was doing there, but to Kretschmer it looked suspicious.

Mattera collected Chatterton and Ehrenberg, and full-throttled it out to the island. They found Webber's crew anchored over the same site that the archaeologist had provided to Cultura—the site they had just ruled out. It enraged both Chatterton and Mattera, but things got worse. As they drew closer, they could see divers in the water.

"Let's fucking ram their boat," Chatterton said.

Mattera wasn't sure if he was kidding. Either way, it was clear to him that Webber's men had arrived to claim that they'd found the *Golden Fleece*, or at least were close. That alone might prompt Cultura to wrest salvage rights from Bowden and award it to Webber, another old-time great who had deep pockets and a first-rate crew.

Chatterton steered the boat closer to Webber's. Drawing to within one hundred feet, he lined up a straight shot and reached for the throttle. He looked at Mattera. Then, slowly, he reached for a different weapon—his cell phone—and began shooting photographs. He emailed the pictures to Bowden, then followed up with a call. Bowden didn't like what he heard. He told Chatterton he worried that Webber's crew might be onto something at Cayo Levantado.

"These are fugazi numbers," Chatterton said. "The wreck's not there."

But that left the matter of why Webber, or anyone else, might be anchored over the archaeologist's site.

To Chatterton, the answer was simple: buzz. Word was out that Bowden was hot after the *Golden Fleece*. Anyone who could make it look like they were contributing to finding the wreck might petition Cultura to award them some or even all of the salvage rights. If they found so much as a piece of shitty old wood—and there were mountains of them sunk around Cayo Levantado—their case would appear even stronger. If they had investors, even a rumor that they might get the *Golden Fleece* could bump their stock price.

"I don't know Webber's motives," Chatterton told Bowden. "Maybe his guys are just out for a swim and a suntan. But you need to get him the hell out of here."

Bowden called Cultura. Officials there said Webber had been granted permission to test equipment in the area. But when Bowden asked why Webber might be over the same spot where the archaeologist reported finding the *Golden Fleece*, his contact could only say he would look into it.

That evening, Mattera drove to Santo Domingo to buy supplies. Chatterton went with Kretschmer and Ehrenberg for dinner at Tony's. There, they saw several members of Webber's crew at a table drinking beer. Just the sight of these men irked Chatterton; even his favorite local restaurant wasn't off-limits to intruders.

Chatterton sat down with his back to a wall, in a place where he could see the entire restaurant. One of Webber's crew called out to Chatterton's table.

"Treasure pussies."

Chatterton just stared at the men. Another of Webber's crew called to him.

"What are you looking at, asshole?"

"Fuck you," Chatterton said.

"I should come over and kick your fucking ass," another one called out.

"Come on over," Chatterton said.

He looked to Ehrenberg and Kretschmer. They were two of the smartest and most capable men he knew. They had options in life. They weren't making much money here, and conditions were difficult. And they certainly weren't bar fighters. But both of them clenched their fists and pushed their chairs back from the table, ready to rumble. They were all in this together.

"They're drunk, we're not," Chatterton said. "We're carrying guns. They're holding their dicks. Seriously, who's got the advantage here? If they make a move I'm going to beat the crap out of them with my Smith and Wesson."

And then it became clear to Chatterton. If the other crew provoked a fight, it gave them a claim against Bowden. He could hear them now, crying to Cultura: "Bowden's rogues attacked me in a fine dining establishment!" So he and his guys could not be the ones to make the first move.

"We're gonna sit here and eat our dinner," Chatterton told Kretschmer and Ehrenberg. "But if they come over, we gotta do what we gotta do."

But no one came over. Finally, Webber's crew left, mumbling tough as they walked onto the street.

"They talk like Popeye," Chatterton said, "but inside they're all Olive Oyl."

Everyone laughed. The crisis had been averted, but no one slept well that night. If Webber's boat was still at Cayo Levantado the next morning, it would be a strong indication that Cultura had endorsed his presence and dismissed Bowden's complaint. If it was gone, the area still belonged, however tenuously, to Bowden.

The men went out at sunrise. Mattera steered while Chatterton stood at the rail on the side, binoculars in hand, looking for interlopers. He spotted a boat just off the western beach at Cayo Levantado.

"Sonofabitch!" Mattera yelled.

He gunned the engines.

"You don't come into another guy's house and take his stuff . . ."

Peering through binoculars, Chatterton put up his hand and called for Mattera to slow down.

"It ain't Webber," he said.

Mattera cut power. As the boat settled, Chatterton got a steadier view of the offender. She was a university vessel they knew, doing research on whales. Webber's boat was gone.

The men returned to their storage shed beneath the villa, doing maintenance and repairs, waiting for Bowden to come to his senses and finish salvaging the sugar wreck.

The next morning, Mattera received a call from a fisherman friend, who reported that there was a new salvage boat anchored off the western beach at Cayo Levantado, one the locals hadn't seen before.

Mattera and the others rushed to the island. Anchored over the archaeologist's site—and where Webber's crew had just been working—was a vessel belonging to American salvors Bowden had put to work on a different wreck.

Mattera cut hard to the left and maneuvered until his boat was cheek to cheek with the other. Standing on the bow, Chatterton called to their crew. To Mattera, he looked like a seventeenth-century pirate ready to board a merchant vessel.

"What in the hell are you doing here?" Chatterton yelled.

"We're diving a wreck," said one of the men.

"I know you're diving a wreck. The question is why are you diving a wreck in our area?"

The captain stepped forward. Chatterton remembered being introduced to him by Bowden. And disliking him.

"I am a citizen of the city of Samaná," the man said, "and I can dive wherever I want. Besides, we have permission. You better talk to Bowden."

That statement slammed Chatterton. What if Bowden had sent this crew to search for the *Golden Fleece*? What if he'd told them to survey the area and find the pirate ship? If that was the case, Chatterton and Mattera were already out; Bowden just hadn't told them yet.

Mattera dialed Bowden by cell phone but got no answer. For now, he and Chatterton were helpless to do anything about this new crew; they were just diving and there was no law against that. Mattera dropped anchor and parked just off the invading boat's bow, waiting to hear back from Bowden.

When Bowden finally called back, Mattera told him about the new crew, and asked him straight out: Did you send these guys out here?

"Let me take care of it," Bowden said.

"Did you send them?"

"No. But I'll take care of it."

Mattera ended the call. Chatterton asked if he thought Bowden was behind the new crew.

"He said he wasn't," Mattera said. "But I don't know."

Chatterton and Mattera could do little more than watch the rival divers. It was bad enough that these invaders wanted to cash in on others' hard work. It was worse that they didn't care anything about Bannister, a man who'd never have wanted to be found by men like them.

The new vessel left a few hours later. Things were clear now. Word was out about the *Golden Fleece*, everyone wanted a piece, and more would be coming. If Bowden didn't claim the pirate ship soon, it was just a matter of time before Cultura awarded rights to the wreck, or to the area, to one or more of these late intruders. But now it seemed obvious to them that Bowden wouldn't budge. He wanted them to return to Cayo Levantado.

And then, at dinner that night, Chatterton and Mattera conceived a simple and powerful solution to the entire problem. Rather than wait for Bowden to finish work on the sugar wreck, they would do it themselves, without asking, looking for any artifact that would prove the wreck to be the *Golden Fleece*. A smoking gun. Half the world already seemed to be looking for the pirate ship without permission. Why couldn't the guys who actually put in the hard work and spent money and put their families on hold get an unimpeded shot at the wreck, too? They would go the next morning.

But when they awoke, no one made a move for the boat. In their excitement, neither man had considered that Bowden might see this as mutiny, or that Cultura might consider it an affront, or, most of all, that it wasn't an honorable thing to do.

But they couldn't return to Cayo Levantado, either. They tried to think of something constructive to do, something better than just wasting time. For a few days, they drove their boat around the bay, looking for nothing in particular. Then, one morning, they just didn't go out. Fuel was too expensive, or another pump needed fixing, or it rained. Chatterton had business to do in the States. Mattera had his dive center to run. Ehrenberg needed a break. Kretschmer wanted to visit family. "See you guys soon," they said to one another, but to each of them, it sounded like good-bye.

In Maine, Chatterton spoke to his friends in the television business, every project they discussed sounded promising. He checked his portfolio; he was already into his treasure-hunting adventure for several hundred thousand dollars, a serious dent to his net worth. He couldn't keep burning money like this without earning income or seeing a return. Things were getting tight.

On Staten Island, Mattera went to his internist, who warned that his blood pressure was dangerously high. When Garcia-Alecont called from Santo Domingo to tell Mattera there was talk of more treasure hunters descending on Cayo Levantado in search of the *Golden Fleece*, Mattera didn't even ask questions.

Carolina flew in a few days later to spend time with her fiancée. To her, Mattera looked more than just tired; he looked beaten. When she asked how he was doing with things—with Tracy, the *Golden Fleece*, John Chatterton—he told her a story.

To hone his diving skills while in high school, he took jobs cleaning and changing propellers on boats at Great Kills Harbor, the nicest marina on Staten Island. The work sometimes required him to stay underwater for hours at a time, but the pay was good and the water shallow. One Saturday, while cleaning the last boat, he glanced at the air gauges for his tanks, and saw only five hundred pounds of air remaining, about eighteen minutes' worth—not much, but enough to finish the job. He kept scrubbing, dreaming of ways to spend the four hundred dollars he would clear that day, a king's ransom in 1980.

Suddenly, shards of pain shot through his left arm and into his head, a burning so hot it buckled his knees. He jerked away but his arm wouldn't move; a rusty two-inch bluefish hook had plunged all the way into his wrist. Blood flowed into the water, making ribbons of brown. Mattera knew better than to pull again—the hook was tied to fishing line tangled around the propeller—so he reached for a knife to cut himself free, but no matter how hard he worked the line wouldn't give, and he realized then that it was made not of monofilament but of stainless steel, used by fishermen to stop sharks and bluefish from biting clear through. He checked his air. At this rate, he had just a minute or two left to breathe.

He looked up toward the surface. He was less than a foot underwater, yet could not move any higher. He tried to ease the hook out of his wrist, but the barbs on its shank had anchored next to a vein and he dared not pull it farther. He checked his tanks again. Near empty. Now he had to make a decision. He could rip the barbed hook out of his wrist, or he could use his remaining few breaths to try to untangle the line. If he chose the former, he might bleed to death. If he chose the latter, he risked running out of air and drowning just inches from the surface.

Mattera grabbed the hook in his right hand, took a final deep breath, and pulled as hard as he could. Skin and veins tore, and the water exploded red around him. Now free, he kicked to the surface, throwing off his mask and regulator and gulping air. Bystanders converged, throwing him towels and offering to drive him to the hospital, but immortal at seventeen, he assured them he was okay.

"Listen to me, honey," a woman said. "If you've ever trusted anyone in your life, trust me now. You're going to bleed to death if you don't go to the hospital. You have to go."

He took a towel, wrapped it around his wrist, and ran to his car. At Staten Island Hospital, with Mattera still in his wet suit, doctors cauterized the vein, gave him a tetanus shot, and told him he was lucky to be alive. That night, he bought two pairs of professional pruning shears, European models that could cut through anything, and he brought them to every dive he made after that, the deep and the shallow, the routine and the impossible.

Mattera fought a lump in his throat as he looked into Carolina's eyes.

"I'm drowning again," he said. "We're a week away from getting the *Golden Fleece*. But it's not happening. I'm inches from the surface but I can't pull the hook out."

A few weeks later, in mid-February 2009, Chatterton and Mattera agreed that they needed to talk. Both were headed back to the Dominican Republic, so they made a date for lunch the next week.

In Samaná, they set out for a restaurant about fifteen kilometers down the road. Neither said much as Chatterton drove the white pickup truck through a street crowded with crooked houses, chicken coops, and hanging laundry. Every block or so, he weaved around an open manhole, the cover stolen and sold for scrap.

From out of nowhere, a man riding a motorcycle pulled in front of the truck and began waving.

"Look at this guy," Chatterton said. "He's pissed."

"What did you do to him?" Mattera asked.

"Nothing."

"You didn't cut him off? Run over some chickens? Flip him the finger?"

"Nothing."

The agitated rider swerved back and forth a few more times.

"John, he's got a gun," Chatterton said.

Mattera looked over. He could see the weapon, a nickel-plated Beretta 92. Expensive.

To Mattera, all this was bad news. Either the man was emotionally disturbed, or he was looking to rob two gringos who'd wandered out too far in the country. Drug smugglers lived in these parts, hidden in the hills. They would kill two rich-looking Americans without blinking.

Mattera unholstered his Glock nine millimeter.

"Keep him in front of us," Mattera said. "Don't pass him or let him get to our flanks."

The biker began flailing his gun, screaming obscenities and demanding that Chatterton pass, but Chatterton wouldn't do it. The man slowed his bike to twenty miles per hour, then fifteen, bobbing and weaving, trying to slip behind the truck, but Chatterton slid with him, refusing the flank. It occurred now to Chatterton to stop, but he didn't know who else might be lying in wait; in a moving truck, at least they had three thousand pounds of momentum.

The biker slowed to five miles per hour.

"Watch his hands," Mattera said.

Driving only fast enough to keep the bike upright, the man now waved his pistol over his left shoulder, toward the truck. People crowded the street to take in the spectacle. Mattera cracked open his passenger door and wedged his foot in the space, then pointed his Glock at the biker's torso.

"Stay behind him. I've got him framed."

"Give the word and I run him over," Chatterton said.

Women screamed, children ran, barking dogs descended as the motorcycle inched forward at just two or three miles per hour, the white truck just ten yards behind, guns drawn on both sides, the biker and Mattera screaming at each other in Spanish, a thousand obscenities as the men continued their crawl. Mattera didn't want to shoot, especially near a crowd, but the guy was giving him less choice with each passing moment.

"Drop the gun now!" Chatterton yelled, but the man kept waving his weapon and screaming.

Mattera's finger flexed alongside the trigger guard.

"If he points it at us I'm going to drop him," said Mattera.

"I'll hit the gas and finish him," Chatterton said.

The motorcycle stopped. Slowly, the man got off the bike and stepped forward. This was Mattera's best chance, but it would only be there for a fraction of a second. He carried baggage from things he'd done in his life, just because killing was justified didn't mean it was easy to live with, he had the tactical advantage here, the protection of his truck, and the enemy in front of him, and how would they explain this to police, he'd seen guys die for thinking things over too long, and now Chatterton revved the engine.

"Pon tus malditas manos en tu cabeza!" Mattera yelled. Put your fucking hands on your head!

Slowly, the man tucked the gun into the back of his pants. Spinning around, he ran back to his bike, gave a half salute, then drove off the road and up into the mountains, dirt and dust flying from his wheels. A moment later, he had disappeared.

For a minute Chatterton and Mattera drove in silence. Then, one of them said, "Man, we were good," and the other said, "Hell, yeah, we were."

Chapter 16

THE BATTLE

In a booth at the restaurant, the men replayed their showdown with the motorcycle desperado. They'd intended to use the time to address the obvious—that things weren't working out for them—but neither had the heart to think about quitting on the other on a day when they'd had an adventure like this.

The partners didn't see each other for several days after that. Then Chatterton called and told Mattera it was time to talk. They met at the villa and sat on the veranda, holding sweating cans of diet soda, each waiting for the other to quit.

"Give me three days," Mattera said. "I have one more idea."

The men looked over the channel toward Cayo Vigia.

"I thought we might be done," Chatterton said.

"We might be," Mattera replied. "But not yet."

A few days later, Mattera was on a flight bound for New York. On airplane tray tables, he usually balanced three or four books, a notebook and pens, and a snack. This time, he just looked out the window, nothing in front of him, watching the ocean pass below.

In Manhattan, Mattera pushed into the stacks of the New York Public Library on Forty-Second Street, pulling out as many volumes on seventeenth-century naval warfare and weapons as he could find. None made mention of the Royal Navy's engagement with Bannister, but if taken together, they could be assembled into a picture of the battle, an accounting that put Mattera into the throat of the fight. He took notes on it all, searching for clues in the rubble.

By his previous research, Mattera already knew how things started. Acting on orders from the governor of Jamaica, two Royal Navy frigates, the *Falcon* and the *Drake*, sailed into Samaná Bay to catch the pirate captain Joseph Bannister and destroy the *Golden Fleece*. The navy captains expected to find the ship on the careen—being cleaned of barnacles and other sea growth—as she lay beached on her side at an island.

Mattera had always believed the advantage to lie with the navy. The frigates could carry fifty-eight cannons between them (the *Falcon* forty-two, the *Drake* sixteen), while Bannister had perhaps thirty. But it wasn't until Mattera opened his books that he began to understand the extent of the navy's upper hand.

The frigates were designed to be nimble and quick, lie low in the water, and carry heavy guns. They also happened to be beautiful, with sleek and muscled lines, the hunting dogs of the English fleet. The largest of them, like the *Falcon*, was powerful enough to fight in the line among England's mightiest warships. Between them, the *Falcon* and the *Drake* carried about 250 men, at least double the size of Bannister's crew. In addition to agility and speed, these three-masted frigates cut imposing figures. The *Falcon* was about 130 feet long, the *Drake* about 125, massive ships for a Caribbean deployment. The *Golden Fleece*, at a length of perhaps 100 feet, was a baby by comparison. By size alone, the frigates carried a statement of intent from the governor of Jamaica: The *Golden Fleece* was going to be destroyed, and Bannister was going to die.

But the advantage only began with the ships. While pirates aboard the *Golden Fleece* probably had rare occasion to fire their cannons, gunners aboard the frigates practiced constantly. The navy captains, Charles Talbot of the *Falcon* and Edward Spragge of the *Drake*, were military commanders trained in the art of war. Bannister, by contrast, had been a merchant captain trained in the art of moving hides and dried meat. In terms of provisions, weapons, and ammunition, the navy ships were much better supplied. Best of all for the frigates, Bannister was pinned down on an island. Pirates often were best at running, but there was nowhere for Bannister to go.

Mattera, however, had thought enough about tactics and conflict during his career in security to know that the pirates had advantages of their own. Bannister had placed two cannon batteries on the island—one of ten guns and the other of six—and no doubt had hidden them behind trees and in bunkers of logs or mud or sand, making it difficult for the navy to see his men or hit his guns. They would be firing their weapons from an elevated position on land, not the pitching and rolling decks of a ship. The pirates would be fighting for their lives, always a strong motivator. Most of all, they were being led by Joseph Bannister, a man who'd already proved he could pull off the impossible by cheating the hangman and restealing his ship at Port Royal.

Delving further into the books on his table, Mattera could see how the battle must have unfolded. The frigates would have sailed into Samaná Bay on the prevailing wind, hugging the peninsula along the northern shore, the only area deep enough and sufficiently free of reefs to allow safe passage for ships so large. With a stiff wind, they might have made nine or ten knots (ten or eleven miles per hour), their Red Ensigns flying in the breeze at the sterns, the Union Jack (like the modern British flag, but without the red Irish diagonal stripe) hoisted on the bowsprit over the bow.

Entering the channel near Cayo Vigia, where Chatterton and

Mattera believed the engagement occurred, the frigates would have been prepared for action, their gun decks cleared of tables, hammocks, and other tools of life at sea. At midafternoon, they would have been less than a mile from the *Golden Fleece* but still wouldn't have seen her. Tucked into a crook in the island, the pirate ship was invisible to all but those who came close enough to be ambushed.

By now, pirate lookouts would have sounded the alarm and Bannister would have ordered gunners to their stations. Some of them manned cannons, others muskets. The only question was when to fire on the navy ships.

The frigates drew closer, to within a quarter mile of the *Golden Fleece*. At this point, it was unlikely that Bannister had gotten his ship off the careen and back into the water, but it would have been too late to matter either way. Sailing into the channel, navy lookouts would have spotted the pirates through their telescopes. And the pirates would have known they'd been seen.

It was impossible for Mattera to know exactly what happened next. If he were Bannister—and he knew they thought alike—he would have fired on the frigates at this point, aiming for their bows, which were less well protected than their sides. Whether Bannister did this or, rather, allowed the frigates to move in closer to give his gun crews a better shot, one thing was certain: The two sides were no more than five hundred yards from each other, and the distance was closing fast.

Now, the navy captains had to decide how close to get to the pirates before they committed to fight. There was risk and reward no matter which way they played it.

Cannons were not accurate in the 1680s, especially at distances of more than a few hundred yards. Most often, they didn't need to be; warring ships of the age commonly battered each other from point-blank range, which might be as close as fifty feet. Sometimes, they didn't fire until they saw the buckles on the enemy's shoes. And that was not just an expression.

Shooting cannons at a distance was especially difficult. Gunpowder was inconsistent in both quality and quantity from shot to shot, which affected the speed at which the ball left the muzzle, and therefore the gunner's ability to fire with precision. Cannonballs were made about a quarter-inch smaller than the diameter of the bore, to assure that they didn't jam during discharge and blow up the gun. That meant the ball bounced off the sides of the bore while being fired, and flew out at some small angle—not a severe one, but often enough to make it hook or slice like a golf ball, and almost impossible to put on a bull's-eye.

When cannonballs did find their targets, they could cause devastating damage. Weighing at least six pounds, and often much more, they could tear through the thick hulls and masts of enemy ships, sending huge wood splinters flying into anything, and anyone, nearby. Mattera was surprised to learn that the secondary impact from splinters was the cause of most human casualties from naval cannon fire. Slower flying cannonballs often did the most damage because they didn't penetrate as cleanly through wood, which meant cannons fired from a distance might be the deadliest of them all.

To Mattera, it was clear that the navy captains chose to fight up close. According to records, they'd been hit by musket fire; that wouldn't have happened if the frigates had been more than about 150 yards from the island. But that was the outer range of effective musket fire. When Mattera envisioned the start of the battle, he saw the two sides even closer than that.

Closing in on the *Golden Fleece* at the island, the frigates would have turned sideways—broadside—to fire. Most of their cannons were positioned along the ships' sides, and while this made them a bigger target when fighting, it also allowed them to deliver maximum fire. This is how navies were built to do battle in the Age of Sail—broadside to broadside—a brutal and close-up affair.

Mattera knew from the records that Bannister fired first. But it wouldn't have taken long for the gunners aboard the frigates to throw open the ships' shuttered gun ports and bring their guns to bear. Operating cannons was a muscular and dangerous business. Lives depended on which side could do it best.

Most cannons of the day were made of cast iron, and fired round iron balls. Many guns were named for the size of their shot; hence, a cannon that fired a twelve-pound ball was called, simply, a "twelve pounder." The *Falcon* carried twelve pounders, six pounders, and a few "sakers" (cannons that fired balls weighing five and a quarter pounds). The *Drake* was more lightly armed, having several sakers and some three pounders. Bannister likely had some of them all (he would have carried several as a merchant captain, and no doubt had been stealing more since he turned pirate). Whatever the caliber, the weapons could inflict devastating damage to enemy ships and personnel. It was the job of each cannon crew—often comprising three or four men—to make sure its own gun delivered.

Mattera hardly could imagine a better showdown than the one between the navy and pirate gunners. The navy seamen were better trained, but the pirates had the high ground, and didn't have to fire from a moving ship.

On board the frigates, boys as young as ten ran gunpowder from dry holds belowdecks up to the gunners. Most often, the powder was contained in a sausage-shaped canvas bag known as the cartridge, which was loaded into the bore of the cannon. The size of the cartridge depended on the size of the ball to be fired; usually, the gunpowder weighed a little more than half what the cannonball did. (A twelve pounder, for example, would require about seven pounds of gunpowder.) Wadding, made from old rope or canvas, was pushed in after the powder, then shoved down to the breach (rear) along with the cartridge by a long piece of wood called a rammer. Next, the cannonball was loaded, followed by more wadding and ramming.

Now the gun captain took center stage. Careful not to cause sparks, he pushed an iron poker into the cannon's vent (a small exhaust hole near the breach), puncturing the gunpowder cartridge inside. Then, using a much finer gunpowder, known as serpentine, he filled the vent to the top. Only then was the weapon ready to fire.

Pulling on thick ropes attached to the gun's wheeled carriage, the navy crew muscled the cannon forward until its barrel protruded out of its port. Now, despite the pitch and roll of the ship, despite the concussion of other cannons, despite taking enemy fire, the gun crew aimed as best they could. All that remained was for the gun captain to step forward with his linstock (a long pole with a smoldering match at the end) and put it to the touchhole, and the weapon would fire. If ever there was a time to pray, it was now.

A cannon, even loaded properly, could explode on firing, killing anyone in the vicinity. Backblasts could burn, deafen, or concuss nearby crewmen. Open gun ports made gunners more vulnerable to enemy cannon fire. Even if perfectly fired, a three-thousand-pound cannon's violent recoil could crush a slow-footed crewman who failed to get out of its way.

Moving the match to the touchhole, the gun captain ignited the serpentine powder. A moment later, the world thundered as a black ball, yellow flame, and gray-white smoke shot from the cannon's mouth, and the gun flew back in protest, held down only by ropes tied to the ship's inner hull. On the island, pirates with good eyes might see the cannonball streaking at more than seven hundred miles per hour toward the *Golden Fleece*—or toward themselves.

At the same time, shooters on both sides loaded their muskets (a process similar to loading the cannons, complete with wadding and rammers) and took aim at their targets. The effective range of these long-barreled guns was little more than one hundred yards, but no one was looking for bull's-eyes. Instead, they would have fired in volley, sending dozens of shots at once in the general direction of the enemy. Just one heavy lead ball could tear off a man's arm. Dozens raining down from the sky could test even the bravest man's courage.

The battle was on. To destroy the *Golden Fleece* and the pirates' gun emplacements, the navy gunners likely fired classic round cannonballs. Against people, however, they might have fired any number of nasty variants, including chain shot (two balls, or half balls, connected by chain), bar shot (similar to chain shot, but connected by a bar), and canister shot (metal cans of musket balls or rocks that sprayed shrapnel). Returning fire, the pirates probably used round cannonballs aimed at the frigates' hulls and masts.

By now, the navy warships were likely anchored at both ends to keep them steady and fighting near to each other, bringing the maximum amount of firepower to bear on Bannister and his crew. It was rare, during the Age of Sail, for ships to fire full broadsides all at once because it strained the timbers of the vessel. But both the *Falcon* and the *Drake* likely fired several of their guns together, pummeling the island and whatever targets they could find.

It was essential for the frigates to take out the pirate cannon batteries, which Mattera believed had been placed by Bannister at the top of the eastern tip of the island. The elevation alone—more than a hundred feet over the shoreline—would have made aiming heavy cannons on the frigates even more difficult through narrow gun ports. Often, to aim high, a ship had to anchor farther away from its target—thereby reducing its accuracy. To Mattera, elevation alone meant advantage.

But perhaps the biggest problem in hitting the pirates with cannon fire came from the pitching and rolling of the ships. Fighting from the water, cannoneers often had to wait until the moment their vessel came level to fire. In this way, they were aiming the ship more than the guns.

Both sides likely missed with most of their shots. Those that connected, however, would have done grave harm. The *Golden Fleece*, minus at least half her guns (which had been moved onto the island) and possibly still careened on the sand, was likely damaged early on, though she might have been unmanned during the battering. Navy seamen, struck by musket balls and wood splinters, would have begun to fall. Those hit in the head or neck or torso often died, immediately if they were lucky. The injured who survived were moved to the ship's surgeon or barber for bandaging or, if the wounds were more serious, amputation. It was here, before the surgeon and his saw, that the grievously injured man's fate would be decided.

Seamen doing battle in the seventeenth century expected to lose limbs. Navy surgeons had seen every gruesome injury and removed mangled arms and legs often. By Bannister's time, there were few places in the world more advanced in trauma surgery than the dank and unsterile quarters of a navy fighting ship. If one had to be separated from a part of his body, this was the place to be.

Amputations were performed frequently, but the surgeons

did not go into them lightly. The operation "cannot be performed without putting the Patient to violent and inexpressible pain," wrote Pierre Dionis, a prominent French surgeon of the time and author of a surgical textbook. Nor were surgeons under any illusions about the outcomes; there was a good chance a patient would die after amputation, but it was near certain he would die without it. So they did what had to be done.

Speed was paramount. Delay increased the risk of blood loss, infection, shock, and delirium. It often exposed the patient, and his wound, to onboard nibbling rats. And it allowed him to contemplate what was to happen on the operating table; sometimes the imagination could be even crueler than the bone saw. Delay also deprived the surgeon of perhaps his most effective tool—the patient's own adrenaline. That hormone, in addition to acting as a painkiller, could provide a man courage, and he would need it, because in the late seventeenth century there was no anesthetic. At best, a man might be given a bit of alcohol to drink, and then not too much, for fear it might inflame rather than calm him.

Shipboard surgeons had little time to explain amputation to injured men, but what they said was likely honest and direct. John Woodall, an English author of an early-seventeenth-century text on surgery, recommended, "If you be constrained to use your saw, let first your patient be well informed of the eminent danger of death by the use thereof, prescribe him no certaintie of life, and let the worke be done with his owne free will, and request, and not otherwise."

The patient would have to be held down. For this, the surgeon called on several assistants, the stronger the better. Moving the wounded man onto the operating table (often just a board balanced on two chests and covered by a piece of canvas), the assistants would take their positions and plant their feet. One held the patient from behind, others restrained his extremities, and still another held down the ruined limb, often over the edge of the table, so that the surgeon could do his work.

Until now, the surgeon had taken great pains not to show the patient his tools; sometimes, the sight of a bone saw or curved knife could be more terrible than the cut itself. Only after the patient had been secured would the surgeon bring out his instruments. They included an amputation knife, a bone saw, forceps, needles, bandages, and cauterizing implements. They were made as clean as possible for the time, often with a mixture of vinegar and water.

Many surgeons chose to include a bit of healthy flesh above the wound to ensure removal of all damaged tissue and bone. No one, however, wanted to take more of the patient's limb than was necessary. Having chosen the spot, the surgeon tied on a tourniquet (perhaps a rag torn from the patient's own clothes), then steadied himself against the movement of the ship. Every surgeon hoped to make a quick, clean cut, but that could be interrupted by the temper of the sea.

The surgeon first went to work with his knife, making a circular cut through to the bone, and fully around the limb, clearing the way for the bone saw. If possible, he would do it in just two strokes, one on top, the other underneath, a procedure that might take just a minute or two if done right. By now, the pain would have been excruciating for the patient. Some would have gone into shock.

Trading knife for saw, the surgeon went to work on the bone. Using gentle strokes at first, he made sure the teeth took hold, then used long, powerful strokes to cut through the bone, as clean and as fast as he could. Only when it was nearly severed did he revert back to gentle strokes to prevent the bone from splintering.

When the limb finally came free, the surgeon or an assistant tossed it into a nearby bucket of water or sawdust, which might still contain the severed parts of previous patients. The contents of the bucket would be thrown overboard and likely eaten by sharks.

Now the surgeon had to stop the bleeding, not just because the patient could die from it, but because the sight of it could overwhelm him. To do so, the surgeon cauterized the wound with medicines, acids, blazing irons, or binds. Next, he stitched up the flesh, pulling extra skin over remaining bone, then bandaged it. If all had gone well, the amputation might be complete in under five minutes. If the ongoing battle was hot, as it likely was between Bannister's men and the frigates, the surgeon would have wiped down his tools, taken a breath, and called for the next man to be placed on his table.

Having destroyed the *Golden Fleece*, the frigates were free to direct the full force of their fire on the small ship Bannister was reported to have with him, and on the pirates themselves. But now Mattera could see it: The Royal Navy could fire forever and it still would be difficult to kill Bannister's men. Dug in behind sand, mud, and trees, the pirates were protected from cannon and musket fire, which were absorbed with little more than a thud.

And that's how it must have gone for the next few hours, navy seamen shooting and dying from their powerful ships, but unable to put down the pirates. On board the frigates, supplies of powder and shot dwindled, and hulls and masts were battered and damaged by pirate cannon fire. To the navy captains, it had to look like Bannister, who was standing just across the channel, was oceans beyond their reach.

Unless they got to the island.

By storming the shore, the frigate crews could engage the pirates hand to hand, using swords, pistols, muskets, pikes, hatchets, and fists to do what their cannons could not. Better trained than Bannister's men, and outnumbering them by at least two to one, the navy was likely to decimate the pirates in any face-to-face meeting on the island.

The problem was getting there. The frigates were too big to sail into the shallow water at shore. That meant crewmen would have to row to the island in longboats, perhaps thirty to a vessel, leaving them virtually helpless against sniper fire—a miniature version of Omaha Beach. The Royal Navy prided itself on its willingness to fight, even under brutal conditions. Suicide, however, was another matter. If Talbot and Spragge considered a landing, they likely didn't consider it for long.

Instead, the navy seamen reloaded their weapons and pounded the island wherever they saw evidence (mostly from smoke and flames) of pirate gunfire. In this era, the rate of cannon fire was slow—it took five or six minutes for gunners to reload—but it was not imperative that the frigates fire rapidly, as the pirates no longer had a means of escape now that the *Golden Fleece* had been battered. Instead, the gunners strived to be accurate, to whatever extent that was possible.

All the while, the pirates fired back. It didn't need to be much, just enough for Bannister to remind the navy he was still armed and supplied—and to wear them down and to keep them from storming the island.

As darkness settled over Samaná Bay, the fighting would have died down; it made little sense for either side to spend powder and shot on targets they couldn't see, but both sides would have maintained a continuous watch. Navy crews would have gone to work repairing damage and preparing for the battle yet to come.

During breaks, they probably wolfed down salt beef, salt fish, salt pork, peas, cheese, biscuits (often infested by weevils), and beer (one gallon per man, per day). If there were even a few minutes for sleep, they took it.

It might have been during the night that the navy tended to its dead. The English were religious and would have done all they could to perform a burial service. Given the size of the crews aboard the frigates (about 180 on the *Falcon*; about 75 on the *Drake*), there likely was at least one chaplain between them. To the best of his abilities, that chaplain would have performed some kind of service. Crewmen would have doffed their caps as the bodies were pushed overboard.

Mattera couldn't wait to read more, but the library closed, so he met his childhood friend John Bilotti at Elaine's, the famed restaurant near Second Avenue and Eighty-Eighth Street in Manhattan. They ordered mussels and clams, and Mattera described all he'd learned about the drama of doing battle at sea in the seventeenth century. Mattera and Bilotti agreed that the Royal Navy was one hell of a tough outfit. But neither man would have joined that crew in the seventeenth century.

"We would have been pirates," Bilotti said.

"We were pirates once," Mattera replied.

When it came time to leave, Bilotti asked Mattera how things were going. Mattera could not lie to his friend. He was hemorrhaging money with nothing to show for it. He was working with an old man who wouldn't get out of his way. And his partner was losing his mind.

"I know you don't quit," Bilotti said. "And I'm not saying you should. But you and I both know. Sometimes a guy's gotta get out."

For a moment, Mattera didn't know what to say. Then he told his friend that in a few months he was going to turn forty-seven, the age at which his father died.

"So I can't quit now," he said.

Mattera resumed his research the next morning, just as the Royal Navy crews resumed their fight. Talbot and Spragge had to make a decision. They'd done their best to sink the *Golden Fleece*, but they also had orders to capture or kill Bannister. They could do that more easily by drawing closer to the pirates, but they risked further damage to the frigates if they dared.

Historical accounts didn't say how close the frigates moved in on the second day of the fighting, but Mattera knew one thing for certain: The navy seamen stayed on their guns, slugging it out, firing cannons and muskets, suffering more casualties, until evening came and the frigates ran out of gunpowder and shot. It was then that Captains Talbot and Spragge made the only decision they could: sail back to Jamaica and plead their case to the governor. Molesworth would not be happy. The frigates had suffered twenty-three dead and wounded, and no one had laid a hand on Bannister. That kind of failure might cost the captains their lives.

On return to Port Royal, Talbot and Spragge were "much censured," but spared more serious punishment. Molesworth must have concluded that they'd unleashed hell on the island and done all they could, because the two men's careers continued, as Bannister later would find out.

Packing up a pile of photocopied papers and notes, Mattera left the New York Public Library and caught a taxi to the airport. He felt like he'd just left the battlefield himself.

He met Chatterton a few evenings later in Samaná. He described what he'd brought back from New York: a historically accurate vision of the fight between Bannister's pirates and the Royal Navy frigates. Chatterton sat riveted. But he knew Mattera hadn't made the trip to New York just for a story.

"So what's the upshot here?" Chatterton asked.

"I don't know yet," Mattera said. "But I'm close."

The next afternoon, Carolina arrived for a visit, but Mattera was still working. He'd asked Kretschmer to meet him at the dive center, just below the villa. He sensed that Kretschmer, fed up with the tension among the crew, and months of fruitless searches, was about to quit for good, and he couldn't afford to lose him. When Mattera arrived, he could see Kretschmer already in the shed, at work on an engine.

Mattera didn't want to go in just yet. He needed to use the right words with Kretschmer, so he stood on the beach to think it over. Across the channel, he could see the spot where the *Golden Fleece* would have careened, the woods where pirate snipers would have hidden, the hill on the eastern edge where Bannister would have placed his cannons.

And then he saw something he'd never seen before.

"Heiko!" he yelled.

Kretschmer came running from the shed.

"Drop everything," Mattera told him. "Get Carolina, she's up in the villa. I see it now. I know where to look."

Chapter 17

ANOTHER WAY

M attera and Carolina waded into the water and walked to the Zodiac, carrying a picnic basket full of sandwiches, wine, cold water, and suntan lotion. On board, they joined Kretschmer, who had already loaded his share of picnic treats: a handheld metal detector, a shovel, and a hatchet. Mattera carried two cameras around his neck. Carolina wore a giant floppy hat.

Driving the Zodiac at tourist speed, they headed across the channel toward the eastern end of Cayo Vigia. They landed on a tiny section of sand, unloaded their gear, and did their best to look like they'd come from the nearby resort. Carolina posed for Kretschmer's snapshots; Mattera assembled a fishing pole. When they were sure no one was looking, they ducked into the dense woods and began hiking up the steep hill.

It took twenty minutes for them to fight their way past tangled overgrowth and bird-sized insects to a point more than a hundred feet over the water. Looking out over the channel, Mattera could see the world through Bannister's eyes. In all the Caribbean, there was no better place to careen a ship or to win an unwinnable battle. From here, pirate cannons could hit any target, but anyone shooting back would be doing it blind.

Kretschmer assembled the metal detector and put on the headphones. Running the unit over mud and brush, he listened for hits but heard nothing. The group pulled themselves through the overgrowth, trying to suck in the bits of fresh air that managed to penetrate the dense jungle. Even Carolina was sweating now, but the group kept moving, bent over and dripping, all of it a fevered dream.

Kretschmer stopped.

"I've got something," he said.

He moved the metal detector, slowly, over a patch of dirt and mud about three feet square. Beeps in his ear adjusted his aim, until he arrived at a spot.

"Here," Kretschmer said.

Mattera grabbed the shovel, Kretschmer the hatchet, and the men went to work digging on hands and knees. As the hole got bigger, Kretschmer pushed the metal detector down into it to refine the direction of the dig. But no matter how much dirt they removed, there was more underneath. They kept at it, for thirty minutes, digging, chopping at roots, listening to the metal detector, and digging again, until the blade of the shovel finally collided with something solid at a depth of about a foot, something it couldn't move.

"Whoa, whoa, whoa!" Mattera said.

Now using a hand spade, Kretschmer chipped away sections of dirt from the sides of the hole until a shape began to emerge, a little less black than the mud, but as round as the top of the moon.

"There it is," Mattera said.

Wedging the hatchet behind the object, Kretschmer muscled and leveraged until the thing finally came loose. All three picnickers stared into the hole. Lying free at the bottom was a six-pound cannonball.

"The last time someone touched that was in 1686," Mattera said.

He reached into the hole and pulled out the cannonball. The

weight startled him. He could tell it was a six-pounder, but only by holding it could he feel its destructive potential.

The group celebrated with hugs, kisses (Kretschmer wiped off Mattera's), and a glass of wine. Carolina spread out the blanket she'd brought so they could sit and enjoy a toast. Kretschmer wondered aloud if Bannister could have imagined this scene—two treasure hunters and a beautiful woman drinking wine on the site of his battle. Mattera assured him that Bannister could.

When they finished, they hiked back down the hill, running the metal detector as they fought not to fall. Halfway down, they got another hit, and dug up another cannonball, this one even bigger than the first.

After everyone posed for photos with the cannonballs, the group made its way back to the beach, then across the bay to the villa. Mattera dashed off an email to Chatterton. In the subject line, he wrote, "Buddy, we got it."

But Chatterton wasn't there to receive it.

He'd set out in the Range Rover to pick up supplies. On an unimproved road near the back bay in Samaná, he'd hit a hole filled with jagged rock, tearing a gash into the sidewall of his tire. He managed to drive onto the beach, but when he tried to change the tire, the jack collapsed and bent, and the wheel sank up to its fender in sand. Chatterton checked his cell phone—no signal. It might be miles to the next town. He started walking.

Down the road, he found four local men, one of them elderly, playing cards outside a small shop. They didn't have a jack, nor did they know where to find one, but told Chatterton they would help with his car. He tried to explain that the Range Rover was heavy, but they didn't seem to understand. Walking back to the vehicle, the elderly man motioned for Chatterton not to worry.

The Dominican men studied the truck, muttering in Spanish too fast for Chatterton to understand. Soon they were gathering supplies: a large tree branch and a pile of rocks. "I'm in the Stone Age here," Chatterton thought. The men went to work. Using improvised levers and fulcrums, and a big rock as a hammer, they bent the jack back into shape. "No way," Chatterton thought, but soon the jack looked nearly new. When they got it under the truck, however, it gave way and collapsed again, this time beyond repair.

Chatterton began to thank the Dominicans and reach into his pocket, but none of them wanted his money. Instead, they went out collecting again, farther away this time, bringing back heavy palm branches and giant rocks. Chatterton tried to explain that the jack couldn't be saved, but that's not what they had in mind. The men used the stems to dig a hole under the truck's strut assembly, then replaced sand with rocks. Chatterton grabbed his own leaf and jumped in to help them dig. A space began to open under the flat tire, and the truck's frame came to rest on its rock support.

Now Chatterton could see the beauty of this plan—it was right in front of him. And it struck him that he'd often seen this kind of approach in Dominicans—that they rarely had what they needed, and often had nothing at all, but they didn't seem to notice that or at least be much bothered by it. Instead, they focused on what they did have—if not a jack then a branch, if not money then time—then cobbled together a solution, a different way of getting there. He'd long cursed their *mañana* culture, swore that these people were going nowhere because they didn't go at full speed, but as he watched the old man flip off the ruined tire and replace it with the spare, he could see what he'd admired about Dominicans all along—that they didn't worry for the future because they knew there was always a way to arrive.

The men shoved piles of rocks under the truck to give it purchase, then Chatterton backed it off the beach. He insisted they take the money in his pocket, about twenty dollars, and they did, *gracias, gracias*, then walked back to where they came from, a place where they were dirt poor, able to figure their way as things came to them, looking happier than anyone Chatterton knew.

It was morning before Chatterton received the cannonball photos from Mattera. By that time, he was on his way to catch a flight to Miami, to take care of personal matters he'd put off for too long. The flight lasted more than two hours, much of which he used to gaze at the images his partner had sent him.

When he landed, he called Mattera, who told him about the discovery, and about how things looked from the top of the island, a worthy place for the "veriest rogues in these Indies," as the governor of Jamaica had referred to Bannister and his crew.

To both Chatterton and Mattera, the cannonballs proved that the battle had occurred at Cayo Vigia, and that the so-called sugar wreck, located less than two hundred yards off the island, was the *Golden Fleece*. It was imperative that Bowden resume salvage on the sugar wreck immediately, not just to prove the wreck's identity, but to put an end to the parade of interlopers at Cayo Levantado. Yet, Mattera was reluctant to tell Bowden about the cannonballs. He knew Bowden didn't want anyone working on land—an area that went beyond his lease rights.

"Let me talk to him," Chatterton said. "I'll go in person."

Mattera saw all kinds of risk in the idea. Chatterton could lose his cool and blow up at Bowden. Or Bowden might become frustrated with Chatterton and finally pull the plug on the pirate quest. Until now, Mattera had been a buffer between the two, but he'd be eight hundred miles away from this meeting. Still, he agreed to it.

"John, call me when the meeting's over. And keep that famous Chatterton temper under control."

Chatterton laughed.

"What temper?"

He sat down with Bowden a day later at a Denny's restaurant in Miami and detailed Mattera's adventure. He took Bowden all the way to the top of the hill at Cayo Vigia, just as Mattera had described it to him. To Chatterton, Bowden looked more excited with every detail.

"How many cannonballs did Mattera find?" Bowden asked.

"Two. In an hour. Can you imagine what else is up there, Tracy? Weapons, bones, treasure—who knows? Give the island to Cultura. They get shipwrecks all the time. They get galleons. How many pirate islands do they get?"

Bowden looked uncomfortable. In the past, he'd warned Chatterton and Mattera that his lease didn't extend to the land, and he didn't want to anger Dominican officials by working beyond the lease boundaries. But now Chatterton tried to reassure him: At the end of the day, would Cultura really be upset with him for unraveling the mystery of a historic pirate battle?

"This is your island, Tracy," Chatterton said. "The *Golden Fleece* is your idea. Only now, you don't just have a pirate wreck to offer; you have a pirate *camp*. How many of those are there in the world? Give Cultura the island. And let's finish the sugar wreck."

But Bowden still didn't look sold, and Chatterton believed he knew why. The sugar wreck debris field lay in forty-four feet of water. Treasure hunter William Phips had seen the wreck of the *Golden Fleece* in twenty-four feet, just months after her sinking. That disparity, Bowden often had told Chatterton and Mattera, troubled him.

"I don't think the sugar wreck is right," Bowden said.

Chatterton sat there for several moments.

"All right, Tracy," he said finally. "Thanks for your time."

From his car, Chatterton called Mattera and reported on the meeting. It was clear, he told his partner, that Bowden would never finish salvage of the sugar wreck no matter what the evidence showed, because he believed it was too deep to be the *Golden Fleece*. After that, there was nothing left to discuss.

Mattera knew this must be the end for Chatterton. He'd lived with the man for two years, knew him better in ways than he did his own brothers. You couldn't ask a person like that, one who'd been willing to swing a sledgehammer around live explosives in a sunken U-boat, to stand down from something that was speaking to him, something great and rare he believed he could reach.

"So, I guess that's it, John," Mattera said.

But Chatterton didn't hear him.

"I think there's another way to do this," Chatterton said. "I'm coming back."

Chapter 18

THE *GOLDEN FLEECE*

The team didn't know about Chatterton's plan when they boarded the *Deep Explorer* toward the end of February 2009, but one thing was clear: He'd returned to the bay to search. The magnetometer, in storage at the villa, had been unwrapped and carried aboard. Lying in its wooden cradle, it looked like an old friend to the men.

Chatterton fired the engines, then put the boat into a swooping arc away from the villa and on course for the sugar wreck. Mattera feared this might happen — that he or Chatterton would finally be pushed too far by Bowden's obstinacy and take matters into their own hands. Mutiny, however, was not an option. The partners liked and respected Bowden and considered him a friend. The pirate project had been Bowden's idea, not theirs, so to go rogue now would dishonor them. And they despised claim jumpers. Mattera was about to remind Chatterton of all this when his partner cut the wheel hard to the right, bypassed the sugar wreck, and set course straight for the island. Two minutes later, they were there.

"What are we doing?" Ehrenberg asked.

"The cannonballs are irrefutable," Chatterton said. "They prove Bannister was at this island. That's the first solid evidence in more than three hundred years, since Phips was here. But we've been so focused on the sugar wreck we never magged the shore along the island. That changes today."

"What are we looking for?" said Kretschmer.

"I don't know," Chatterton said. "I think we take whatever the island gives us."

And with that, the men started a magnetometer survey along the shore. Their work was difficult—the island had an irregular shape and quirky dipsy-dos, and modern debris threatened their sensitive equipment. Chatterton kept the survey tight until all of the island's coast had been covered, even the back side, where everyone knew nothing had happened.

Survey complete, the team returned to the dive center to process the data. Ehrenberg began to see anomalies on the middle part of the northern side of the island, where Chatterton and Mattera believed the battle to have occurred. Everyone's instinct was to gun the Zodiac back to the island and dive the hits, but they waited on Ehrenberg's data, and by the end of the day they had their survey, a map with electronic Xs in places no one had ever looked.

The men would have mortgaged future treasure for another eight hours of daylight, but they had no choice but to wait until morning. And they needed to call Bowden anyway. They sensed they were getting close to something important, and he would want to know. Mattera reached him by phone. Bowden said he would be there soon.

The next morning, the team moved the boat to the northern shore of Cayo Vigia. A handful of tourists were strolling the bridge that connected the nearby resort to the island, watching the sunrise as if this had always been the most peaceful place on earth.

Kretschmer anchored the boat, then backed in and tied a line from the stern to a palm tree onshore. Then he and Mattera lifted the Zodiac from the roof of the boat, dropped it into the water, and used it to hover over the targets from their survey, marking each one of them with a buoy. Chatterton and Ehrenberg suited up, then splashed to check out each hit.

In the water, they spotted a mass of stones in the mud, clustered together into the most perfect shape in the shipwreck hunter's world, the *pile*. This was ballast, assembled from rocks to give a ship stability in the water. It was not accidental, and it was not done by nature. It was from a shipwreck. And it was almost exactly where Bannister would have careened the *Golden Fleece*.

In the mud around the pile, Ehrenberg and Chatterton began to see gallon jugs, many intact, at a depth of around twenty feet. Some appeared to have writing embossed on the sides. Ehrenberg moved one of the jugs toward his mask until he could read the writing: *Pearl Street—New York*. Other bottles were similar—beautiful and likely from the nineteenth century, too new to have come from the Golden Age of Piracy.

But maybe these bottles didn't belong to the wreck that lay underneath the ballast; perhaps they'd come from a passing ship. The men moved more rock, looking for older artifacts, but they found only more bottles. They spent the rest of the day discovering nothing significant. On the way back to the villa that afternoon, no one said much more than "Damn, I thought we had her."

By the time the men set out for Cayo Vigia the next morning, Bowden had anchored his own boat over the sugar wreck. If Chatterton and Mattera didn't make good at Vigia now, there was nowhere left to look.

In the water, Chatterton and Ehrenberg pushed handheld metal detectors over the shallow bottom, searching for the source of the remaining hits on the survey. Soon, they were hearing faint beeps, and they followed these bread crumbs of sound to a new rock pile. But when they began moving stones and mud, they found only a steel beam and an old navigation buoy, all modern junk, all just like the stuff they'd spent the last year of their lives finding.

Then something in the distance caught Chatterton's eye, the rippling outline of a pile of stones, lying about twelve feet from shore. As he moved toward it, the shape came into sharper relief. It wasn't just a pile of rocks and stones. It was a pile of rocks and stones in the shape of a sailing ship, one big enough to cross oceans.

He and Ehrenberg drifted over the pile. From above, they had no doubt this was ballast. And it was massive, about fifty feet long by forty feet wide. The shallowest part lay in just six feet of water, but much of the rest sloped downward. Chatterton checked the depth at the other end of the ballast pile. The reading on his gauge: twenty-four feet.

The men found artifacts right away: a paint can, a lawn chair, a combination lock. But for the first time, they weren't worried

Site of the wreck of the *Golden Fleece*, about twelve feet out from the shore.

by garbage. They dug deeper. Near one end of the pile, Ehrenberg found a three-foot-long pipe, almost entirely encrusted in coral. Chatterton swam over and motioned—*let me look*.

Angling it into the sunlight shimmering down from the surface, Chatterton and Ehrenberg could see through cracks in the pipe's coral encrustation and down to the metal, which was not rounded like pipes should be, but forged into the shape of an octagon.

Chatterton left the pipe back on the ballast pile and then swam to the surface. On the boat, dripping and clinging to the ladder, he called to Mattera.

"John, you gotta get down there. You need to look at something."

Mattera was in the water minutes later. Hovering over the ballast pile, he could see five or six of the pipes. He picked one up. By its length and heft, he thought it looked like a musket barrel. Mattera had decades of experience with guns. He looked closer. To him, the object appeared to have been made in the late seventeenth century. That's when he remembered what Phips's men had said about seeing the wreck of the *Golden Fleece*: There were muskets lying on deck.

Mattera swam back to the boat. On board, he scrambled for his cell phone.

"Who are you calling?" Chatterton asked.

Mattera pointed toward Bowden's boat, which was anchored just fifty yards in the distance.

Mattera didn't know what to say first—in his hurry he stumbled over his words—but he finally asked Bowden his questions, which poured out in an unpunctuated stream: Could he and Chatterton recover the pipe and could they bathe it in muriatic acid to remove the coral and get a better look at the metal? He feared Bowden would want to step in and take over himself, but Mattera could not imagine anyone but his own team pulling up first proof of the pirate wreck.

Mattera hung up the phone.

"We're a go to do it ourselves," he told the others. "Tracy's as excited as we are."

Chatterton slipped his regulator into his mouth and fell back into the water.

Three minutes later, he surfaced, cradling the pipe with a midwife's touch. Mattera took it from him—gently—and examined it.

Chatterton (left) and Mattera, with a musket barrel they found on the *Golden Fleece*.

"I've seen them in books and shows and auctions," said Mattera. "I'm no expert, but I'm telling you, I think that's late 1600s."

Mattera snapped a photo of the artifact with his cell phone, and attached it to an email he addressed to antique gun experts and collectors he knew. In the subject line he wrote, "What does this look like to you?" He noted its dimensions and weight in the message field, but said nothing further. Then, he pressed send.

Piling into the Zodiac, and with Mattera cradling the length of iron, the men sped back across the channel to the dive center near the villa, where Kretschmer built a box made of two-by-fours, and lined it with a thick plastic bag. Ehrenberg poured in about two liters of muriatic acid and then, motioning everyone to stand upwind to avoid noxious fumes, took the pipe from Mattera and slid it into the bath. Coral broke loose in the acid, turning the liquid brown. This was shock treatment for an artifact, and likely to damage it, but the pipe could not be preserved in any case without great effort and expense, there were more of them on the ballast pile, and its value, in this condition and without its wood stock, was more evidentiary than monetary.

The last of the coral dissolved in ten minutes. Ehrenberg pulled the pipe from the acid and rinsed it in cold water. Now its octagon shape was obvious.

"That thing wasn't made to move water," Ehrenberg said. "That thing was made to kill."

Mattera took the artifact and brought it close to his face. Etched over the length of the metal were elegant swirling patterns, like those he'd seen on hammer-forged musket barrels from centuries past. He didn't know its pedigree. But he knew it was a gun barrel. And he knew it was old.

Everyone wanted back in the water now, but Chatterton

thought they should wait. It was important to keep Bowden involved, so he had Kretschmer build a small wooden cradle for the gun barrel and secure it using zip ties. Only then did the team get back into the Zodiac and head for Bowden's boat. On the way, Mattera received an email reply from Duke McCaa, a long-time dealer in rare and expensive big-game rifles, and an expert in antique firearms. McCaa had an opinion about the object in Mattera's photo. It was a musket barrel. European. Dating from the late seventeenth century.

A holler went up from the Zodiac. Mattera warned that this was just one opinion, but no one was listening to that, including Mattera, and a minute later they were boarding Bowden's boat. Bowden studied the artifact, turning it over in its wood cradle, moving his fingers over its textures and grooves, looking through its hollow barrel.

"How deep did you find this?" he asked.

"Sixteen feet," Chatterton said. "But we have others that are deeper."

Despite their excitement, Chatterton and Mattera knew the gun barrel would not be enough proof. Even if it were period to Bannister's time, that didn't mean it had come from the *Golden Fleece*. An ironclad case couldn't be made based on just a half dozen musket barrels and a theory. Cultura, and history, would need better proof, something no one could argue with, especially with so many competitors closing in. Mattera reminded everyone they weren't likely to find a bell embossed with the name *Golden Fleece*. Most merchant ships of the era didn't carry bells.

So a plan was made. Bowden would move his operation to the ballast pile where the muskets had been found. Both crews would work the site, looking for anything that would conclusively prove they'd found the wreck they were looking for. But they would have to wait until the next day to do it. The weather was turning. Chatterton and Mattera had waited a year for this, but neither of them felt like he could wait for another tomorrow.

There was an antidote to that, of course. The team would go drinking that night, because the next day was likely to be one of the happiest—or most disappointing—days of their lives.

By the time they dressed for dinner, Mattera had received more replies to his emails, each confirming that the object in his photo was likely a European-made musket dating to the late seventeenth century. This was cause for celebration, but as the dinner wore on the mood at the table changed. It wasn't just muskets that couldn't be proved to belong to the *Golden Fleece*; it was likely true of whatever artifacts they might find. When Chatterton had finally identified the mystery U-boat off New Jersey, he'd done it by pulling a tag from the wreck inscribed with the submarine's number. But there were no tags on seventeenth-century pirate ships. To get that kind of proof, they would need a bell or something just as good, which meant they'd need something close to a miracle. Of course, this had always been true, but it hadn't really hit them until they'd laid their hands on these muskets.

The next morning was too rainy to work. Inside Mattera's dive center, the men tried to keep busy, but mostly they swore at the sky.

Early that afternoon, Mattera's phone rang. It was Bowden.

"I have news," he said. "Meet me at Tony's."

As Chatterton and Mattera waited for Bowden at the restaurant, they braced to be told that Cultura had awarded rights to the *Golden Fleece* to another company, or had taken back parts of Bowden's lease. By now they'd heard enough treasure-hunting stories to know how many of them ended a day short of the prize.

At Tony's, Bowden opened a Ziploc bag and handed the men a piece of paper. It was a photocopied drawing of the battle scene between Bannister's *Golden Fleece* and the Royal Navy, done by John Taylor, the *Falcon*'s clerk, who'd been aboard the navy ship during the fight. *An eyewitness.* It showed a group of masted ships set against a swirling island backdrop, and had been sent to Bowden by a historian he'd recently commissioned to do research on the *Golden Fleece.* The man had discovered the drawing in a newly published book, *Jamaica in 1687*, by noted historian David Buisseret.

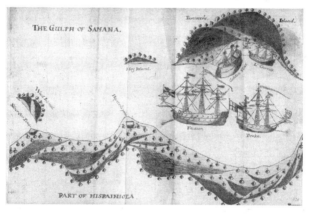

Drawing of the battle between Royal Navy ships the Falcon *and the* Drake, *and Bannister's* Golden Fleece, *by eyewitness John Taylor, June 1686.*

Chatterton and Mattera could hardly believe what they were seeing. The black-and-white drawing, done in striking detail, showed the Royal Navy's *Falcon* and the *Drake*, in a small channel, facing down Bannister's *Golden Fleece*, with another ship, *L'Chavale*, nearby. The vessels were beautifully rendered, but it was the topography that struck the men most of all.

The *Golden Fleece* was tucked into the middle of an island, labeled "Banister's Island," that appeared, in shape, size, flow, and lines, to be Cayo Vigia. The channel's northern coastline, too, was a match for the real thing, as was the western end of the bay. Just to the east of the *Golden Fleece* in the drawing, Taylor had labeled a small landmass "Hog Island." Chatterton and Mattera knew it as Paloma Island, for the hundreds of white doves that roosted there, but it was one and the same. Even the spot on the island where the man placed the *Golden Fleece* matched the spot where the ballast pile and muskets had been found. In this single drawing, it was as if Taylor had reached back through time and told Chatterton and Mattera, "You were right."

And there was more. Taylor had written an account of the battle, which was also in the book, though Bowden didn't yet have a copy.

"I've got a book dealer in London who will overnight me anything," Mattera said. "We'll have it tomorrow."

The men got a table and studied the drawing. It did not show a ship in the area of the sugar wreck, between Banister's Island and Hog Island. But that didn't bother anyone. The sugar wreck— whichever ship she was—had probably sunk early in battle, or was too inconsequential for the eyewitness to draw, or might have been unrelated to the event.

But what of the ship *L'Chavale*? The name was French, but Mattera didn't remember reading about a French ship. He did, however, recall that Bannister had worked with several French pirates, including the infamous Michel de Grammont. And that the French pirates had been loyal to him.

"Maybe that's how Bannister made his getaway," Chatterton said. "Maybe he escaped on *L'Chavale*."

Chatterton and Mattera shook their heads at the luck of it

all—an illustration and account of the battle by an eyewitness. Bowden loved the drawing, too. Yet he still wished for more proof from the wreck itself.

"That," Mattera said, pointing outside toward still-stormy skies, "is up to the gods."

Up early the next morning, Mattera walked down to the beach and looked out over the channel, envisioning the Royal Navy frigates and the *Golden Fleece* where the eyewitness had put them. It all looked like he'd imagined it from his thinking and research. He wondered if the remains of dead seamen and pirates still lay under the mud at the bottom of the channel.

Skies were clear, and soon Mattera and Chatterton's team, along with Bowden's crew, had anchored over the ballast pile at the middle of the island. Soon, there were nine or ten divers in the water.

Much of the day's work was devoted to moving ballast. Some stones were pebble-sized; others weighed more than twenty pounds. They all required work. The smaller ones could be moved by hand or bucket, but there were thousands of them. Larger ones were carried off by lift bag, a device that used straps and an inflatable bladder to move heavy objects underwater. Big stones had to be handled carefully; if dropped, they could break artifacts buried below. Mud, sand, and coral were sucked up by an airlift, a device that used compressed air and a length of PVC pipe to create a powerful underwater vacuum.

As ballast was cleared, the divers began finding artifacts. Many were modern detritus dropped by fishermen, sailors, and tourists. But they also found shards of centuries-old pottery, another musket barrel, and an iron canister, which looked to Bowden like the kind that contained metal shrapnel and was fired by cannons during the Age of Sail.

The men were back moving ballast the next morning. Currents made work difficult in the afternoon, so Chatterton and Mattera invited Bowden to come onto the island to search for more cannonballs. They expected Bowden to decline—his lease extended only to the waterline—but Mattera had had such fun the first time out he couldn't help but ask. An hour later, Bowden was pushing with them through brush, sweeping a metal detector around the eastern end of the island. Chatterton found two cannonballs and half of another, which appeared to have sheared on impact. Mattera tried to remember if he'd seen Bowden smile like that before.

When they returned to the boats in late afternoon, some artifacts had been laid out by divers and rinsed. There were onion bottles (named for their shape) that had once held Madeira wine. One of them was still full. All of it was of historic value; all of it was period to Bannister.

"Save that wine," Ehrenberg said. "We might need it tomorrow."

On March 9, 2009, the men went back to work on the ballast pile. Digging through mud, one of Bowden's crew saw pieces of burnt orange spackled into the dull greens and tans of the surrounding coral and stone. He put several of these orange pieces into his glove, then surfaced and climbed back aboard the boat. When he removed his glove, the pieces spilled onto a table. These were beads, just like the pirates wore, barrel-shaped and each a quarter of an inch long, orange with fast streaks of black, still as bright as the day they'd been made, still capable of terrifying merchant captains who saw them around the necks or braided into the beards of violent men.

But the beads were just signals of what lay below. Divers began to find pikes, cutlasses, daggers, musket balls, cannonballs, sword handles made of coarse bone, and the fifteen-pound wrought iron blade of a boarding ax, the most fearsome weapon of them all, which pirates used to pull target ships close, cut lines, or, with its gruesome and oversized head, hack at opponents during battle. They could have spent hours admiring each of these pieces, but didn't dare risk missing the chance to find more. They discovered Delftware china, smoking pipes, small hourglass-shaped medicine bottles (sealed by lead tops and with remedy still inside), soles of

(ABOVE, TOP) Pirate knife from the *Golden Fleece*.
(ABOVE) Silver treasure coin recovered from the *Golden Fleece*.
(RIGHT) Cereal bowl, with uneaten porridge still inside, from the *Golden Fleece*.

boots, and coins from several countries, as one would expect from pirates, who were egalitarian enough to steal from all nations. All of it was historic. All of it was period to the late seventeenth century. All of it was the stuff of pirates.

Near the end of the day, Mattera found a simple wood plank, about three feet by one foot, and with one distinguishing feature: It was burned. Captain Spragge of the *Drake*, Mattera remembered, had returned to the scene of the battle after refitting in Jamaica, only to find the wreck of the *Golden Fleece* burned to her decks.

"I'm holding a piece of Bannister's ship," Mattera thought. "I'm holding a piece of the *Golden Fleece* in my hands."

The charred top of the wood disintegrated and blew away in the current. It had remained intact for 323 years, just long enough for Mattera to find it.

Topside, the divers were thrilled by the quality of their discoveries.

"What do you think, Tracy?" Mattera asked.

Bowden didn't look cautious anymore.

"This is even better than I dreamed," he said. "Guys, we have the *Golden Fleece*."

The teams celebrated that night with dinner at a fine Italian seafood restaurant. One mystery still lingered as the men raised toasts to long-ago pirates: the identity of the sugar wreck. She'd sunk less than two hundred yards off the island, and was full of period artifacts, mostly Dutch, not one dating later than 1686, the year of the battle. Bowden had always insisted that the sugar wreck, lying in forty-four feet of water, was too deep to be the *Golden Fleece*, and he'd been proved right. The men raised a toast to Bowden. But if the sugar wreck was not the pirate ship, which vessel was she? And what was she doing there?

Bowden had an idea about that. The historian he'd commissioned to research the *Golden Fleece* had uncovered the log of Charles Talbot, the captain of the *Falcon*. Talbot had reported firing not just on the *Golden Fleece*, but on another, smaller ship—a Dutch ship. So maybe the sugar wreck was present during the battle, after all.

"Bannister must have taken a Dutch prize before he got to the island," Chatterton said. "The Royal Navy would've sunk a sitting duck like that right away. Maybe that's why the eyewitness didn't draw her."

"Everything fits," Mattera said. "That's history."

After dinner, the men ferried Bowden back to his boat. But when they returned to shore, they were too excited to call it a night, so they went to the villa for drinks.

Sitting on the veranda under a nearly full moon, Chatterton, Ehrenberg, and Kretschmer could see all of Cayo Vigia, as it must have looked after the first day of battle. Mattera joined them, but he wasn't carrying drinks. Instead, he had a copy of *Jamaica in 1687*, the new book by David Buisseret, which contained not just Taylor's drawing, but his eyewitness account of the battle. Mattera read aloud from Taylor's description:

> About fore in the afternoon, the boats return'd, and informed us that at the bottom of that bay, in the gulfe, Banister was, and another small ship with them, and they were on the careen, and further that they had pitch there tents on the island, and had hal'd their guns ashore and fortified themselves with two baterys, the one of six, and the other of ten gunns. . . .

Being enform'd thereof, the Faulcon and Drake wayed about three a'clock, all things being put in a fighting posture and in less than half an houer we came to anchor within musket-shott of Banister. They immediately fier'd at us (without shewing any ensigne) from their batteries, and with their gunns shott very furiously, and wounded one of our men. Being come to anchor in 5 fadom watter, we with all expedition bent out our best bower, and brought our broadside to bear on them and fier'd with our uper and lower fire of ordnance and our small shot on the quarter deck with good success, soe that we shattered the bowes of the Fleece all to pieces, and utterly distroyed his great ship Fleece and soon beat them from their cannon, which they plied violently against us, with little damage.

Yet they being beat from their small ordnance, did nevertheless with greatest resolution imaginable continue firing with their small arms against us (being befrinded and shelterd by the thick woods) untill such time as the sable night had cover'd the earth with hir silent vaile; then seased they from their obstinat resistance, and all was silent. In this conflict we had three men kill'd outright, and two wounded; what number of Banister's wer slain, we could not learn. Thus night being come, we clens'd the ship and prepair'd all things in redyness to fight the morrow morning. . . .

Thursday the first of July, in the morning before that Aurora had fully withdrawn the sable curtain of night and illuminated this western world with hir refullgent raies, did this obstinat pyratt sound a levet with his trumpets, and fiered fouer cannons and severall volies of shott at us, with little hirt, not wounding one man. Then the Faulcon brought hir starbourd side to bear on them, and soon return'd them satisfaction from the mouth of their cannon, upon which they forsook their batteries, and betook themselves to their small arms, for this our broadside of double and catridge did them much damage, yet still they continued fiering at us graduallie six musquets at a time from the woods about the middle of the island, thereby to withdraw us from distroying their battery (which was built of stones and old trees) with our cannon. Soe we kept all day long fiering at the Fleece, and theirby reducet hir to such condition that 'twas imposible for hir evermore to swim. For oftentimes we plac't 20 shots of our lower fier in hir bowes and quarter, soe that we saw both planck and timbers fly from hir. But as for the L'Chavale the French privater she goot in soe near to the shore that we did hir but little damage.

In fine we demolish't their batries, and fire their ships all to peices. Yet they continued fiering at us with their musquets, and we at them with our cannon, as long as light would admit. This night we had continuall rain with the wind at north and northeast. Now haveing little wind we wayed our best bower and (with the Drake) warp'd off in the night, 'till we were out of their shot, (for we could lie here noe longer, because we had verey litle powder and shoot left). But now the wind encreaseing we came to anchor about two cables' lenght to the westward of Cabbadg Island in 75 fadom water near Hog Island.

Saturday the 2d we had aboundance of rain, thunder and lightning, with the wind at east, soe that we could not turn out of the Gulph of Samana at break of day. Banister fiered severall great and small shot, but hurt us not, soe we kept warping out untill we goot about two miles from the island. . . .

Sunday the third we had abundance of rain, thunder and lightning, tho' the sun shin'd for the most part, with ye wind at east, and northeast by east. This morning we heard a great noise from Banister's island, and saw a great smoak, which continued about half an houre. I suppose they blow'd up somwhat and fired their great ship.

When Mattera finished, the others made him read it again. They loved the drama of it all, the pirates' toughness, how it gave Bannister his due. The writer hadn't accounted for many of the navy casualties—by official count, there were twenty-three dead and wounded—but they couldn't blame him for putting a hometown spin on events. And they learned things no one but an eyewitness could have told them: that Bannister had fired at the frigates even as they were sailing away. And that it was Bannister himself who had burned the *Golden Fleece*.

Mattera checked the book's index for further mention of Bannister. There was just one more story, this one of the pirate captain's demise. According to the account, most of Bannister's men deserted him after the frigates withdrew, and he was forced to give over his command to the captain of the French pirate ship, who spirited him and some of his crew off the island. After stealing a small ship, the French captain put Bannister and his men aboard, gave them some provisions and weapons, and sent them away.

To "ease his dejected spirits," Bannister sailed to the Mosquito Coast, where he was welcomed by Indians. Soon, all but six of his remaining men ran away with his ship, leaving Bannister at the mercy of the natives. Captain Spragge in the Royal Navy's *Drake* tracked Bannister to this hiding place, where he found the pirate captain disguised as an Indian, roasting a plantain in a wigwam. One of Bannister's men fired a musket at Spragge, but missed and slightly wounded another navy man. Bannister, along with three of his cohorts and two boys, were taken prisoner and put aboard the *Drake*. In sight of Port Royal, Bannister and the other pirates were hanged, their bodies dumped in nearby Gun Cay.

But something seemed wrong with this part of the story. It was neither consistent with historical accounts of Bannister's character, nor with the spirit Taylor himself ascribed to the pirate captain in battle.

"You think Bannister really surrendered without a fight?" Mattera said. "This guy? Who stole his own ship twice? Who stood toe-to-toe with two navy warships?"

"Well, they hung him," Ehrenberg said.

"Did they?" Mattera asked.

He allowed the question to linger. Then, he laid out his thinking.

The English government wanted Bannister dead. He was a top priority. He'd embarrassed them, not once but twice, by stealing his own ship and then by cheating the hangman under their noses. Then he defeated the Royal Navy in battle. Maybe Spragge did catch him on the Mosquito Coast. But maybe not. Maybe Bannister got away after the fight with the frigates. Would the English want to admit that, and risk making him a folk hero forever?

Chatterton picked up Mattera's thinking.

The navy supposedly hanged the pirates on a ship off the coast of Port Royal. But who saw it? How did the witnesses know it was Bannister? For all anyone knew, it was an unlucky Indian chosen by the navy to stand in for Bannister. The bodies were cut down and thrown overboard, so who could say?

Mattera opened the book and again read the last line Taylor had written about Bannister:

Thus wee have given you a full account of the overthrow of the misserable Banister, who not long befor was a welthy captain of good repute in Jamaica, and might have lived long and happy had not he turned pyrat.

To Mattera, that sounded like a warning to would-be pirates, directed by the powers that be.

"So what do you think really happened to him?" asked Kretschmer.

Chatterton imagined that Bannister might have taken on a new identity, put together a fresh crew, and continued pirating, taking even bigger ships, maybe moving operations to the Mediterranean or the American East Coast.

Mattera saw him as perhaps captain of a great whaling vessel, taking on an opponent even more dangerous than the Royal Navy.

"Or maybe he retired as an English gentleman," Kretschmer said, "living a quiet life in a house by the sea."

Chatterton and Mattera thought about that one. They looked across the channel. Under the moonlight, they could see waves breaking over Bannister's wreck.

Then, each together, the partners said, "No way."

EPILOGUE

Salvage continued in earnest on the ballast pile at Cayo Vigia. Every artifact recovered by divers was period to the *Golden Fleece*. Over two months, Chatterton, Mattera, Bowden, and their crews discovered gold wedding rings, silver and bronze coins, a small gold statue, boarding axes, thousands of beads, a brass gun barrel, knives, smoking pipes (some with the owner's initials scratched into the handle), jewelry, china, and a small bronze statue, beautifully crafted, of an English gentleman, wearing a top hat and holding a firelock musket, his dog standing guard by his side. This piece, the men liked to imagine, had belonged to Bannister himself.

Divers often couldn't wait to get the artifacts topside for cleaning. Blackened Delftware china dishes, washed in mild soap and water, showed their true colors: blue and white, blue and yellow, and, rarest of all, red and black. All of it was delicate and valuable, worth perhaps three thousand dollars a plate, maybe more, given its provenance. A pewter bowl, after gentle rinsing, revealed lumps of leftover porridge still inside. Museums and auction houses would have desired any of these pieces; collectors would have paid handsome sums. Few people got a chance to acquire verifiable pirate booty—and no one knew if it would ever happen again.

Chatterton and Mattera stood to gain financially by these recoveries. By handshake, Bowden had agreed to give them a percentage of the salvage. But after accounting for expenses, neither man knew if he'd break even. For now, everything recovered from the site would be cataloged, preserved, and stored at the laboratory at the Oficina Nacional de Patrimonio Cultural Subacuático. When salvage was complete—and that could take months or even years—a division would be made between the Dominican government and Bowden. It would then be up to Chatterton and Mattera to arrange their own division with Bowden. In this business, parties often selected their artifacts in rounds, in the way professional sports teams draft players: Bowden might choose a boarding ax and a sword, Chatterton a flintlock and a handful of beads, Mattera a pistol and piece of Delftware china, then back to Bowden again for another round. All of it would be done according to the percentages of their agreement.

In May 2009, Mattera and one of Bowden's crew began to uncover the hull, or lowermost section, of the pirate ship. Chatterton joined them soon after. As they removed ballast,

Hull of the *Golden Fleece*.

they could see that the ship's beams had remained intact, and the entire lower portion of the hull was still there, a miracle. If the wreck had sunk almost anywhere else, she would have long since disintegrated. But the water around the island was much less salty than in the surrounding waters, and had a freshwater stream nearby (yet another reason Cayo Vigia made for such an effective pirate stronghold—access to drinking water). Also, the sand and silt under which the *Golden Fleece* was buried was of a very fine consistency and acted as a preservative for the ship and her artifacts. Hovering over the site, the men could see the *Golden Fleece* as she had been, steadfast and muscular, a ship as tough as either of them ever had seen. A few days later, they found a cannonball on the wreck marked by the broad arrow, a symbol of the Royal Navy—just as the treasure hunter William Phips reported seeing on the wreck months after the pirate ship sank.

Representatives from the lab, along with archaeologists, visited the site later that month, inspecting artifacts and taking a tour of the island. They snapped photos and congratulated the men on the discovery. None had any doubt about what had been found. By now, divers had recovered thousands of artifacts. Not one dated later than 1686, the year the *Golden Fleece* had been lost.

Cannonball recovered from the *Golden Fleece* wreck site. Note the mark of the broad arrow, a symbol used by the Royal Navy.

News of the find spread quickly through the treasure-hunting and archaeology communities. Those who managed to see the artifacts at the lab or even aboard one of the salvage vessels tipped their hats to Chatterton, Mattera, and Bowden. But perhaps the best endorsement came from the great treasure hunter Bob Marx, who had discovered the lost city of Port Royal, Jamaica. He called Mattera on the boat after he opened emailed photographs of the Delftware china and the pewter cereal bowl. "Goddamn it, you got it," he said. "I wish you guys were here to see my smile."

The men couldn't stop smiling themselves. They'd found a Golden Age pirate ship, the hardest and rarest and most exciting thing an explorer could find underwater, or maybe in all the world. Sometimes, in the middle of lunch or after working on the boat, one would turn to the other and say, "We did it." And the other would answer, "Yes, we did."

It was around this time that Mattera flew back to New York to visit family and friends. His last stop was at Moravian Cemetery, at the bottom of Todt Hill Road on Staten Island. He spoke aloud to his father there, bringing him up to date on Carolina and the kids, and on the Mets, who were playing good ball that season.

"And one more thing, Dad," he said aloud. "I found a really cool pirate ship. I wish I could tell you about it. It was an adventure. You'd love it."

Months of salvage remained to be done on the *Golden Fleece*, but Bowden and his crew had that in hand, so Chatterton and Mattera turned their sights back to treasure hunting, this time to the *San Miguel*, the early Spanish galleon they believed could be the most valuable treasure ship ever lost, loaded with gold, priceless Inca and Aztec works of art, and glorious contraband. The prizes from the *San Miguel* might be worth more than five hundred million dollars at auction. But the finders of the great ship wouldn't just be treasure rich; they also would have discovered the oldest known shipwreck in the Western Hemisphere. Instantly, the wreck would become important to historians, archaeologists, universities, and governments, its name—and the names of its finders—known the world over. Many treasure hunters dreamed of riches. Others imagined black-tie openings at museums or a dedicated auction at Sotheby's or Christie's. Still others yearned to make their names legend. For the finders of the *San Miguel*, every one of those dreams could come true.

So Chatterton and Mattera made a deal with Bowden to go after the *San Miguel*, which they believed to be sunk in one of Bowden's lease areas, a discreet and searchable place less than a hundred miles from Samaná Bay. But they knew it would have to happen fast.

In early June 2009, a U.S. magistrate judge in Florida directed Odyssey Marine Exploration, the publicly traded salvage company that had recovered half a billion dollars' worth of silver coins from a centuries-old Spanish warship, to return the treasure to Spain. That was the kind of writing on the wall Chatterton and Mattera had been warned about early in their partnership. Tides were shifting against treasure hunters, even as the partners began their new quest.

The men spent the next two and a half years in search of the *San Miguel*. It drained most of their savings. They'd expected to cash in on the pirate booty by now, but most of the artifacts from the *Golden Fleece* were still at the lab awaiting division. Expenses mounted. They lost their survey boat in a storm, which alone cost them more than one hundred thousand dollars. They raised the vessel, and it sunk again, this time with both of them aboard.

But the years and money seemed worth it. They tracked the *San Miguel* to a picturesque area on the eastern end of the country's north coast. There, they found a sixteenth-century anchor that appeared, in detail, to be a match for one carried aboard the galleon. Soon after, they found broken pieces of pottery, which also had likely come from the *San Miguel*. Hundreds of pebble-sized ballast stones lay nearby, the kind used to fill space between larger ballast rocks on galleon-sized sailing ships. Given all he and Mattera had learned about *San Miguel*, they had little doubt they were closing in on the great treasure ship.

And then, just as the men prepared to salvage the site, a business dispute arose between them and Bowden. Months passed as they tried to work it out. Eventually, lawsuits were filed. Chatterton and Mattera could hardly digest their position. They believed they were sitting on top of the most valuable treasure ship ever lost, but couldn't bring her up while rights to the wreck remained in dispute.

The legal battle continues to this day. If Chatterton and Mattera prevail, they will go back to work on the wreck site. If they do not, the *San Miguel* might remain undiscovered forever.

Most of the artifacts from the *Golden Fleece* remain at the lab. The divers have asked officials there to postpone a division until the dispute with Bowden is settled. Given the rarity of the find, it's difficult to put a precise monetary value on the booty recovered from the pirate ship. By some estimates, the collection might be worth several million dollars.

But even if a single piece from the *Golden Fleece* never got sold, the men had their prizes. Chatterton had found the rarest and most exciting kind of shipwreck in the world. Mattera had pieced together the story of one of the Golden Age's great pirate ships, changing how history understood her adventures and her final days. Best of all, they'd found Joseph Bannister.

Each man also got something else from his discovery, something different from shipwrecks and pirates, even if he didn't expect it at the time.

For Chatterton, it was the chance to learn from the Dominicans. He had arrived in Samaná believing there was just one way to do things—straight ahead and by sheer force of muscle and will. Then he began watching the locals. Many of them were near destitute but made do with whatever scraps they could gather. If they didn't have a jack to change a tire, they used rocks and sticks. If they needed to dive deep to catch fish, they built an air supply system from an old paint compressor and a garden hose. To Chatterton, even the poorest among them seemed to have all they wanted, not because they didn't desire much, but because they always found other ways to get what they needed, always found other ways to go.

That idea helped Chatterton break through on the *Golden Fleece*. But it also stayed with him after he found the shipwreck. He'd long dreaded the day when he would be too old to keep diving, to do what he was meant to do. He knew that his partnership with Mattera, made at age fifty-five, was in ways an effort to have one last great adventure before it might be too late. After watching the Dominicans, he didn't believe in too late anymore. He knew the day was coming when he could no longer strap on the tanks. But when that day came, he would find other ways to get the feeling a great shipwreck gave him. The water was a big place, and he would find other ways to go.

For Mattera, the *Golden Fleece* answered a basic question: Was it ever too late to follow one's heart? Months into his search for the pirate ship, Mattera's view on the matter had been dim. He'd spent several years and more than a million dollars to go after a dream—first of treasure, then of pirates—but had yet to find anything important. Worse, it had begun to occur to him, as the failures and stresses piled up, that there might be nothing out there for him to find.

That's when he discovered Joseph Bannister, buried in historical records almost no one had touched for centuries. The pirate captain had been in his thirties or forties when he'd abandoned a respectable career and a future assured in order to do something daring, something that called to him. To Mattera, Bannister's calling was democracy, but what mattered most was that Bannister had answered.

Things went badly for Bannister at first. Then he began a singular adventure, one of swashbuckling and daring that culminated in doing the near impossible—defeating the Royal Navy in battle. To Mattera, the lesson was clear: A person had to go when his heart told him to go. Even if he didn't know how the journey would end.

Mattera was never the same after that. He fought through frustrations and challenges in Samaná, spent even more of his money, then found the *Golden Fleece*. He kept a cannonball from the wreck, a reminder to listen to his heart when next it asked him to go.

By 2013, Chatterton had moved back to the United States, while Mattera, now married to Carolina, remained in Santo Domingo. In the spring of that year, Chatterton made a trip to the Dominican Republic to visit Mattera. The men had planned to take it easy

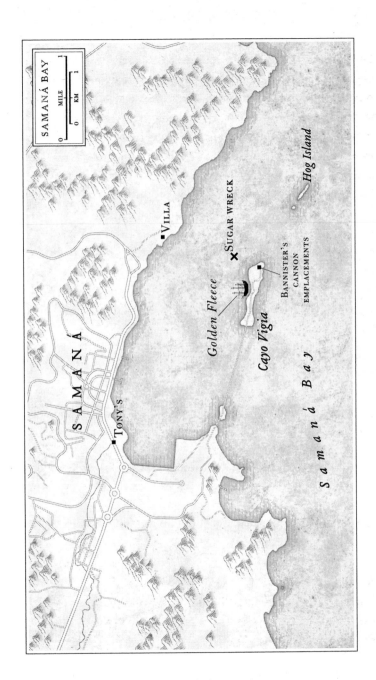

SAMANÁ BAY

0   MILE   1

0   KM   1

SAMANÁ

TONY'S

VILLA

SUGAR WRECK

✕

Golden Fleece

Cayo Vigía

BANNISTER'S
CANNON
EMPLACEMENTS

Hog Island

S a m a n á   B a y

that weekend, lounging around and eating grilled octopus, as they had in the early days, when every shipwreck in the New World might be theirs. Instead, they drove to Samaná, where they took the Zodiac across the channel and anchored over the *Golden Fleece*. It was tourist season. The beaches should have been crowded, but that day it was quiet. Only Chatterton, Mattera, and Bannister were there.

ACKNOWLEDGMENTS

I am grateful for the help and support of the following people:

Kate Medina, my editor at Penguin Random House, for her unwavering belief in me, sharp instincts about story, and the kindness she has shown me through the years. I have learned much from Kate about writing, and even more about what it means to have a beautiful heart.

I also wish to thank the following people at Penguin Random House:

Derrill Hagood, editorial assistant, who worked with me on this book tirelessly and cheerfully, and was the engine that always kept the project in motion.

Deputy copy chief Dennis Ambrose has worked wonders on my manuscripts — and talked diving with me — for years.

I've been very lucky to work with Sally Marvin, director of publicity at Random House, and Tom Perry, deputy publisher at Random House/Dial — the best in the business at what they do — and I count them as friends. I can't begin to describe how much their encouragement has meant to me.

Gina Centrello, president and publisher, Random House Publishing Group, has believed in me from the start, which helps me believe in myself.

I would also like to thank these terrific people at Penguin Random House: Barbara Bachman, Laura Baratto, Sanyu Dillon,

Richard Elman, Kristin Fassler, Karen Fink, Carolyn Foley, Sarah Goldberg, Ruth Liebmann, Poonam Mantha, Leigh Marchant, Tom Nevins, Allyson Pearl, Bridget Piekarz, and Erika Seyfried.

Flip Brophy, my literary agent at Sterling Lord Literistic. A writer couldn't hope for a more loyal and fierce champion. People always tell me I'm lucky when they learn that Flip is my agent, and they're right. She is like family to me.

John Chatterton and John Mattera spent more than two years answering all my questions—in person, on the phone, in airplanes, on boats, standing knee-deep in Samaná Bay, wearing scuba gear, on the L trains in Chicago, sneaking in for free breakfast buffets at my budget hotels, crammed into Chatterton's Mini Cooper in Florida, on treacherous roads in the Dominican Republic, inside the homes of legendary treasure hunters. I'd known Chatterton to be a great storyteller from working with him on *Shadow Divers*; Mattera was a revelation. He spoke cinematically, painting pictures as much as recounting events, and his instinct for story structure is excellent. It didn't surprise me to discover that Mattera is a terrific writer. It's been a privilege to read his work, and to know both of these stand-up guys.

Carla Chatterton and Carolina Garcia de Mattera were always gracious to me in sharing memories of their husbands' pirate hunt. It takes a special kind of person to support an explorer's journey.

Victor Francisco Garcia-Alecont, former vice admiral and chief of staff of the Dominican Navy, answered my questions with insight, patience, and good humor. In Santo Domingo, he and his wife, Lcda. Francisca Perez de Garcia, made me feel like part of the family.

Captain Tracy Bowden welcomed me into his home in Florida, where he described his life as a shipwreck diver, treasure hunter, and explorer. Since time began, it seems, men have set out in search of treasure; almost none of them succeeds, and of those who do, few have succeeded like Bowden. His stories of salvaging treasure are gripping, but even better is when he talks about the life of a treasure hunter—how lonely it can be, the strain it puts on one's life, the voices a person hears at night eighty miles offshore when anchored over a mass grave. Bowden was a pioneer, and I was lucky to hear him tell me about his odyssey.

Howard Ehrenberg is one of the smartest guys I've met. Even better, he's an adventurer, and his curiosity is an inspiration. It's hard to imagine the search for the *Golden Fleece* being possible without Howard's mastery of the cutting-edge technology and equipment—or his easygoing nature. It's equally hard to imagine how I would have filled in the details of the story without him. No matter how many times I called, Howard was available to explain things to me. Thanks, too, to Howard's wife, Megan Ehrenberg, an excellent diver (and very nice person) in her own right.

Heiko Kretschmer met with me in Santo Domingo and in Samaná. I'd heard about his tireless work ethic and ability to fix nearly anything, but what I didn't fully appreciate until meeting him was his fine mind. He added nuance and specifics about the search for Bannister's wreck that no one else could. His own story, of fleeing East Germany at age eighteen aboard a train for a better life in the West, is worthy of its own telling. As with Ehrenberg, the successful pirate search wouldn't have happened without him.

I don't know that I've ever met a better storyteller, or a nicer man, than treasure hunter Carl Fismer. He opened his home to me, showed me good breakfast places in the Florida Keys, and took two years' worth of my phone calls. Whenever I talked to Fizz, he made it feel like I was doing him a favor, rather than the other way around.

Robert Marx met with me at both his home and office in Florida. By then, I'd read several of his books, but nothing prepared me for meeting the famed treasure hunter. (For starters, he told me not to use the term *treasure hunter*: "Lots of guys hunt for treasure, but how many find it? I'm a treasure *finder*.") And it got better from there. I stayed for an entire day and didn't have a boring moment. Jenifer Marx, Bob's wife, was delightful. I'd read her excellent book *The Magic of Gold*, published by Doubleday, and was honored to meet her.

These men sat down with me and brought the world of treasure hunting and wreck diving to life: Dave Crooks, president of the Sunken Treasures Book Club; Joe Porter, publisher of *Wreck Diving Magazine*; Kim Fisher and Sean Fisher at the Mel Fisher Maritime Museum in Key West; and (by phone) David P. Horan of Horan, Wallace & Higgins LLP.

I can't offer enough thanks to Professor David Buisseret, senior research fellow at the Newberry Library, for the help he gave me in researching Joseph Bannister and the *Golden Fleece*. I think it's safe to say that without Buisseret's work, little would be known about the pirate captain and his ship. By a stroke of good luck I found Professor Buisseret living near me in Chicago; even better, he made himself available to me, at his home, in coffee shops, by phone, whenever I needed him, and always with grace and warmth. It's been a pleasure watching him work and a privilege knowing such a fine man.

Naval historians Sam Willis, Jonathan Dull, and Frank L. Fox all spoke to me by phone and helped me understand the subject of seventeenth-century naval warfare, ships, weapons, and tactics. I leaned especially hard on Fox, who astonished me with his vast working knowledge of these subjects, and his ability to answer whatever question, no matter how obscure, I put to him.

Whenever I reached out to Fox, he was always there, and for that, and his warm demeanor, I'm grateful.

In the Dominican Republic, thanks to the minister of culture, José Antonio Rodríguez; the vice minister, Luís O. Brea Franco; and the director of the ministerial cabinet, Carlos Salcedo.

Many thanks to these people for their feedback on chapters and ideas, and for talking writing with me: Dick Babcock, Andy Cichon, Kevin Davis, Ivan Dee, Katelynd Duncan, Jonathan Eig, Joseph Epstein, Robert Feder, Brad and Jane Ginsberg, the Glover family, Ken Goldin, Elliott Harris, Miles Harvey, Ryan Holiday, Len and Pam Kasper, the Kurson family, David Shapson, Joe Tighe, Randi and Rob Valerious, and Bill Zehme.

Mitch Lopata of Lopata Design in Skokie, Illinois, did beautiful work on illustrations, photos, and charts. Carolina Garcia de Mattera, Celia Reyes, and Virginia Reyes provided fast and sharp assistance with Spanish translation.

I was aided in some of my research by the superb work of Av Brown of Your Man in the Stacks, and Dr. Andrew Lewis of Andrew Lewis Historical Research. Copy editor Michelle Daniel did fine work with my manuscript. Todd Ehrhardt, a great guy, supplied photos of Samaná Bay and helped me dig for treasure there.

Dr. Steven Tureff means the world to our family. We couldn't hope to know a kinder or more caring man.

A special thanks goes to "Superman" Sam Sommer. He was one of the first people to whom I told the pirate story. The look on his face helped me believe. He will be missed.

Thanks, also, to Ken Andre, Stuart Berman, Mitch Cassman, Pat Croce, Dr. Michael Davidson, Dr. Samuel Goldman, David Granger, Peter Griffin, Rich Hanus, Jordan Heller, John Jacobs, Richie Kohler, Jeff Lescher, Jon Liebman, Ann Marie Mattera, Dana Loren Mattera, Robert Neiman, Gil Netter, Scott

Novoselsky, John Packel, Tracey Patis, Scott Rosenzweig, Dr. Dan Schwartz, Chris Seger, Jaynie Smeerin, Jason Steigman, Gary Taubes, Mark Warren, Dan Warsh, Dr. Phillip Werner, Victor and Sally Reyes, and Virginia Reyes.

My family has supported my writing since I quit law and took the leap onto the page. Much love to Jane, Larry, Sam, and Mike Glover; and to Ken, Becky, Steve, Carrie, and Chaya Kurson. My mom, Annette Kurson, died while I was writing this book, but I always felt her with me. She and my father, Jack D. Kurson, were the two best storytellers I've known. I wish they were here.

A special thanks to my brother, Ken Kurson. He was never too busy to read my drafts or talk to me about writing, baseball, or life.

Finally, my deepest thanks to Amy, Nate, and Will Kurson. They are my world and my truest loves. Both boys edited my work, and I (mostly) took their suggestions. They also stayed up late with me, even on school nights, allowing me to structure the story aloud for them, helping me see Bannister and the *Golden Fleece* through their wide eyes. Amy is my best friend, editor, confidante, and soul mate. When I need her, she drives with me to the place that hangs over the road to get snacks and talk, even at five in the morning. I can't imagine a book, or a life, without her.

NOTE ON SOURCES

This project began over late-night burgers at a steak house in New Jersey, where divers John Chatterton and John Mattera told me of their quest to find a pirate ship—and a pirate captain—unlike any history had known. Over the next two and a half years, I spent hundreds of hours interviewing the men, in person and on the phone.

I also made two trips to the Dominican Republic with the men. In Santo Domingo, I handled piles of treasure and priceless artifacts, interviewed experts in archaeology and nautical history, and read books in buildings that dated to the sixteenth century. In Samaná, on the country's north coast, I saw Bannister come to life. It was there that the divers took me by boat to search the bay and investigate islands, hike into treacherous jungle, and wade into shipwreck-laden waters, all as they had done in their search for the pirate captain and his ship, the *Golden Fleece*. "You've gotta know the place to know the pirate," they told me, and they were right.

Captain Tracy Bowden, and crewmen Howard Ehrenberg and Heiko Kretschmer, granted me interviews, both in person and by phone. Victor Francisco Garcia-Alecont spoke to me in cafés and at his home in Santo Domingo. Carla Chatterton and Carolina Garcia de Mattera met with me to share memories and give insight into their husbands' adventure.

The business of treasure hunting, along with its rich history, legend, and lore, were explained to me in Florida by Carl Fismer,

Robert Marx, Sean Fisher, Kim Fisher, and Dave Crooks. I am convinced that treasure hunters are the best storytellers.

The fast-changing state of international maritime, admiralty, and salvage law was laid out for me by attorney David P. Horan of Miami, who prevailed in the Supreme Court of the United States on behalf of Mel Fisher, the treasure hunter who discovered and salvaged the *Atocha*, the richest shipwreck ever found.

Much of the historical research that appears in this book was done originally by John Mattera as part of his team's search for the *Golden Fleece*. I consulted all of his sources, along with my own (including interviews with experts), to confirm Mattera's work and to fill in details where necessary.

Much of what is known about Joseph Bannister comes from the correspondence of the governors of Jamaica in the 1680s, contained in the *Calendar of State Papers, American and West Indies*, now at the British National Archives in England, and in the manuscript collections at Colonial Williamsburg, in Virginia. Many of the relevant letters, along with other details on the English government's pursuit of Bannister, can be found in two stellar books by historian David Buisseret: *Port Royal Jamaica* (written with Michael Pawson) and published by University of the West Indies Press; and *Jamaica in 1687*, from the same publisher. It was the latter book that provided the eyewitness drawing and account of the battle between Bannister and Royal Navy frigates, and which confirms the discovery of the shipwreck at Cayo Vigia to be that of the *Golden Fleece*. Professor Buisseret also spent dozens of hours with me, in person and by phone, answering questions, assisting me with research, and pointing me in good directions. His assistance was invaluable.

(A note on spelling: Sources contemporary to Bannister often spelled the pirate captain's name "Banister." Modern sources, including those written by historians David Buisseret and Peter

Earle, almost always spell it "Bannister." The reason, as explained to me by Buisseret, is that seventeenth-century spelling was quite random, and that the latter spelling has become more conventional and more readily familiar to modern readers.)

On the Golden Age of Piracy, *The Buccaneers of America* by Alexandre Exquemelin, originally published in 1678 (and later published by Penguin Books), was essential reading, an eyewitness account of pirate life by a man who sailed with Henry Morgan, and it's a page turner. Peter Earle's *The Pirate Wars*, published by Thomas Dunne Books, gave a first-rate and highly readable account of how and why navies did battle with the buccaneers. *The Invisible Hook*, by Peter T. Leeson and published by Princeton University Press, provided a compelling look at the economics of pirate life, and shed new light on why, beyond the obvious reasons, pirates might have chosen such risky lives. As a general primer, David Cordingly's *Under the Black Flag*, published by Random House, was indispensable and a pleasure to read. Two fun and useful books about pirate language, terms, and sayings added color to an understanding of the era: *The Pirate Primer* by George Choundas, published by Writer's Digest Books, and *The Pirate Dictionary* by Terry Breverton, published by Pelican. Also useful were *The History of Piracy* by Philip Gosse (published by Burt Franklin); *Pirates of the Caribbean* by Cruz Apestegui (Chartwell Books); *Pirates: Predators of the Seas* by Angus Konstam (Skyhorse); *Villains of All Nations* by Marcus Rediker (Beacon Press); and *Pirate Hunting* by Benerson Little (Potomac Books).

Seventeenth-century naval warfare, weapons, ships, and tactics is a rich and exciting subject. Much was learned by reading Jonathan Dull's *The Age of the Ship of the Line*, published by the University of Nebraska Press. Mr. Dull was also kind enough to grant me a telephone interview, which was very helpful. I referred often to *The Oxford Illustrated History of the Royal Navy*, edited by J. R. Hill and published by Oxford University Press; *The Line of Battle: The Sailing Warship 1650–1840*, edited by Robert Gardiner and published by the Naval Institute Press; *The Command of the Ocean: A Naval History of Britain, 1649–1815*, by N.A.M. Rodger, published by Norton; and a small pamphlet by Albert Manucy titled *Artillery Through the Ages*, published by the U.S. Government Printing Office. In addition to Mr. Dull, two other experts granted me interviews: I spoke via Skype to British maritime historian Sam Willis, and by phone on several occasions to naval researcher Frank L. Fox, whose vivid and cinematic descriptions helped me envision the kind of fighting that took place between Bannister's pirates and the Royal Navy. Fox, also an expert in the work of Dutch marine painters Willem van de Velde the Elder, and his son Willem van de Velde the Younger, directed me to copies of drawings done by these men of the navy frigates *Falcon* and *Drake*. After months of reading about these great ships, it felt like a small miracle to be given illustrations drawn by men who had actually seen them.

In learning about the rarity of finding and identifying sunken pirate ships, I relied on an April 2005 article from the *International Journal of Nautical Archaeology*, "'Ruling Theories Linger': Questioning the Identity of the Beaufort Inlet Shipwreck," by Bradley A. Rodgers, Nathan Richards, and Wayne R. Lusardi. I also read Barry Clifford's *Expedition Whydah: The Story of the World's First Excavation of a Pirate Treasure Ship and the Man Who Found Her*, published by HarperCollins; *X Marks the Spot: The Archaeology of Piracy*, edited by Russell K. Skowronek and Charles R. Ewen, published by University Press of Florida; and a review of the Skowronek and Ewen book by Michael Jarvis in the journal *Caribbean Studies*, volume 36, number 2, July–December 2008.

(During the writing of *Pirate Hunters*, I checked media for reports of new pirate ship finds. As expected, there were almost none. In 2011, researchers at Texas State University discovered cannons and wreckage in Panama they thought might belong to one of Henry Morgan's ships, but, like almost all suspected pirate wreck finds, no conclusive evidence of the ship's identity was uncovered.)

On the subject of amputations at sea in the seventeenth century, there is an excellent website: The Pirate Surgeon's Journals (piratesurgeon.com). The author of that page cites several Golden Age sea-surgeon texts, which a research assistant helped me access via Gale's Eighteenth Century Collections Online and Google Books. They were *The Navy Surgeon; or, Practical System of Surgery* by John Atkins, London, printed for Henry Woodgate and Samuel Brooks, at the Golden Ball in Pater-Noster-Row, 1758; *A Course of Chirurgical Operations, Demonstrated in the Royal Garden at Paris* by Pierre Dionis, London, printed for Jacob Tonson, within Gray's-Inn Gate next Gray's-Inn Lane, 1710; *Chyrurgic Memoirs: Being an Account of Many Extraordinary Cures Which Occurred in the Series of the Author's Practice, Especially at Sea*, by John Moyle, London, 1708; *Chirurgus Marinus: Or, the Sea-Chirurgion. Being Instructions to Junior Chirurgic Practitioners, who Design to Serve at Sea in this Imploy*, by John Moyle, London, Three Bibles on London-Bridge, 1702. More recent texts, also useful, were John R. Kirkup's *A History of Limb Amputation*, published by Springer; and John Ashhurst's *The International Encyclopaedia of Surgery: A Systematic Treatise on the Theory and Practice of Surgery*, volume 6, published by W. Wood, 1886.

To learn the history and lore of Samaná, I consulted Encyclopedia Britannica online, and *History of the Panama Canal— Its Construction and Builders* by Ira E. Bennett, published by Historical Publishing Company. I also read "Historical Synthesis of

Biophysical Information of Samaná Region, Dominican Republic," by Dr. Alejandro Herrera-Moreno, Center for the Conservation and Eco-development of Samaná Bay and Its Surroundings, 2005. (This paper notes that 34 percent of fishermen in the Dominican Republic operate in Samaná, the majority of whom work from wooden rowboats or kayaks. It is these fishermen who often know more about the location of old shipwrecks than archaeologists, historians, and treasure hunters combined.) Finally, I referenced an obscure book, *Samaná, Pasado y Porvenir*, by Emilio Rodriguez Demorizi, published by Sociedad Dominicana de Geografia, second edition (1973). Mattera discovered the volume in a small Dominican hotel; despite the warning stamped inside, *"Por favor no retirar de esta area"—Please do not remove from this area*—he borrowed the volume and later gave it to me. Written mostly in Spanish, it mentions Bannister and makes some interesting claims, few of which Mattera or I could substantiate in the historical record. For more information, please visit my website at robertkurson. com/piratehunters.

For information on Port Royal, Jamaica, the "Wickedest City on Earth," I relied on the book by Pawson and Buisseret, *Port Royal Jamaica*; Buisseret's *Jamaica in 1687*; Cordingly's *Under the Black Flag*; Breverton's *The Pirate Dictionary*; Earle's *The Pirate Wars*; and Buisseret's *Historic Jamaica from the Air*, published by Ian Randle. Robert Marx was kind enough to talk to me in Florida about the historic excavation he did at Port Royal in the 1960s. I also watched a useful documentary produced by National Geographic, *Sin City Jamaica*, from 1998.

Captain Tracy Bowden's historic work on three Spanish galleons was chronicled in two *National Geographic* articles. The first, "Graveyard of the Quicksilver Galleons," was written by Mendel Peterson and published in the December 1979 issue. The second,

"Gleaning Treasure from the Silver Bank," was written by Bowden himself in the July 1996 issue. Bowden was kind enough to answer questions about these wrecks for me in person, too.

On the history of shipwreck and treasure hunting, I was helped by Joe Porter, Dave Crooks, Robert Marx, and Carl Fismer. I also read *The Devils Gold* by Ted Falcon-Barker, by Nautical; *Pieces of Eight: Recovering the Riches of a Lost Spanish Treasure Fleet*, by Kip Wagner as told to L. B. Taylor, Jr., published by Dutton; and two books by Robert F. Marx, *The Lure of Sunken Treasure*, published by David McKay, and *Shipwrecks in the Americas*, published by Dover.

These excellent books helped me understand the wreck of the Spanish galleon *Concepción* and the generations of treasure hunters, including William Phips, who searched for her: *The Hispaniola Treasure* by Cyrus H. Karraker, published by the University of Pennsylvania Press; *The Treasure of the Concepción* by Peter Earle, published by the Viking Press; and *The New England Knight: Sir William Phips, 1651–1695* by Emerson W. Baker and John G. Reid, published by the University of Toronto Press.

For the life of shipwreck historian and researcher Jack Haskins, I relied on the memories of his closest friend, Carl Fismer. Everyone should have a friend who remembers him like Fizz remembers Jack.

Many of the events in the book were recounted to me by the participants from their memories. If there was doubt about the order of things, I used my best efforts.

Mattera continued to research Joseph Bannister and the *Golden Fleece* even after the discovery of the pirate captain's wreck. Among his finds were logbooks from Captain Talbot and Lieutenant Smith of the *Falcon* for the dates that Royal Navy ship did battle with Bannister; letters by English officials and others noting the fight and its aftermath; even a log entry reporting word of Bannister's hanging off the shores of Port Royal. All of it added bits of detail and color, and was consistent with what Mattera had learned during his search for the *Golden Fleece*. For details and illustrations, please visit my website at robertkurson.com/piratehunters.

Finally, during my trips to the Dominican Republic, I saw and handled artifacts from the wreck of the *Golden Fleece*. Those I did not observe in person I saw in excellent photographs taken by Mattera and Ehrenberg. Mattera's collection of old maps and charts of Hispaniola and Samaná Bay, which hang on the wall of his apartment in Santo Domingo, also helped take me back in time to the era and place described in the book.

I even did a little treasure hunting of my own.

On a steamy spring morning, Chatterton, Mattera, Kretschmer, and another accomplished wreck diver, Todd Ehrhardt, hiked with me through dense jungle at Cayo Vigia, then up the island's steep eastern tip, where Bannister's pirates had dug in for their fight with the Royal Navy. We hung on to branches to keep from plunging to the rocky shore below. At the top of the island, we saw the channel just as Bannister would have seen it. With cannons and muskets, we could have hit any target in any direction. Kretschmer unpacked an Aqua Pulse AQ1B metal detector and began sweeping it back and forth over the mud. Moments later we were digging, with a hatchet and small shovel and ax. I don't know how long we worked. I don't know who did what. I just know that I didn't fear falling anymore, and that when we reached the bottom, we had four or five cannonballs between us. As a writer, you can do research and ask questions and make notes. But nothing puts you inside a story like finding your own cannonball from a pirate fight.

Index

About the Author

Robert Kurson earned a bachelor's degree in philosophy from the University of Wisconsin, then a law degree from Harvard Law School. His award-winning stories have appeared in *Rolling Stone*, *The New York Times Magazine*, and *Esquire*, where he was a contributing editor. He is the author of the 2005 American Booksellers Association's nonfiction Book Sense Book of the Year *Shadow Divers*, and *Crashing Through*, based on Kurson's 2006 National Magazine Award–winning profile in *Esquire*. He lives in Chicago.

www.robertkurson.com